NEW & COLLECTED POEMS

Ruth Fainlight was born in New York City, and has lived mostly in England since the age of 15. Her father was born in London, and her mother in a small town on the eastern borders of the Austro-Hungarian Empire (now in Ukraine). She was educated at schools in America and England, and at Birmingham and Brighton colleges of art, and married the writer Alan Sillitoe in 1959. She was Poet in Residence at Vanderbilt University, Nashville, Tennessee, in 1985 and 1990, and received a Cholmondeley Award for Poetry in 1994. She is a Fellow of the Royal Society of Literature.

Her many books include poetry, short stories, translations, drama and opera libretti. Her poems have appeared in numerous anthologies, and her stories in books including *The Penguin Book of Modern Women's Stories* (1991), *Caught in a Story: contemporary fairy-tales and fables* (Vintage, 1992), *Contemporary Jewish Writing* (University of Nebraska Press, 1998) and *The Penguin Book of the Beach* (2001).

Her poetry books include: *Cages* (1966) and *To See the Matter Clearly* (1968), from Macmillan in Britain and Dufour in the USA; *The Region's Violence* (1973), *Another Full Moon* (1976), *Sibyls and Others* (1980), *Fifteen to Infinity* (1983), *Selected Poems* (1987) and *The Knot* (1990), all from Hutchinson and Century Hutchinson; *This Time of Year* (1994) and *Selected Poems* (1995) from Sinclair-Stevenson; and *Climates* (1983), *Sugar-Paper Blue* (1997), *Burning Wire* (2002) and *Moon Wheels* (2006) from Bloodaxe Books. *Fifteen to Infinity* was published in the USA by Carnegie Mellon University Press. *Sugar-Paper Blue* was shortlisted for the Whitbread Poetry Award. Her latest poetry book is *New & Collected Poems* (Bloodaxe Books, 2010).

She has also translated two books of poetry from the Portuguese of Sophia de Mello Breyner, and collaborated with Alan Sillitoe on *All Citizens Are Soldiers*, a translation of Lope de Vega's play *Fuenteovejuna*. Her translation (with Robert J. Littman) of Sophocles' *The Theban Plays* was published by Johns Hopkins University Press in 2009. Her own poetry has been published in Portuguese (1995), French (1997, 2000, 2006), Spanish (2000, 2004, 2009, 2010), Italian (2003) and Romanian (2007) editions.

She has published two collections of short stories, *Daylife and Nightlife* (André Deutsch, 1971) and *Dr Clock's Last Case* (Virago, 1994). Her libretti include: *The Dancer Hotoke* (1991), a chamber opera by Erika Fox (nominated for the Laurence Oliver Awards in 1992); *The European Story* (1993), a chamber opera by Geoffrey Alvarez; and *Bedlam Britannica* (1995), a Channel Four *War Cries* TV opera directed by Celia Lowenstein with music by Robert Jan Stips.

RUTH FAINLIGHT

Ruth Fainlight

NEW & COLLECTED
POEMS

for dear Christine,
much love
from Ruth

BLOODAXE BOOKS

ISBN: 978 1 85224 885 7

First published 2010 by
Bloodaxe Books Ltd,
Highgreen,
Tarset,
Northumberland NE48 1RP.

www.bloodaxebooks.com
For further information about Bloodaxe titles
please visit our website or write to
the above address for a catalogue.

Supported by
ARTS COUNCIL
ENGLAND

Cover design: Neil Astley & Pamela Robertson-Pearce.

Printed in Great Britain by
Bell & Bain Limited, Glasgow, Scotland.

in memory of Alan

ACKNOWLEDGEMENTS

This book includes poems reprinted from the following collections by Ruth Fainlight: *Cages* (Macmillan, 1966; Dufour, USA, 1967), *To See the Matter Clearly* (Macmillan, 1968; Dufour, USA, 1969), *The Region's Violence* (Hutchinson 1973), *Twenty-one Poems* (Turret Books, 1973); *Another Full Moon* (Hutchinson, 1976), *Sibyls and Others* (Hutchinson, 1980), *Climates* (Bloodaxe Books, 1983), *Fifteen to Infinity* (Hutchinson, 1983, Carnegie-Mellon University Press, USA, 1986), *The Knot* (Hutchinson, 1990), *This Time of Year* (Sinclair-Stevenson, 1993), *Sugar-Paper Blue* (Bloodaxe Books, 1997), *Burning Wire* (Bloodaxe Books, 2002) and *Moon Wheels* (Bloodaxe Books, 2006).

Acknowledgements are due to the following publications where some of the poems from the *New Poems* section first appeared: *Answering Back*, edited by Carol Ann Duffy (Picador, 2007), *Artemis, The Guardian, Jewish Quarterly, Manhattan Review, Poetry Review, Salt, The Times, The Times Literary Supplement* and *Wasafiri*.

Some of the poems were first published in these artist books: *Twelve Sibyls*, with woodcuts by Leonard Baskin (Gehenna Press, USA), *Pomegranates*, with mezzotints by Judith Rothchild (Éditions de l'Eau, France), *Feathers, Leaves/ Feuilles, A Postcard from Tunis* and *Nacre*, with mezzotints by Judith Rothchild (Éditions Verdigris, France); *Sheba and Solomon*, with drypoints by Ana Maria Pacheco (Pratt Contemporary Art, UK).

The poems by Sophia de Mello Breyner were first published in *Marine Rose* (Black Swan Books, USA, 1988). 'The Islands' first appeared as the English section of a trilingual edition: Portuguese, French, English, of *Navigations* (Imprensa Nacional, Casa da Moeda, Lisbon 1983). The translation of 'Your Hand, My Mouth' is reprinted from Victor Manuel Mendiola's *Selected Poems* (Shearsman, 2008). The three Messengers' speeches are from a new translation of *Sophocles' Theban Plays* by Ruth Fainlight and Robert J. Littman (Johns Hopkins University Press, USA, 2009).

CONTENTS

THE REGION'S VIOLENCE (1973)

II *Others*

POEMS FROM CHAPBOOKS

FROM *Twenty-one Poems* (1973)

THE KNOT (1990)

THIS TIME OF YEAR (1993)

MOON WHEELS (2006)

TRANSLATIONS

New Poems

(2010)

The Empty Lot

I

Between my aunt's house and the backs
of those with their low roofs
on the next block
lay an empty lot.

The summer weeds were tall enough
(in fall, the goldenrod)
to close us off.
The field seemed boundless –

neutral ground – almost a barrier.
No one but I chose
to enter that space.
It was my empire.

II

To stand waist-high
in the surf of weeds,
bare feet and dusty toes
a hilly terrain for ants,
heels burrowed by chiggers,
legs scratched by dry stalks
and burrs, bitten by ticks,
the sun burning my shoulders
and small flies circling my head
as I dragged the back of a hand
across brow and under chin
to wipe away the sweat:
bliss – although
I did not know it yet.

III

Even in winter, when cold scythed
all growth flat, a tangle
of rotted leaves, shattered stems
and muddy snow

kept us isolated
in our small house
on that unpaved street
at the edge of town.

And after school, until
the grown-ups got home from work,
my brother and I, alone,
could fight and talk.

We were strangers – in wartime –
with nowhere else to live, and few
neighbours so far from the centre.
How lucky I was.

Midland Contemporary

I

If you stand on the path leading out of the village,
with your back to the airport buildings, the pylons
hidden, the bright motorway signs too far
on the left to enter your field of vision
and the last row of houses too far to the right,

the vista towards that distant line of hills
sloping gently down to the muddy stream
in the shallow valley that lies before you, gives
little evidence of the present moment – seems
a perfect nineteenth-century English landscape.

But the moment you shift your head from that one angle
or let yourself hear the traffic-roar: the endless
stream of cars, the HGVs, the freight-planes
lifting off and the holiday flights landing,
you know exactly when and where you are.

It is this interdigitation of rural and
global, industrial and contemporary – this
evidence of encroachment by an augmenting
population and its wants: consumption and
mobility – which fascinates and appals.

II

Cattle in the shadow of cargo hangars
and new-built terminals. Virgin, Easyjet
and DHL. Sheep with fleeces darkened
to the tarnished silver of clouds emerging
from the power station's cooling towers.

And past the highway's wire-link barrier –
and barely noticed by that Mondeo's only
passenger – discordant acres of acid
yellow rape fields coruscate like molten
metal through an open furnace door.

Diversion

These days, I seem positioned
on an adverse camber, sliding towards danger
rather than away.

Straddle the nearside lane
they say, but I never remember, nearside
or offside, which is which.

Free rescue – await recovery.
I'd be glad to wait, but rescue from what?
Do I want to recover?

Better perhaps to keep my distance
from the soft shoulder until that sign,
the yellow and black of incident-tape,

then follow the traffic ahead
back to the motorway and hope
for safety – or maybe disaster?

Dawn Blue

Bright against dawn blue
when the blind is raised
and framed by the window bars:
a full moon, pure disk marked
with the Sea of Tranquillity
and Archimedes' volcano.

Haze of cloud: a mauve veil
drawn across a woman's face
softening its contours. A flock
of pigeons races up and down
the street. The moon fades.
The veil whitens and thickens.

Between a church steeple
and roof-tops opposite
the moon becomes a vague imprint
of its first clear image:
not hammered silver foil
but crumpled tissue paper.

How quickly it moves, like a child
who runs to hide behind a wall
and giggling, calls: 'Where am I?
Come and find me!'
The sky has paled, and the birds
flown off to another street.

Windows

The room had seemed completely dark
until, as if a padded curtain
slid across the window, a sepia
wash from a sable brush clogged
with pigment puddled onto a sheet
of paper as thirsty as a blotter,
or a metal blind clicked into place,
the air curdled, blackness condensed.

Neighbours were turning off their lights.
Windows, opposite mine, at different
levels on the other side of the street,
became rectangles of watery
tones, like an early Klee. As each
lamp faded and the distillation
of darkness proceeded, I felt myself
break free, plunge deeper into space.

Insomniac's Moon

Insomniac's moon,
mineral and organic,
with its phosphorescent
mushroom-punky glow,
its halo of acid orange
rim of gassy blue

the blue and orange
that flash from a prism
or the bevelled facets
stabbing that image
into sleepless eyes
from a mirror's edge,

like a drop of milk
pearling from the breast
of the harsh moon-mother
which I try to catch
between parted lips
before it dissolves

with other ancient dreams
of love and sleep,
or the blue and orange
of fading bruises,
into the oceanic dark
circling the universe.

Their Story

To hear their story told
by harpist and poet
to live it all again,
those battles of heroes:
the Heiki and Genji
Achilles and Hector
Balder and Loki,
becomes the last pleasure
of the defeated dead.

Ageing

I

Since early middle-age
(say around forty)
I've been writing about ageing,
poems in many registers:
fearful, enraged or accepting
as I moved through the decades.

Now that I'm really old
there seems little left to say.
Pointless to bewail
the decline, bodily and mental;
undignified; boring
not to me only but everyone,

and ridiculous to celebrate
the wisdom supposedly gained
simply by staying alive.
– But maybe, to have faith
that you'll be adored as an ancient
might make it all worthwhile…

II

Ageing means smiling at babies
in their pushchairs and strollers
(wondering if I look as crazy
as Virginia or Algernon –
though I don't plan to bite!)
Find myself smiling at strangers.

It means no more roller-skating.
That used to be my favourite
sport, after school, every day:
to strap on my skates,
spin one full circle in place,
then swoop down the hill and away.

When I saw that young girl on her blades,
wind in her hair, sun on her face,
like a magazine illustration
from childhood days, racing
her boyfriend along the pavement:
– then I understood ageing.

A Different Form

When food goes rotten: white spots
on the cheese and green streaks of mould,
sooty black spores on slices of bread,
and fingers sink shockingly
into the underside of a piece of fruit
when you lift it from the bowl,
wrinkled and collapsed; like

the soft, crumpled face of that woman
swathed in layers of scarves, talking
to someone only she can see and
plucking pieces of lint out of the air – or
the age-blotched arms of a gaunt old man
squinting at the sun, harsh silhouette
against a sea as bright as tin; try

not to forget that what is consuming
the bread, cheese, fruit, the elderly brain
and flesh, has the same immortal
energy as the one about to be born,
that matter can change but never die,
that nothing is wasted – although
each time it takes a different form.

Borrowed Time

I feel a bit crazy tonight,
my mood heightened, unstable:
maybe because it's full moon,
or maybe because we're living
on borrowed time. But borrowed
from whom? Maybe the moon –
it could be the moon who allows
you to live beyond your due.
This morning the doctor said
he's amazed you're still alive.
I'm not. Why should you die?
Far more reason to live,
so much still to do.
We both look up at the moon,
and silently I beg:
be as generous as you can,
kindly usurer,
give me endless credit.
Later I'll pay my debts
(I already know
the price will be cruel). Please,
let me borrow again, let us gaze
at you again – and again –
new moon, crescent, full,
in a clear or clouded sky.
Do not allow this moment
to be, or to become, even
maybe, the very last time.

The Wedding Chapel

My Nashville apartment
was near the campus and
opposite the Wedding Chapel.
If only I'd made friends
with someone local
I might have been invited
to a ceremony –
but I knew no one.

Weekend afternoons
I would sit by the window,
watching them enter,
one couple after another.
I could only imagine
exactly what happened
in the chapel, from the look
on their faces, afterwards.

Sometimes music
from inside would reach me –
interesting, what they chose
(maybe old songs from
the Bluebird Café) – notes
which blew across the road
like the gold and silver stars
and moons of the confetti.

It made me feel older, lonely –
but lucky – because I knew
that even though I stayed
the whole semester in Nashville,
when I got back home,
my husband would look at me
as wonderingly as if
we still were bride and groom.

Facts About Ants

The fierce grip of black ants' mandibles
clipped together the gaping sides of a wound
in my ancestor's thigh. As the jaws clamped
shut, the writhing bodies were twisted off.

To cure her rheumatism, my great great
grandmother was eased into a tin bath
where a nest of ants had been boiled. Their
formic acid made the water dark as iodine.
(These days, more likely, she would order
Chinese Ant-venom Extract on-line.)

Tons of cement were poured down the vents
and chimneys of an ant city, to map the structure.
Then, with the same care it was built, the earth
around was dug and shifted, to uncover

galleries, garbage pits, pastures where workers
milk honey-dew aphids, air-conditioned
fungus gardens and larvae nurseries,
the queen-mother's chamber. No single mind
conceived this triumph of the collective.
I contemplate it with awe and fear.

A colony of forty thousand ants
has the same number of brain cells as a human.
Ant brains are the largest among insects.
Each has the processing power of a computer.

'Go to the ant, you sluggard, consider its ways
and be wise,' are King Solomon's words
in the Book of Proverbs. But ants yawn.
In Japan, they say that an ant-hole will collapse
an embankment; in Africa, that not even
the sharpest ear can hear an ant's song.

Pain Figure

The head is enormous,
every feature magnified:
rabbit-eyes, puffy lips,
swollen tongue, aching teeth,
and the hands like padded
gauntlets, fingers extended,
legs and feet water-logged
as if moon-booted:
Dr Frankenstein's vision,

limbs, appendages and organs
doubled, quadrupled in size
to indicate their sensitivity
to pleasure and pain, record
the network of nerve-paths
which carry the signals
like bristling roots that spread
from the stem of an ivy:
centipede-feet grappling a wall,

that blue and purple drawing
from an antique book, a figure
with the proportions more
of a rubber doll, an embryo
or acupuncture model
than a normal human:
recalling which, awake through
the small hours, I feel myself
become its living version.

Dixit Dominus

Antonio Vivaldi is smiling with pleasure,
peering over the painted balustrade
(birds and cherubs in steep perspective
circling his head as they rise to Heaven)
on a painted ceiling – or so I imagine,
while listening to a performance
of his newly-discovered piece of music:
glorious sounds we hear together.

If those annotated sheets of paper –
fragile treasure – survived for centuries,
then inconceivable that their creator
does not enjoy this harmony
of voices and instruments, this blend
of ecstatic vibrations, now, from his cloud
in the sky, or seated beside me – both
of us sharing it, smiling with pleasure.

Dixit Dominus: the work recently identified (2005) by Janice Stockigt
of Melbourne University as a composition by Antonio Vivaldi.

Nacre

I *Pearls*

I

What other gem grows in a living creature
underwater

is made from crystalline substance
iridescent nacre

layer upon layer secreted, exuded
by the mantle tissue

when one small grain of sand or parasite
embeds in the pulpy flesh

that fills a mollusc shell, to coat the irritant
and form a pearl.

II

Sometimes this happens – but rarely.
And few have much value. The magnificent pearls,
with their orient nacre, were saved
for queens and emperors. Entire villages
holding their breath: how many divers' lives
lost in the oyster beds for a royal crown?

III

Caligula named his horse a consul
then garlanded it with pearls.
Cleopatra, to flaunt her power
before Mark Anthony, dissolved
a pearl, the worth of a king's ransom,
in a glass of wine and swallowed it.
With one of his mother's pearl earrings,
General Vittelius
financed his most ambitious campaign.

IV

To decide if she would visit him,
Sheba set riddles to test Solomon.
Across the Red Sea and the desert,
in an envoy's sealed wallet,
among the other presents
she sent a hollowed moonstone
and an unpierced pearl.

Pearls were Krishna's wedding gift to his girl,
and part of Hindu marriage ritual
is the piercing of an undrilled pearl.

II *Venus*

What was the grit in the oyster
that formed beautiful Venus,
who came floating shoreward
on an oyster-shell, her flesh
as lustrous as the orient
on a royal pearl?

Some say she was engendered
by the fertilising foam
from the severed genitals
of Uranus. Some,
that the pulpy tissue inside
a mollusc is like a vulva, and
the gleaming pearl becomes
a clitoris. Whichever, flesh
or nacre, incarnates treasure.

III *First Forms*

A pearl swells
inside an oyster shell
by augmenting strata
of milky nacre,

as a girl's chest
buds warm flesh
in the first form
of perfect breasts.

IV *Shells*

For ashtrays, she uses the shells
where the pearls were formed
that now circle her smooth neck.

The warm sift of ash
down their nacreous curve

when he taps his cigarette:
the slow slide of pearls
against her satin dress.

Later she takes her earrings off
and lays those pearls in another shell.
But the necklace stays on –
until he opens the clasp
under perfumed curls
at the nape of her neck.

V *Clam Chowder*

   I

Aunt Ann's clam chowder:
that creamy broth
glistening like nacre
could never be kosher.

I loved its unctuousness,
the shimmer of grease on top,
like a fat bishop
in his shiny robe and mitred hat,

and the detritus of shells
on the kitchen table
to hide from the neighbours –
(O sinful Jewish daughter!)

   II

But when lunch was over
and the plates washed up,
and she changed her dress
for the Ladies' Club,
I thought she looked best
if she wore that brooch
with a pearl in the centre
that had been her mother's,
and the pearl ear-studs.

Plunging both hands deep inside the tin,
buttons would slide through my fingers like sand.
I picked out the shiny ones: nacreous
mother-of-pearl, round, oval and square,
cut with patterns elaborate as snowflakes,
edges serrated like the puckered lips
of a cowrie shell, a tightened chamois purse,
or a whale's curved mouth with its bony fringe.

Cowrie-money: those button-necklaces
I loved to thread with the glinting buttons cut
from Mother's worn-out frocks. Were cowries
only valued for tone and shape? Her gaze
was powerful enough to make me doubt
myself, and seemed as distant as a whale's.
As my inheritance, she left her button box,
some necklaces, and three cowrie shells.

Before the Fall

How exactly right the garden looked,
half still in sunlight, half in slanting shadow,
the lawn recently mown

All the trees in the orchard vivid with fruit:
plum, pear, crab, apple, damson,
shrubs in full bloom

Children's voices over the hedges, laughing
not squabbling, birds singing, dogs barking,
Mozart on the radio

And that scarlet rose with golden stamens bared
and layered petals arching back and open,
about to fall...

An Ancient Ritual

If a friend (even an acquaintance)
was threatened by serious illness,
she went on the alert:
an animal scenting. Visits etcetera
became frequent, obsessive.
It took years to understand that
the patient was irrelevant.

She was performing an ancient ritual
of obeisance and acknowledgement
to another class of being,
a different power:
to placate and divert from herself,
if just for one moment,
that fearful, focussed attention.

Last Year's Sicknesses

Those overwhelming states of possession
        drenches of passion
as powerful as drunkenness or migraine
    or anaesthetic

when body's urgencies annihilate
        the borders of self
that era of ecstasy, anger and pain
        equally intense

now seem another person's memories
        no more a part of me
than last year's sicknesses – and everything else
        I need to forget.

Slow Wet Flakes

Spring snow falls
in slow wet flakes
   loose
      starry
         shapes

the pattern
   on a cotton
kimono
of faded indigo
              stretched

across the sky
     as if
it were the back
of an enormous
       woman.

The Shower

Water that pours so freely
from the shower-rose over her head
as she stands in the bathtub,
splashing against the wall
tiled gleaming white
and the bright shower curtain,

slicking her shoulders
like a libation of perfumed oil
slowed for a moment
by the points of her breasts
then streaming faster
sluicing the belly and hips

of this confident woman,
a lavish fall of water
swirling around the tub
and circling away down
the pipe into the drain
then who knows where,

becomes a thin drip of water
through holes punched in a pail
hung on a mud brick wall
which puddles into the ochre earth
around the feet of a girl
on the other side of the world.

Triptych

The right panel could be one of
Goya's *Capricios* or *Disasters*...:
a prisoner, arms twisted
awkwardly back as if broken or strait-
jacketed, placard pinned to his chest:
Renegade, Infidel, Heretic,
(whatever they made him confess),
in a cart that jolts through jeering crowds
towards Cathedral Square
to hear sentence pronounced.

The left side is the china figure
I saw in a local shop window:
a woman, hands tensely clutched,
the dunce-cap jammed onto her head
scrawled with ideograms I cannot
read but know are accusations
against an 'enemy of the people',
blood-stained clothes and bruised face
as meticulously painted as
the blooms of a hundred flowers.

The central image for contemplation
is the photograph of a naked figure,
hooded, draped in a blanket,
balancing on the narrow top
of a wooden box with arms outstretched,
electric wires clipped to his fingers,
circling his neck, snaking under
the cloth: a man being tortured.
Nothing has altered.
It keeps happening.

Collateral Damage

To be killed by a rocket
I need not be its target
just another statistic
charged with adrenalin
caught in the crossfire
between two armies
with their own stories:
collateral damage.

Water, Fire, Blood

To rule the mountain is to rule the river.
You can't step into the same river twice.
Water under the bridge. The bridge
that arches the flood. Open the flood-gates.
To walk on pulsing embers or thin ice.
Lick your lips and think of mother. Blood
is thicker than water. A river of blood.
Water covers a multitude of sins.

A world in a drop of water. Plain as water.
Water finds the lowest level. Water
wears away the hardest stone. Silent
waters. The waters of affliction.
Under a livid sky, a parting flood.
Mid-ocean volcanic eruptions,
conflict of water and fire. Ice and fire.
Unmelting ice. Fire that cannot be quenched.

Still water runs deep. Names written
on water. The blood congeals. The same tide
touches both sides of the ocean. A tide
in the affairs of men. Cast your bread
on the water. The water of life. The polar caps
will melt and, drop by drop, each stalactite
and stalagmite dissolve, before you reach
the river's source, the mountain peak.

Tongue-tied

A tarnished silver napkin ring
with a quartered red and golden shield
marked RMS *Antonia*
fixed to its filigreed band, a spoon
with a stem of twisted darkened brass
and a crowned, scroll-topped oval crest
painted with minute bright figures:
      horse, cow, flag-topped tower,
      scales of Justice; the smooth curve
      of its bowl filled by a turreted palace,
      and in finely-drawn black letters
      against a blue enamel sky
      the three words: *Legación*
      Argentinia, Montevideo,
plus a few photographs –
are the only evidence
that my father ever lived
in South America.

But why he went to Buenos Aires,
barely twenty, what he did,
and when he left for New York City –
no one still alive to ask, or
answer. I know he married, because
soon after, I enter the picture
and introduce a few hard facts.

> But really, he told me nothing; not one
> story of aunts or uncles, school friends,
> girl-friends; nothing. He was dead
> before I learned his mother – the other
> unknown grandmother (nor did
> my mother's mother live to see
> her daughter's child) was one of nine.
> I must have many second cousins.

Family: a word that terrified me.
I ran away as soon as I could –
although now I feel deprived.

And I suppose my father
had his own reasons for silence.
How far back to go,
when did it begin?
A search as hopeless as
trying to date Original Sin.

> From grandparents to grandchildren
> spans five generations. So much
> I should like to know. But
> that inborn habit of silence
> leaves me ignorant and tongue-tied
> at those very moments
> when words are most essential.

A painted spoon and a napkin ring
are poor inheritance
without the story to explain them
and enchant the listener –
even if I must invent it.

Cages

(1966)

Dawn Chorus

There comes a moment when the tide turns:
Light has won again. The birds stop singing
For a long moment, then begin again
On a more casual note. They've done it:
Dragged back day, tipped cool light
Over the lock of dawn with the nervous force
Of their throats. Some strength of mine
Was sapped to bring that toneless even glare
And settle the question: after each dawn's
Struggle, in the clear white of exhaustion,
Insomniacs float down wide canals of sleep.

The Angels

They're poised like statues, civil, dignified,
Interested, even, as photos on tombstones are
By a stranger who peers curiously.
The soil is stony, friable. Dry roots break
As I clutch out to stop my downward slide
Into the pit, the place they're solemnly
Admiring. Why don't I cry for help? They seem
So courteous. One would surely bend
From his shallow ledge, reach out a hand.
But my tongue stays still as the empty sky,
As their faces in the stern unwavering light.

Cages

Dawn wind and rising sun get trapped by the trees
Stain my eastward windows into Moorish lamps
Cages of light fretted like stilled twigs
That flicker again as the candle flame stirs.

Whipping and flashing shadows on the grainy wall
The branches make a wicker cage. Who is in it
Me or the sun? Caught like a golden stag
He twists his horns in panic but cannot free them.

Neither candle flame nor stag, the sun's globe
Shudders clear and the wind dies.
Whatever the cage, our shared urge
Is fierce enough to burn the bars away.

Equinox

More than a week of storms –
Storms and sickness –
Between now and my last clear view of the moon.

In two more nights she'll be full.
Thunder, bruised clouds, a sea like melted stone,
Confirm her waxing arrogance.

Full moon had no such heralds through the summer,
Nights of stars, moon discreet somewhere
In all that glitter. Now the stars have no chance.

This is her season of power, she is everywhere.
The wind scoops mock moons,
White crescents of waves on the violent water.

Three times magnified, she flashes through streaming
Cloud like a wrecker's beacon;
Her lurid halo makes the sky seem hollow.

Time is slowed by storms – more will happen
Before she gains full circle than between
One full moon and the next in calm weather.

The Brothers

The prince who lay in his filth
Almost dead when they found him
In the ruined castle,
Untrained to clean himself,
To lift a hand for food or drink,
Demands a wry respect.
He died soon after.

His fatal inadaptability
Has troubling meaning set against
The evolutionary virtues
Of his brother prince,
Who lived in rice-fields,
Led the horde that sacked the castle,
Became the people's hero.

Self-confessed

The prince went everywhere
In his disguise. He'd answer, Nothing,
When they asked him what he did
And who he was. But who are you?
He'd say. In his disguise
They did not know he was a prince,
Were pleased to answer carefully
Yet somewhat scornfully
To this small man who confessed himself
As nothing.

The prince heard who they were
And what his people did.
He felt he'd learned enough.
I am a prince, he said, the next time
He was asked. How is it
That you did not see?
I thought you'd recognise me
Through my humble cloak, your prince.
It was a sort of test, he added wryly,
But now I think perhaps I am the one
Who failed, made into nothing,
Self-confessed.

Hope

One always hopes the luck will hold:
The photos turn out clear and sharp
When they're developed
Though one doubts the camera was steady;

Hopes one's instincts were accurate,
Will have no consequence,
Though honest thought about the past
Can make one giddy.

But luck has no use for hope,
Despises those who think
That hollow-eyed men with big hands
Will not insist the pay be bloody.

The Ante-room

Reaching, I think, the end
Of my testing, I find
I've still got left
More tether to unwind.

I'm only in the ante-room
Of waiting, have learned nothing yet.
Old selves I must assume
Again before forget

Hang dead as empty coats.
Like poetry, the certitude
For my next step grows.
Open the door of solitude,

I'll find the strength
To be alone,
To learn the height and width and length
Of this room of stone.

A Child Asleep

To see the skull beneath the skin
Of a child's head
Is seeing death clear.
The power that makes those bones appear
Will not spare anyone.

I watch my son asleep
And cannot stop
The general pain
Pass out from me to him again
I cannot spare him for I am not spared.

The Screaming Baby

Mouth stretched into the ancient rictus,
The screaming baby: formidable
To the newly-delivered mother. Too pure
An expression of something completely felt
Not to inspire fear; with no memory
To weaken or blur eyes snapping
An anger no adult could muster, and which
Animals are exempt from. A creature
Throbbing with such elemental power that
The cringing woman must adore or kill him.

The Infanticide

I left my baby there among the trees,
Rain-rusted leaves, decayed stalks,
Twigs husked with grey and white moss.
The black mulch makes a soft bed.
Perhaps he will not cry, lulled
Till I am far enough away
By sky's dazzle, the touch of ferns and air.
From the top of the woods I hear nothing.
Silence is like a plastic sheet over
His stretched mouth, stifling his thin alarm,
Powerless to stop the mist.
I left my baby there among the trees.
Now the forest gods can have me.

The Shriving

Like a log's heartwood being consumed by flames
Something is working inside me, crumbling away.
Soft ash thickens as the wound widens,
Hides the gnawing red core you can't see –
But if you'd touch me, how I'd burn you.

The dead black charcoal is gouged away
And the suave fire slides deeper, vanishes
Like water into cracks of earth.
Maybe I'm being shaped into a boat
To be launched out of this jungle on my journey,
All doubt purged away.

Stones

They stand on the sloping beach
And throw stones at the sea
That sink in its heaving mass
Without trace,
Impotent against
Indifferent female force
Rarely beautiful but always powerful
Whether raging or asleep.

All he has made and fought away from
Lies behind each man's throw
And its viciousness:
Absolute challenge
To the old female
In her shapeless wrinkled coat
That sometimes slides to show
The body of a goddess.

Weed dark with water
Plasters her thighs –
Black, crimson, green –
The wet white flesh between
Unbruised by even one lucky hit.
Cast against Fate, that Venus
Far below the frothing waves,
The stones always fall short.

Autumn Stirring

(i.m. S.P.)

What agitates and makes her walk just now?
The autumn stirs her.
She doesn't want to die,
And never once intended it.

Even at the moment of suffocation she knew
The spores she left would germinate
And mark the trail to follow.
For months she had her talons in my throat,
Hovered above me nightly.
I thought I was hungry for death
When the dead most wanted to devour me.

Those who kill themselves are angels,
Survive the longest,
Have found the way of power,
Despising all oblivion.

Those who meditate upon the angels
Go mad. Why is that?
The dead are angels:
Black shapes with outspread wings
Whose dusty pinions beating in our faces
Infect us with their agitation... and
Magic misery to poetry.

The Chain

I

When I first learned of the death of my sad sister
I wanted to conceive a daughter –
A restitutive rite that might allow
the atoms of your shattered soul to reassemble.

Still at night, sometimes, as I lie
Deep in the bed, on my side, like a corpse,
Knees drawn up, as if huddled for new birth
Into the black world where snail-slime,
Phosphorescent, glistens along the path
You followed underground,
I feel compelled to make this act of love
And give your spirit rest in living flesh.

II

When I lie sleepless beneath the hidden ceiling,
That black shape, as a child would draw
Its mother, arms outstretched, is you.
You've come to get me and to comfort me.
Cold stars, those constellations of faces,
Regrets like shreds of dirty protoplasm,
Will have no power against you. Death
Is the big mother. In her embrace I'll sleep.

III

Down you come, take back the blood
I tried to scratch from your breasts.
You'll suck me drier than I could manage
When I first imagined death.

The Ghost

A ghost woke me, eve of the Feast of the Dead,
Rainy night in June on the African coast.
Rattling shutters, fireworks, shots or thunder –
Something broke into a blurred dream of myrtle,
Blue-washed plaster, headstones and white robes.

Defeated by neon the ghost faded –
While rain, unconfined by its ancient courses,
Unseasonable on the scrubby, stippled hills,
Fell over the whole country, wet me
As I stood on the terrace, rushed into her grave.

The Arab Fluter

Good for the poet to be marked, apart, for ever,
Like the Arab fluter with a hole pierced in his throat.
He, a great flute himself
His throat opened to take
Air in for ever;
No human need of breath
To end his note.

Some Thoughts on Death

Like everyone else, I suppose,
I think about death most when I can't sleep.
But the only dead I've seen was an unknown woman
Who fell, not even at my feet,
But ten yards back, at Notting Hill Gate,
One rainy shopping morning. Curiosity
Made me turn as I sensed a crowd
And there she was, a decent middle-aged lady,
Liver-splotched hands twitching
In the yellow mud of the reconstructions,
Her hat in a puddle. I barely saw it
When a policeman strode over – a young boy –
'Hasn't anyone called an ambulance?'
When I came back she was dead.
Quite different for the few minute's lapse.
Flat. She looked so flat.
Her head had moved slightly
In the dizzying fall into lifelessness,
The poor blotched cheek and nose
Now visible and meaningless, a smear of blood
Dirtying her hand, dry on the wet road.
I gave my name as witness,
But heard nothing about it
And felt nothing about it
Except surprise at how little I did.

But when it becomes difficult to sleep,
That ignominious death on a busy street,
The traffic, shoppers, workmen in the rain,
That flat body hugging the sealed-off earth,
Spreads its thin arms in a protective gesture
Against more grandiose horror –
My own protection from the final knowledge.

White Nights

No moon on white nights in Finland.
Birch trees frail as tin
Bar the lake's dull mercury.

A grey wolf gulps troll-faced clouds.
Three suns smoulder between the islands
As fire meets water, slow and shuddering.

But no sight of the moon
Unless this livid sky
Is the scarred surface of her other side.

New Moon and Full Moon

That dim presence hidden
By the reefs, behind
A shifting curtain of weed,
Dream-furling of limbs
In the fume of its own ink:
The black squid of the future,
Now chalky-white and leprous,
Screams down from the full moon
And hissing clouds a month later.

Her glaring eye,
The awful heat of moonlight,
Leave shrivelled flesh and bleeding nails,
Veins clogged with the drift
Of her powders, white sediment
Of madness. Now the moon wanes
But should not be trusted:
A black umbrella twitched
Over the staring face of the present.

Mooncity

At twilight, windows melt,
House after house open to the night
With only that slow liquid
Trembling like fire or membrane
Protection from the moon's rays.

Walls splay out from vertical
Their angles gone, streets exposed
Like white bone glinting in a dark wound.
Ape-ghosts gibber from the scaffolding.
The moon swings with them.

Ashy Moon

Seared, scarred, sealed by the ashy moon
Who advanced through the wavering glass
Between slats of shutters tamped
With dry, frail dust of summer streets:
Outmoded and romantic defenses
Against the malignancy of the cat-goddess
Who rips a barrier of mosquito-net contemptuously,
Passes like X-ray through lovers' caresses and arms,
Enters the womb like an instrument
Or the ice-hot hands of guilt and obsession,
Then sows bright mercury seeds of death
To blossom through all my future days
With that pure force of life characterising her –
Like blue flowers from the ash of Peace Square.

One Phase of the Moon

My moon shines obdurate as scar tissue,
A circle cut from steel sheeting. She's dry,
Slick as cellulose multi-coated,
Queen of dust and bones, strung up
In the hollow of a dead black sky.

Between the sun and streaming water
Hangs my moon. Right now she can't see either,
Denies her light reflects from anywhere,
Forgets that she can clothe with moving tides
Sea-hidden bones no matter where they lie.

Song

The moon waxes full
Waxy cheeks
Gleaming with fatness
Like wax like a wax figure
Full faced
Cheeks lacerated
Like a weeping wax Madonna
In a dark church
Wax tears on her cheeks
And daggers in her heart
Like the pins in the magic figure
Meant to cause weeping
Like the weeping moon

The Old Bear

The old bear dragged from a high cave
Where he'd slept all winter:
The fat of summer feasts, October pickings, gone
Burned slow to keep alive.

He gazed through thin air
Across valleys and peaks
For the first time seeing the whole range
And its endless climbing:

An old man thinking of his life
Who knows nothing else will happen,
The fat of pleasure worn
From bones of marriage and all other ties.

For a long time the bear sat in the sun
Wondering whether to kill,
Begin again or go back,
Lie down in the dark cave and die.

Old Man in Love

The goods accrete as he gets older:
Land, children, fame,
He's weighted by a lengthening list
Of things that name him,
Tethered firm to age and death.

The work left to complete
Like secret money he can draw on
Might help escape, but surer still
He hopes, is anguish, severance.
He seeks destruction in the gaze of love.

The Black Goddess

Distant, half hidden by the cave's mouth,
The goddess gleamed whitely.

Is it because you or she
Have reached a certain age
That she stands outside, in silhouette?

One time she showed the sun to you,
Now she obscures it,
And ancient vanity deceives you both.

Learn that her fitting role must be
To lead you to the sanctuary
And kiss your eyes most tenderly
Before she binds them.

A Painting
(in the style of Marc Chagall)

The roses are blue, incandescent with death,
As soft and as bruised as a mouth in the dark
And each swollen petal is meshed with pink veins.
There are four of them dying in a small jar,
Their luminous mauve the only colour in a moonlit room.

Held in a maze of fine scrolled metal,
Inside the secret house of a mosquito-net,
Two lovers lie, dazed by the scent of decay.
In the night, the many small beasts cry and sing,
But they are silent, their arms touching tranquilly.

The moon, who creates for their pleasure alone
Patterns of white in the threads of the net,
Sentimentally softens her light to mystery
And wistfully rounds the flesh of the girl.
The man is in shadow, lapsed in a dream of blue roses.

Time Theory

I love you ever lovers cry
Disintegrated by pleasure's grace

The moment like a black cone rises
Expanding timelessly in space

Paolo and Francesca clasp
Insatiate mouth to eternal face

The Night Flower

A cruel wedge cleaves me, root
Spurting sweet bright colours of hysteria,
Outrageous night-growth that burgeons
Under the moon's scalding glitter.

With dawn the dense leaves wilt,
Choke everything but one flower, matrix
For that corrosive seed, whose dream
Is a towering cedar of pure pain.

A Fable

Where she lost the ring they never know;
Her circumscribed activities were easily traced
But nowhere in the room could the ring be found.

How she lost the ring neither could understand;
Crumpled gloves, sides of chairs, even the sink
And the waste-paper basket were searched.

They turned to the empty bed. The hunt
Ceased for a while as, trapped by the billowing sheets
And laughing, they embarked on another quest.

But not in the bed, either, did the ring appear.
How such a well-fitting ring could slide
Unknown from her finger seemed almost mysterious.

For a few more days she looked, and glanced
At her strange, bare hand occasionally. Then,
Except as a joke, they acknowledged the ring was gone.

*

A ring meant nothing to them; they would not accept
Such a thing as a symbol of love
Or of anything else. He did not even consider

Buying another. And yet, the loss did not fade,
For it seemed that something between them changed
As she studied her empty hand. Ideas

She had hotly denied took root in her mind,
And he who had thought himself rational
Longed for a miracle. They were lost in a forest

Where the menacing trees that kept them apart
Constantly grew, and the ring, their only link,
Was lost as they. So now there is nothing to do but wait

For the transfigured prince, changed to a toad, who must wake
And set out from the heart of the forest
Bearing that ring in his mouth which will free them all.

Everyone Dies

Every time my parents went out I thought they would die.
I never looked for their return.
I imagined it all so clearly; after receiving the news
And a suitable pause for crying

I planned to sell the house. Loaded with cash
I'd banish my brother into an orphanage.
He might as well be crushed by those churning wheels:
In one black fantasy I'd kill the lot of them.

The shadows would get thicker. They were still not home.
Now surely they must be dead and it was all my fault.
Because whoever faced me in the bus or train
Could read my evil thoughts

I knew that mind was paramount. Of course I had done it,
Driven the car that flattened them into the ground.
Alone, there seemed suddenly nothing to do
With all my longed-for freedom.

Some time during the evening I'd want to go to the bathroom
And there on the stairs, like Chinese paper dragons
Which even in my terror I guessed were paper,
Monsters waited to snap at my heels as I ran up higher.

If my mother or father came in while I was trapped
How I adored them.
They were the hall light I wouldn't put on:
I had been punishing myself.

When I set the same death-car back into lumbering motion
When my husband was late, despair
Like a photographer's black cloth
Dropped over the new head I thought I'd been growing.

I still was killing them off. And now my son
And my fear when he went to play in the park.
As the hour grew later I fatefully put on mourning
Sure I would never see him again.

The stone wheels, pocked by ceaseless use,
Grind on. I can see them turning so clearly,
As close as if about to be dragged between them
To meet that freedom. My turn is coming too.

Four Verses

I *Ultimate Day*

Frail artefact, the gold-leaf bracken,
Tenuous as flame in sunlight,
Cuts stark against mouldering ditches,
The shivering ghost of the summer.

Sole marks of distance in a flat land,
Haystacks age into royal purple.

This ultimate day, colour of copper
And fire, burning haulm of autumn,
Is the dying throb of fertility's pulse.
Tomorrow the coldness will burst
In barbaric panoply over the marshes,
Steel; iron; weapons of death and winter.

II *Langdale Tarn*

Winds blow of which we know nothing
High in the black ice of the sky,
And beneath the green ice of the tarn
Unknown currents move the reflected clouds.

III *Ligurian Winter*

The leaves of the olives
Are tarnished silver
And their wet-soot branches
Are blotched with mould.

The wet mimosa
That has been axe-slivered
From grey lead branches
Weeps frozen gold.

From the ash dead hilltops
Clouds like smoke are sliding
Through rust-needled branches
Of pines gone iron cold.

IV *Dead Weed*

Dead weed beneath my feet
And pebbles flung up, dragged back
With grating lonely roar.

Dead weed beneath my feet
Black sea, grey sky, and white surf
Crashing to the shore.

Dead weed beneath my feet.
Stone that will be sand,
Sand that was stone before.

To See the Matter Clearly

(1968)

Gloria

However she's personified
Or represented,
I won't forget
How space expands
Until it can contain
A million goddesses or concepts.

Sophia, Anima, or Kali,
Black or white, death or wisdom,
The central fire
Or all-engulfing water,

My muse is in myself:
As past and future
Only exist
By my own need to think them,
This power is manifest
In her resplendent figure.

She makes me dance,
She frightens me at night
With horrors,
Leads me to the burning-place.

She stands behind the mountains
Like the sun,
And lifts her arms to show
That they are flesh,
That all this valley is alive
Because she wills it so.

The Muse

My muse is in myself: what does that mean?
I do not see myself as that great queen
I am at such pains to describe.

*

If such a question forms itself,
Can it be meaningless? Yesterday noon
The massiveness of mountains frightened me:

That solid rock could be bleached flat by sun,
Suspended for so long in static plunge
Down through clear air to edge of sea.

Surely the hour will come when they must crumble
And topple down the keystone of the gate
That leads to her domain.

*

This table where I'm writing must exist
When I don't see it – that dull twist
Of thought, I know, is finished.

But something in this room's more real
Than all that it contains, myself included.
Perhaps the muse sustains us for a game,

Plays with our feelings like a skein,
Draws memory from the table's wood
And brings the tree alive within my brain.

*

It seems my muse becomes more powerful
As I try to define her, spreads
Her influence beyond the moon and night,

That world of blood and clouds which until now
Has been the only place we've met,
And manifests herself in full sunlight.

*

73

In wood and stone I image her
Who in my own soul lives and grows:
That strength must be expressed when known;

As some use flesh and one beloved name
To clothe the force which they themselves contain,
The Muse invoking when they summon it.

The Chain

The chain links back and forward
No beginning is apparent
No part superior.
Chain, dance, or wheel.
To accept any emotion
As the real implies the truth
Of every sentiment.
Chain, wheel, or dance.
We cannot stop one part unless
Prepared to let the whole collapse,
That shudder of arrest which snaps
The links apart.
Wheel, dance, or chain.
We gave up freedom
When we joined the dance
And laid our own limbs
Down upon the wheel
And held our wrists out willingly
To take the chain.

Unseemly

I left my race and family
To learn about myself: that
Was my explanation. So I became
Unseemly and dishonourable.

I called myself a poet, reasoning
That poets are inhuman;
Use grit of others' suffering,
Even their own, to aid digestion.

In dreams I kill my child, welcome
Embraces of the incubus,
Do it for the experience.
Poems are my consolation.

Sleep-learning

All that I try to save him from
Is what he dreams about.
I watch his face
Each night emerging clearer,
Stern son who reads my dreams:
The dreams I had
And those my brother had
And which my parents learned from theirs,
Moving behind mauve lids
That seal his eyes.

He dreams I want to leave him,
Roams through night forests, desolate.
And I dream I've abandoned him:
First punish, then atone.
Next morning both our faces
Mark the change:

Mine with the guilty look of those
Who knowingly succumb to dreams,
And his the gaze
Of someone learning.

Fever Hospital

The fever pustules first appear
In creases and the hidden parts.
The war is far away, I am safe here.
I sit at home, I live where there is peace.
My child plays submarines and guns
Though I discourage him. But every day
He senses what I read in the newspapers.
Perhaps he knows more than I do.
He trains himself for his expected future.

The fever symptoms break in me
As fascination with destructiveness.
I watch the others – and let them act
What I am too fastidious
To execute myself: those drenching
surges of maliciousness, the dreams
Of torture – (while I disinfect
My fantasies by playing victim).

If I must purge myself of fever
By surrogates: the monkey-man,
The fascist, the politician, even
The householder and his dull omissions,
I spread the sickness just as much.
I mould the world as if I pressed
My form into a bed of wax
And called that shape my opposite;
As if external evil makes me good.
The country is at peace – at least I claim
That I am, though my dreams are troubled.

My child imagines dangers everywhere,
Demands to know the natural weapons
Of each creature, its protection.
For he was born into this fever hospital
And learns geography to make quite sure
Just where the tanks and airplanes are
Enacting the realities of power
Which I try to disclaim. It is no good.
The fever breeds within my blood.
This hectic flush must signal quarantine
To every corner of the universe.

Water

Water fills up empty places,
Smoothes all irregularities
Of surface, penetrates
As dew, as rain, as seeping tides,
Inexorably undermines,
When dammed compounds its power,
Insistent leveller.

The Spirit Moving on the Face of the Water

At first it seems to flow forward,
But sea's as rooted as a wheatfield,
Slides from crest to trough forever,
Heaves its shining mass
But never throws the rider.

Suspended in the bowl of continents
Ocean dreams of margin,

Nirvana of dissolution,
Spray flung onto stone –
The heavenly beaches of evaporation.

Waves goad the water
With the shape of freedom.

Fire

How hard at times to start the fire
Though wood is meant for burning.

How slow the fire takes hold, the wood seems iron.
Delighted children crowd around the chimney.

Dark smoke rose sluggishly above pine forests
But trees were safe – it was flesh burning.

I cannot stop my mind from dwelling on
Incineration, holocausts
Of witches, human torches, reeking light
That flickered on the faces of those watching
Such grim entertainment, without protest.

The napalm fire falls from the sky,
And those who did not aim it, nor have seen
Slow torture (the man may die, but
What he knows can be passed on and used),
Feel jealous. They stare into the flames
And plan their private pleasures.

Moloch extends his metal arms.
With old newspaper photos of the martyrs
I light my cigarette, and muse on those
Who saturate themselves with petrol
As if they cannot wait. The sign is fire,
It is ascendant, roars for ceremony.
The instruments lie heating in the braziers.

Wide-eyed

Blind chance, blind fate,
Blind destiny, blind guides,
Blind paths and alleys.
Blind hope and blind malevolence.
Blind faith. Blind Justice
Clutching at her scales,
Blind love. Wide-eyed jealousy.

Love and Justice

Justice holds scales, she weighs
All words and gestures, knows
The value of each action:
How some appreciate, while others
Drain away the capital
Of trust and good report.

Love watches whom he loves
And learns the traits that mark her,
Her singularity.
Whether they mean that she is good
Or evil, is no concern of his;
Let Justice be the judge.

The Midas Touch

Because love makes me feel a fraud,
My mind can't lose its habits of accountancy.
However much I check the books I know
Nothing I do deserves reward.

I calculate relationships
In columns clearly double-lined,
And dole my love out grudgingly,
As if a rare commodity,
Disturbing when defined.

I cannot balance what they mean to me
– Who claim they love me –
And what I give them:
Know love cannot be weighed,
Nor offered as a surety,
Nor tested like a doubtful coin.

Oh, to dissolve my ire
Like pearl in vinegar,
And shed my fear,
A final, burning tear
To melt the gold-dust from my face;
To lose my killing touch
And earn love's grace.

To See the Matter Clearly

Through reason's telescope the figures
Seem distinct and small.
A jeweller's precision must have
Formed the cunning limbs, instilled
The counterfeit of feeling that
Articulates those manikins.
Their piping voices barely reach
My ear, and eye is strained
By such elaborate enamelling,
The play of each expressive feature.

It's easy, though, to change the focus,
Be overwhelmed by giant agony:
Huge soft pitted faces mouthing
Pain, and clumsy yearning gestures.
Shift glass again, turn down the sound,
Retreat to that high vantage point
Of reason, leave them
Thrashing in the undergrowth
That through the telescope
Shines beautiful as jewels.

Bacchante

Addicted to exhaustion, nicotine
And quarrelling at night
Vibrations from nerve-circuits
In her legs and feet

Inappropriate rituals
Of a maenad's courtship
A violent raver

Drench with the urge to leap
From twisted sheets and blankets
Overturning ashtrays and dregs
Of coffee left in saucers

Run frenzied round the bed
Till poisoned by her fantasy
She sees him absolutely Orpheus

The Weather

She said: 'A perfect day.' 'Too fine,'
He answered. 'Though should it stay
So cold, less chance of change.'
'Perhaps,' she murmured dubiously.

Analogies drawn from the weather
Seduce by presupposing unity
Of passion and environment:
So fateful and significant.
If she stayed cool, his words implied,
That might avert catastrophe.
But she still wondered if instead
Her self-control was understood
Only as lack of ardency.

'Goodbye,' she said, as casually as
She could muster. She thought he loved her
Most when she showed most indifference.
But if she let him go like this,
Her kiss so sweet – they might indeed
Be talking of the weather.

Night Mare

I shut the moon behind the door:
Bathroom floor so light I could not sleep
So I had closed the moon away.
But she was straining
And the door was creaking.

Alone in bed I felt so cold,
Full moon in winter's coldest time
And you had gone away. Full moon
Was my love's enemy:

You spend full moon with her
New moon with me. Perhaps
New moon has more potentiality
But I was cold with fear.

Naked behind the door, black hair
Around her head like branches
Of a winter tree, white body
Full and glistening,
The night mare waited,
Pawed the shining tiles and waited,
Menacing, and silently.

Uncertain

Because I talk about my life with you
With you, that changes it. You say I want
Approval, totally. It must be true
That viewing matter changes it. The patterns
Shift as if responding to disturbance.
What I learned from Heisenberg is true:
Viewing matter changes it. Results
Cannot be modified, controlled, predicted.

The mechanism which I once set up
For watching me with you, to magnify
All motives, analyse each thought and action,
Has made the wounds I'm bleeding through.
Examining one's life is sure to change it,
And I'm exhausted by this repetition
Of lessons I already knew: once
Change begins, then everything's uncertain.

Paradise

Against death-fear I can oppose
Only a steel engraving I remember,
Some lost craftsman's detailed labour,
Lines and dots and miniscule cross-hatching,
Clouds open to reveal the august throne,
Massed tiers of angels, chanting cherubim,
Trumpeting the glory that is shown
As one circle of peace on storm-tossed sea,
And there a boat, its sails unfurled,
Saved from the horrid perils of the deep –
Each detail that can be recalled
Of Sunday afternoons with picture books
And half-forgotten pledges: Paradise!
The boat will make safe harbour, all reach home,
In heavenly fields the worm be overcome.

Air

Gills collapsing inwards
Choking suffocation
The last failing bubbles

Its filming eye white-glazed
Brown blood on the green grass
Thick as enamel

That gasping dream
Of lungs and adaptation
That killing air

Old Man, Old Woman

He's sheathed his life with amber of regret,
Aesthetic of avoiding depth
Through calm extension. By rarely acting
He has lived the longest. He made an ally
Out of time, a pact to let
Wounds heal by just enduring them
And all desires slowly fade to death.

Her face has registered such bitterness
Those fine sardonic lines bite through the muscle.
Only her eyes can change: they sadden
When she wants to smile, and her grandchildren
Whisper that she looks just like a monkey.

A Missing Word

Again that one particular word seems lacking.
Almost on my tongue it still eludes me
Escapes to other time or language
And leaves me stammering, empty-mouthed,
Though sure that it must be exactly
The only word for what I need to say.

All things begin by yielding, loosening.
I see what could be merely crumbs of soil
Nudged at first by a thin swirl of water
Dissolving, sliding, losing their consistency;
Or a great flood surging in full spate –

Earth and water in suspension
Boiling swell of brown disintegrating
Swales and upland all engulfed by swash
Of water every solid sluiced away.

I ease my mouth around the sounds to try them
Though I know they won't assuage me.
Mud still clings heavy to that hidden word.

The Hero's Mother

She put her son into the fire
But he assured her that it did not hurt.
She watched him as the flames climbed high
And his calm face gazed forward,
Smiling, seeming lost in thought.

The fire threw shadows round the cave.
Blackness transmuted into gold.
Until he swooned she held him up.
Now he would be invulnerable;
Her child had the protection of a god.

Sure that she acted for his honour
She did not tremble, felt no fear,
Partaking in this secret rite
Whose meaning in her dream was clear,
But which she lost, waking in horror.

Seven Sevens

I

The wind relies on ceaselessness
The wind disperses everything
The wind may blow with gentleness
Or tear trees from their ancient moorings
But violent or insidious
The wind achieves its purposes
Revealing sky's true clarity

II

Breath like a shell to my ear
Your mouth blows seas and tides
Spangled blood moves up internal beaches
Washes through warm hollows

That wind filters through my bones
As sand escapes between closed fingers
Those waves will carry me far out

III

Convolvulus wind flower neon blue
Deep in its throat the colour of raw meat
Is opposite to such aethereal hue
Convulsive   Tissues clutch convulsively
And tainted beauty darkens glistens
Torn by wind to separate images
Of petals crushed of lips bruised blue

IV

Truth does not imply duration
Pure desire is liberation
From time and other tyranny
Truth of desire is anarchy
The hazard of annihilation
Indifferent to expectation
Or promise of stability

V

I feel your heart where you can feel my finger
That steady throb of life
I'll mark its place with ink between two ribs
Then you can always find it
But mine seems muffled by my breast perhaps
So grant an equal favour
Show me exactly where to plunge the knife

VI

Action sometimes leads to clarity
Reaction brings its own inertia
Stagnation deepens melancholy
Thought-nets dredge through scum of dreams
While the tide ebbs ebbs but yet reveals
No treasure on the dun brown foreshore
Nothing but wet sand and still receding

VII

Whichever way I turn the exit's blocked
I circle rat trapped deep within a pit
My mind whirls round remorse as sharp
As those wires piercing the rat's neck
Remorse sharp teeth the hopeless bite
When reparation is impossible
Remorse and grief weep on each other's neck

Definitions

I

Because I will not look
Refuse to see
How I define myself
By each day's actions,
Insist on moving
With averted gaze;
A false sleep-walker
Without the confidence
Of trance, only
Its irritation,
(Those avoidance tactics),
I hide behind
Accelerating need
For poetry;
As if to speak the problem
Is to solve it.

Meanwhile, the roof slopes steeper.
The somnambulist
Must draw upon
Her deepest strength
To carry on
Nocturnal wandering.
Frail curtains flutter
From her open window.
The house seems calm.

She hopes that all are sleeping.
That no one will wake up
And shut her out.

There is no dignity
In such a role:
An easy prey
To all night creatures
And ambiguities
Of moonlight.
The landscape changes
Under those deceptive rays.
But she is hypocrite
Because she knows
The house stands solid,
Can draw upon
Her daytime knowledge
To map safe divagations.

Exhausted by these
Shadowy encounters,
I leave the management
Of daily life
Open to hazard,
Know the futility
Of being unequipped
To meet the present
Except through words:
Equivocations,
False relations,
Definitions;
In metaphors
And images
Time and existence
Bleed away.

II

Because I will not look, refuse to see
How I define myself by each day's actions,
Insist on moving with averted gaze:
A false sleep-walker, without the confidence of trance,
Only its irritation (those avoidance tactics),
I hide behind accelerating need for poetry;
As if to speak the problem is to solve it.

Meanwhile, the roof slopes steeper.
The somnambulist must draw upon
Her deepest strength to carry on
Nocturnal wandering. Frail curtains flutter
From her open window. The house seems calm.
She hopes that all inside are sleeping,
That no one will wake up and shut her out.

There is no dignity in such a role:
An easy prey to all night creatures
And ambiguities of moonlight.
The landscape changes under those deceptive rays.
But she is hypocrite, because she knows
The house stands solid, can draw upon
Her daytime knowledge to map safe divagations.

Exhausted by these shadowy encounters,
I leave the management of daily life
Open to hazard, know the futility
Of being unequipped to meet the present
Except through words: equivocations, false
Relations, definitions; in metaphors
And images, time and existence bleed away.

The Region's Violence

(1973)

The Climber

That light before the dawn,
Almost the light of negatives,
All grey, when everything
Shows clear and isolate,
So frail, so separate each twig
Each stone upon her path,
So lonely without colour yet.

The wind is strongest then,
Howls down the mountain side,
Is bitter cold. After the night,
The deepest tiredness assails
That climber who had thought
To reach the heights before
This moment of life's ebb.

Perhaps new day will never come.
Such light prefigures something else,
Another night behind
The distant peaks, or some
Further ordeal, demand,
Upon what strength she cannot feel
But hopes to find.

snow poem

      birds stream over the houses opposite
I watch from my window
      one veers, passes through glass as if it were smoke
settles on my table

      it is snowing
I stare at whirling flakes with such intensity
they drift into the room
      transform it to a paper-weight

snow covers my papers
    the bird prints patterns with his feet
hieroglyphs appropriating
    what I've written

the bird flies up   one flake
    approaches, huge, revealing
    its precision and its symmetry
before it muffles me

God's Language

Angels have no memory,
God's language no grammar.
He speaks continually,
All words variations
Of his name, the world a web
Of names, each consonant
Proclaims a further meaning;
The unacceptable
Also the true, beyond
Time's bondage. Thus angels
Forget all contradictions,
Accepting every statement
As a commentary.
Their purpose is to gaze
Upon God's works, and listen,
Until the day that he
Pronounce the name: Messiah.

Lilith

Lilith, Adam's first companion,
Assumed her equality.
For this she was banished.

God had created her
From the same earth as Adam.
She stood her ground, amazed
By the idea of difference.

Adam and God were embarrassed,
Humiliated. It was true –
They had been formed
At the same time, the two
Halves of His reflection.

Her expectations
Should have seemed justified.
But Adam needed to understand God.
A creature must now worship him –
And be resentful as he was.
God encouraged this.

To guard His mystery, God
Made Adam swoon.
There, when he awoke,
Awaited Eve, the chattel.

Eyes downcast, his phallus
The first thing she noticed.
The snake reminded her of it.

That nagging ache in his side
Where the rib was extracted
(In memory of which
The soldier thrust his spear)
Keeps Adam irritable.

Lilith's disgrace thus defined
Good and evil. She would be

Outside, the feared, the alien,
Hungry and dangerous.
His seed and Eve's fruit
At hazard from her rage.

Good wives make amulets
Against her, to protect themselves.
Lilith is jealous.

The Dolphins

No day, no night,
Tides drift me here from somewhere else.
I find myself at my desk
Or the kitchen, in bed in the darkness.
What time is it, where have I come from,
Why am I returning?

No connection
Between these surfacings.
Like two dolphins twisting silently
In deep water, my thoughts grapple.
They separate to breathe, then plunge
Back into battle.

Out of the taut shield
Of underbelly, suave curve shaped
By three pressures: water, intestine, muscle,
His pale penis, unfurled
Into its own dimension, flaunts
The freedom of a blossom.

Her belly tapers to a faint cleft,
Dimple of generation – which must gape wide
In birth, when clouds of blood
Disperse through water –
A flower, a torn poppy
With falling petals.

Smooth and broad as a baby's battering ram
Of skull, the bulge of their heads.
And the same bland eyes, amused
Perhaps through accident of folds –
Yet so ironic. In love
Their eyes are closed.

Language exists, but
I cannot understand the dolphins' language.
What do they say as they couple?
Below the water's demarcation line
Conflict is muffled. But questions rise
In swathes of air-bubbles.

They cannot survive
In either element alone, unmixed.
Their love is enacted between breaths,
Between leaps, in mid-ocean depths –
Where every contact jolts
The story's ending.

Isolates

Apart from present slights
And the more distant, larger,
Still effective hurts,

They brood about the bomb,
The planet's imminent destruction,
All human insignificance;

Those city isolates,
In parks, on benches,
Absorbed beyond awareness

Of the rain, and how it plasters
Strands of thinning hair
Against their vengeful temples.

Neighbour

Too much happens to some people,
Leaves them no time to deepen.

They are completely different
From the established citizen.

Oh, the houses, the journeys,
That have taken my energies.

But then I was younger
And believed myself stronger.

Now I seem to exist
In a torrent of wind

Incurably foreign
As an insect or Martian,

Cannot understand the purpose
Or note more than the surface

Of my neighbour's true quality –
He remains a mystery.

So little happens to some people
And yet they know a secret

Which sustains them, which I cannot
Learn, or long ago forgot.

Sleepers

That was yesterday. Since then
My part of the world slept.
The village lay, horizontal,
Each lapped by his own dream,

Never more unified, more private.
Apart, side by side (if the walls
Should dissolve or fall they'd seem
Cocoons of dreams, mysterious
To an alien observer),
They're linked to other times,
To distant places, stars –
Their sheeted bodies pledges left
As proof the indwelling spirit
Will surely return; dim floats
On the night's black surface
That indicate the exact spot
Where the dreamer sank down
And will rise; to resume his life,
Name, and relationships –
Tomorrow's limitations.

Lake and Island

A lake is the opposite to an island.
Near the middle of the lake is an island.
Held between mountains, the lake seems an island.
A church stands alone on the island,
Roofless, a fountain of silence
That overflows its brim of time-worked stone,
Replenishes the lake and fruits the island.

Two Blue Dresses

What I should wear outweighs
Almost every speculation,
As if clothes could disguise.
A method to evade other
Uncertainties, and yet

The details of a costume
Recollected serve to fix
The character of past events.

The era of that blue silk dress
Totally different from
The year I fell in love, revived
My aunt's old cashmere blue.
Its bias cut and open-work,
That silver buckle-clasp
Low on the hip, enchanted me
Though out of fashion then.
The very fact became supporting.
I felt a heroine –
And just as well, those first weeks
Of my first, unfortunate,
Short-lived affair.

The stylish frock, all ruched,
Had skirt and sleeves puffed out.
I can remember how
I stood and posed before the glass
Entranced, and half afraid
To see reflected in my eyes
The probability
Of loneliness, but more, the wish
For all that came to pass.
I recognised the destiny
I still attempt to grasp.
I nerved myself to welcome it.

That moment, proud in finery,
Has seared my memory
More deeply than the tears I shed
In cashmere, in despair –
The end and the commencement
Of my girlhood, two
Shop-window mannequins
Who almost seem alive.

My Grandparents

Museums serve as my grandparents' house.
They are my heritage – but Europe's spoils,
Curios from furthest isles,
Barely compensate the fact
That all were dead before I was alive.

Through these high, dust-free halls, where
Temperature, humidity, access,
Are regulated, I walk at ease.
It is my family's house, and I
Safe and protected as a favoured child.

Variety does not exhaust me.
Each object witness to its own
Survival. The work endures beyond
Its history. Such proof supports me.
I do not tire of family treasures.

Because no one remembers who they were,
Obscure existences of which I am
The final product, I merit
Exhibition here, the museum's pride,
Memorial to their legend.

My Hands

Even the most banal demand
From one with hands like mine
Asks too much. My palms seethe –
Blood so close beneath the skin
That plumps their sides, soft flesh incised
By stars and crescents under
Every finger, moon-creased at heel
Of thumb. Sometimes I've wondered
If one day I will show stigmata.

Each palm's centre is a square
Of white. When I strain fingers back
The lines flush red like beading cuts –
A fate new-made each time
I query it. Unless I deem them
Beautiful, my hands must seem
So violent, so timorous,
Stubborn and unreliable.
Therefore those who praise them win me.

My Eyes

A child, already I admired
Those eyes set deep in sockets, skin
Beneath stretched fine and dark and taut
Across the watched nerve's flicker, haughty
Arch of brow and curve of hooded lid.

My eyes look like that now – accusing
Mournful eyes which glare when I essay
A covert glance, eyes which betray
Because they neither show a hurt
Nor disguise curiosity.

But they can weep with such discretion
I forfeit sympathy – as if
I feared the taint of cowardice
More than other definition – insist
On staring out whatever happens.

I use my eyes to guard and to repel.
My eyes are witnesses. I think
I am invisible – except my eyes.
Is there a Perseus brave enough
To gaze unflinching at the basilisk?

Fire Queen

Unseen, snow slides from overladen boughs.
Spume of flakes, flurry of light, cold smoke:
Kaleidescope of crystal and lead and flame.
Then silence again as it sinks,
Weightless, lost, white into whiteness, down
To permafrost encasing molten turbulence.

That core answers the sun-spots, flares
When her impotence most torments – she, with
Her presumptions, her gestures, who has chosen
This place rather than any other
To expose herself to the gnawing ulcer
Of her own nature. Such is her kingdom,

Fire-queen of the absolute north,
Who rules by satire, inertia, disdain;
Touch blunted to ice, ears sealed,
Sight gone, reflection congealed, mirror
Shatters aeons ago, rather than see
Merely a pattern of line and colour, flat

As the diagram of what a face might be –
Which to recognise would mean to accept
The clamour of voices imploring, complaining,
But silent, that rise from her brain like steam
From a tub-full of churning laundry.
But silent. Her thoughts – unspoken, ignored.

Their heat is the power that freezes, motor
Of her repression-machine, refrigerator
Of frightful patience, rigid mastodon-throne,
Sealed and invisible ice-pyramid,
Red-hot iron-maiden of self-hatred
She's trapped inside by refusing to listen.

Screams settle like snow and never thaw.
Branches petrified under their burden
Of murdered desires. She sits like Lot's wife,
Ambitionless as death, perfect, absorbed
Forever by her silent incantation,
Beyond the need for sanction. Or praise.

Pigeons at Villa Belmonte

After he mounted her, wings
Fluttering with joy of domination,
Neck iridescent with coppery
Lombardy green and the terra-
Cotta of the Villa Belmonte (she
Smaller, darker, reserved, the same
Grey surrounding the shutters),
She strutted onto his neck as
If in casual imitation, hopped off,
Then up and down, across, a few more
Times. They bent their heads towards
Each other, seemed affectionate,
Their burbling cries conjugal.

I've read that pigeons caged and left
Will pluck each other bare and bleeding,
That they're more murderous
Than wolves, with no inborn restraint,
No code for peace which might allow
Retreat or dignified surrender.
Strange choice of symbol used for love
And tenderness, and yet, because
They're beautiful, they serve.

The Betrothal

What is this, why do they wrestle in the grass,
Tear aside the clothes that separate their skins?
If she wishes to defend herself, why
Do her limbs melt, why does she strain closer?
Even the earth is more caressing than he.
Crumbling, it blots her cool from his sweat,
Its dryness soothes the chafe of their grinding.
And the rosebay-silk, whiteness unfurling
From split pods, confirms that love is precious.

And he, what is he doing? He's forgotten
Who she is. Something is pulling him down
To the earth's centre, there's an opening;
The grasses seem to be lashing his back,
Forcing him to push deeper and deeper.
Hair in his mouth and a voice distract.
The strength of this impulse to murder becomes
The fervent, whispered phrase, 'I love you'.

Somewhere else love must be real, but not here.
This is beyond them both. They search each other's
Eyes, but only find themselves, minute,
Plunging through expanded pupils to nothing.
Each iris complicated as a stellar map,
Once embarked into that flecked immensity,
Empty silence echoes from the void
In answer to the question, 'Do you love me?'

The field is so deep, its soil a talc of bones.
He's far from her, out between the planets,
But his embrace makes her one with the earth.
She seeks comfort from the dead who support her.
If she could hear them talk, they might explain
What love is – or perhaps the shadow of grass
and rosebay on his back, like hieroglyphs,
Could be deciphered, if she exchange
The rest of her life in payment for the answer.

Silence

When you ask for consolation
From one of them, burnt children
Who were never loved – or so
The explanation runs –
They do not understand. Perhaps,
Like speech, it is a skill
Which must be learned at its specific
Moment. Once past, nothing
Yet known can activate
That latent aptitude.
The child remains both deaf and dumb;
The one you turned towards –
a loud, gesticulating mute.

How they torment, who always
Must retreat, as if attacked
By such demands, whose last defence
Becomes exposure of a pain
They moan and rage is fiercer far
Than yours. Heart-broken, you muffle
Your own complaint, adjusting
To the region's violence,
Leaving grief abused, unspoken –
Until, beyond the reefs
Of hopelessness, nothing seems lacking
In this solitude. You've grown
Accustomed to the silence.

Disguise

She took the brush, began
To paint herself all black.
The bristles dragged in streaks
Between the hairs along her arms.

106

She paddled paint
Over her breasts.
How that would frighten him
When he undid her dress.

Her cheeks were soon blacked out.
One stroke across the brow
Another down her nose
The powder caked her lips
Thickened beneath her chin.
Its taste was bitter.

But she was painted out,
A ghost, a negative,
Released by this disguise
From everything (yes:
Life, Death, Love,
Him; everything).

Last Chance, Last Hope
(i.m. A.G.)

She clung to him like a witch
To her broomstick, like
A soldier to his angel.
She fell into his arms
Like jumping from a burning ship –
Without hesitation – from
A plane spiralling down,
Every control frozen, locked.

She wound her arms around him
Like a woman whom the sea
Has rejected already
Two times, knowing the third
Would be fatal. A small smile
On her lips at the memory
Of the waves, the flames, the shock,

The turbulence; nausea
From the drinks and ointments
They applied to her body
Before that launching.
It seems so distant.

He will support her,
Carry her high and away –
Her saviour, source of delight,
Last chance, last hope,
Her instrument of power –
With nothing left to pay
For other miracles
Should this one fail.

Velázquez' *Christ in the House of Martha and Mary*

You stare out of the picture, not at me.
Your sad, resentful gaze is fixed on what
I only see reflected in the mirror
On the wall behind your shoulder, perspective
Through an archway cut from sandy slabs of stone
The same warm brown as your bodice.
That old servant by your side is whispering
Admonitions and consolation – her
Country wisdom. But your attention lapses
From those words of resignation as much
As from the pestle lax within your hand,
The plate of fish, white eggs and pewter spoon,
Wrinkled chilli and broken garlic cloves
Strewn across the table: this, your world,
Precise, material – all you yearn to leave,
Though fear and duty hold you. You cannot find
Courage for the negligence of faith
To justify an action similar –
And so what right to join your sister there?

Beardsley's *St Rose of Lima*

Levitation's diagram
Charted in lines of black on white.
The jet of energy
Propelling her seems effortless.
Surging drapery conceals her feet:
The image Buñuel once used
When son dreams of his mother,
Woman pure, impossible.
Weight of meat bends back her wrists:
Acceptance of whatever comes.
The cotton robe a plinth of folds
Heavy as moulded plaster,
Wet-pack sheet; face an oval blank
Of ecstasy, the meeting point
Of saintliness, carnality.
Saint Rose of Lima smiles
So meltingly, and Jesus
Seems as beautiful as Tristan.

Tanya

(Ché Guevera's last companion)

How long did you lie hidden by the water's edge,
Nymph of corruption, brittle darkening lily,
Lips drawn back into the major grimace of death;
Nymph of ideology, still unperfected
Never-to-be imago of bright revolution,
With the frail elegance of a discarded chrysalis
In the rushes, a plundered mummy-case,
Or a disinterred sacrifice to Anubis,

As if old legends were true, and the body crumbles,
Detritus of a soul that wings to Utopia
To soothe its frenzy for the unattainable –
Having been unsheathed by the one fatal bullet
Whose searing metal entry metamorphised
Dream and desire and turmoil into rotting flesh.

The Ox

Yet still I tread the same straw
Deeper in the mud, still tethered
Must repeat the circle.
Monotony. But sullen rage
Does not abate (gadflies torment
The ox), increases rather
As my feet grow heavy, clogged,
Their weight a penalty imposed
To make the task more irksome.

I want to build. Straw and mud should
Have become by now the bricks
I need in order to construct
The perfect city – (my sweat
Has baked them): vision which
I follow round the central post
And further down that awesome pit
The only monument as yet
My circling has created.

Self-conquest, Heroes and Dragons

Vain effort, when inspired by vanity,
Vain emulation, driven from such source,
Self-conquest can be easily defined:
Aggression's misdirected force.
Deception thrives on just this conflict.

Vanity and the desire to conquer it
Seep from the same chthonic spring:
Vanity and emulation, intertwined
Like sodden roots, almost block the exit.

False dreams, fear, and vanity:
In vain they are approached with violence.
Such stance implies the hero – dragons breed
Especially to flatter and delude him.

St George may win the maiden, but gains
Nothing else. Meretricious symbol
Of self-conquest: the townsfolk clapping,
The painter ready at his easel.

Vain of his progress, a hermit wields his scourge
More single-mindedly. Thus vanity
Is banished, he consoles the bleeding flesh.
Every night dragons wrestle in his dreams.

Finally, vanity seems intrinsic.
Attempts to overcome it paralyse.
Vanity tells the truth regardless.
Confrontation is a vain manoeuvre:
Another trap of pride.

Rapture

Lead-footed on the ocean bed
He understood reality.
Intoxication comes with movement.
Recklessness is ecstasy.
Bright weeds and fronds caress
His weightless limbs. Air-bubbles
Rise like beads of mercury.
The visions crowd around, pale
Fishes' fins seem angels' wings,
And grottos low in shadowed reefs
Tempt onward beyond range
Of oxygen or energy.
He wrenches off his mask,
Deluded. Drifts upward....

Then

Unused and exhausted
By hours of silence
My body has stiffened
– Unmoving, inert in my chair,
Paralysed, convalescent –
A robot, an idol, a prisoner.
Then some circuit flickers, jarred
By introspection's boredom,
And memories stir, random, unconnected.

My mind becomes victim
Of a hazard profound and meaningless
As the encounter which produced me.
If the fusion of those cells can indicate
Intention, then whatever memory,
Partial as lightning, illuminates my brain,
Is neither more nor less significant.

Oh lovely sand, dun, sliding dry
Through my fingers, leaving a white powder,
Fine as flour, on my sun-browned skin.
Oh bleached wood. I remember your greyness
Utterly now, grain harder and raised.
Beach-wood, dessicated, salt-encrusted.

Why do I see it so clearly? I crumbled a shell,
Looked vaguely around, then walked again.
What association brought it back –
That memory, so trivial, so satisfactory –
To make these hours of silence, stillness, and confusion
The very nourishment to feed my spirit.

I surrender to every resentment and fear,
Accept the recurrence of hate and envy,
The numbness, the passivity,
As part of myself, as my necessity,
The other half of my mind – no dark, no light,
No past, no future: no past if I can feel that sand
And see the waves, weed, foam, and lift my head
And stare – which I did not do then – toward the horizon.

On the Moon

For those in thrall to the moon
Horizons are restricted,
Eye's evidence conflicts
With knowledge and reality.
Steep curvatures, abrupt appearances
And vanishings. Imagination
On the moon takes short breaths
But leaps higher. Shadows are absolute.
No nuance between black and white,
Dust so dry that anything dropped
Is lost, engulfed, without memorial,
And fluid tides swung round
A neighbouring, ambiguous planet.
Beneath the moon's surface
The entire past lies hidden,
Its centre a jumble of toys, tears,
Journeys, buried lovers and friends,
Its core a heart petrified.
Moon's day shifts slow
Across my brain, from empty zone
Of fear to plenitude,
Cauterising its quarters,
Moving between two zeros.

Falling

I must let go, I must relax
My hands, dissolve my fear of falling.
My struggles overbalance me.

And should I fall, although no one
Would rescue me, no Anthony*
With outstretched hand or cloak –

The safety faith might guarantee,
The hope belief would give (along with
Punishment and category) –

The joy to have released my grip,
The stillness in that hurtling,
Might seem to last eternally.

* St Anthony of Padua who, among his many other roles is the patron saint
of builders, and invoked for protection against falls. There is a local legend that
while working on the roof of the cathedral at Palma de Mallorca, a workman slipped
and called out, 'St Anthony, save me!' A great hand reached out from the heavens
and held him suspended in mid-air and a voice asked, 'Which St Anthony?' At the
reply, 'San Antonio Abat', (a saint directly connected to the island), the hand drew
back, the voice thundered: 'Wrong Anthony!', and the wretched man fell to his death.
(a story told by Robert Graves)

A Fairy Story

The princess in the fairy story
Discovered that a happy ending
Had unexpected consequences.
The castle in the wood concealed
A certain chamber. Her knight revealed
A taste for flagellation. And when
He tired of protests and capitulation,
He rode away – until another kingdom,
Dragon, maiden who could not be won
By any simpler method, was stumbled on.

He then would stay, enter the lists.
He loved the risk, the praise, that combat
Or the guessing game where death
Remained the final forfeit. He loved
A distraught princess, never could resist.
Their fear attracted, their wavering spirit.

Once upon a time their taming was
The reason for his quest, but now exhaustion,
Boredom, made him pleased his dragon-
Surrogate could test them first.
If they survived the monster's ardent breath,
That smoky taint made them delicious.

The rescued princesses compared
Sad stories, boasted of their sufferings,
Exaggerating the ordeal.
They dressed each other's hair, changed
Robes and jewels, waited impatiently
To see the girl who next would join them.

One day, outside the crumbling walls
Of some obscure and unimportant
Principality, the knight was bested.
The dragon fled, dragging bruised coils
Through hedges, across muddy plough-land.
The princess would not follow him,
But turned her back and went inside the town.
The watchers were not more nonplussed.

The knight rode home, sent messages
To all his friends. They drank and sang,
Tortured his wives – it was an orgy.
Next day he bade farewell to each
Blood-brother, each noble companion,
Vowed his remaining years to penance
Somewhere far from this vile shambles.

But first, before he set off with his squire
Down that faint narrow path which lured
Deep into the misty forest,
A splendid tomb must be constructed:
Memorial to those princesses,
Obedient victims of his destiny.
The monument still stands, although
The castle fell to ruins long ago.
The knight died on a battlefield.
Their legend: fatalistic, gory,
Fit matter for a fairy story.

Progress

The doctor tightens up a bolt.
His monster winces as the screw bites deeper.
It's pain that makes those arms reach out,
Jerks both legs forward clumsily.
'That's progress!' the mad doctor cries in glee.
Almost he does embrace his creature.
The monster's in a swoon of agony,
The circuits now connected generate
Self-loathing. Doc does not know about
Such variation from his blueprints –
It is an error: introspection
Was not included in the plan.
When pressure is relaxed, the monster
Slumps back, useless to his master,
But praising every god of progress.

The Field

The field is trampled over utterly.
No hidden corner remains unchurned.
Unusable henceforth for pasture:
Sheep and cattle must feed elsewhere.

The field was torn by battle, dull
Explosions, trenches dug for shelter,
Vehicles which wheeled, reversed,
Hunted down the last resistance.

The field is strewn with bones and metal.
Earth which had not felt the air
During millenia, is now revealed
To every element and influence.

The undersoil surprises by its richness.
In battle's lull, at night, the farmer crawls
To estimate what might be salvaged
Of his lone field's potentiality.

If he survives, the field holds promise
Of great abundance, a yield
Unprecedented as all he hopes for.
The field is fertile. He must survive.

The Lambs

The lambs are separated from their mothers.
Bleating is louder than birdsong or engine.
And on the marsh, the mother sheep are restive,
The shepherd warns us, for their lost young ones.

The children ask if they will recognise
Each other, later in the year, at pasture
In some green field where they are put together?
I say I wonder, and both fall silent.

Throughout the night they huddled by the hedges
Moaning, awake – and yet the children slept
As peacefully as lambs should, undisturbed:
My own child, and the one whose mother's dead.

At last the wind drowns out their agitation.
Quiet again, the house seems usual.
Why do I feel obliged to make
A soothing story from such harsh truths?

The White Bird

After great grief, how slowly
Ordinary feelings then return.
All daily matters must be learned again
After such strain, such effort.

Uncertain yet if more than life was saved,
Remembrance of bird-song is salvaged.
Perhaps it was a message, but
Survival's concentration deafened.

It might be madness, this conviction.
Crisis engulfs. Surely not one bird
Could last on that mid-ocean rock
When battered by so fierce a tempest.

Hope is a white bird, but fear saw only
Hurtling water mounting upwards,
Green wall blocking land and sky,
The terror of reversed direction.

When storm abates, all drifting wreckage
Must be gathered and examined. While
Waiting for that bird to sing again,
Hope strengthens and adorns her shelter.

Freedom Defined

Freedom cannot be seen against hostility,
        it fades and bleaches out,
        pales to the camouflage of hatred.
Freedom includes delight at recognising
        that there is hardly anything
        to be desired.
Freedom, the great desire consuming every other.
Freedom has no companions or relationships.
Freedom for any purpose becomes limitation.
Freedom from needs is death.

Freedom from love is death.
Freedom from time is immortality –
        the realm of animals and saints
                        – or death.

Words and Letters

Comic or tragic, prose
Or poetry, I use
The same few letters.
They are my tools, also
The raw material.

I seek the words which will
Define the Word: scoop out
The clay with clay, hack stone
With stone, drill deep for metal.
Each force must meet another
Equal force, the paradox
Where truth confronts a truth
As logical, and yet
Totally dissimilar.

Beneath the words are other
Words, behind the marks
Upon this paper other
Shapes, between the letters
Links which might dissolve
So easily, and then unite
Into quite other words,
Assume a pattern
Just as satisfying.

The letters dance before
My eyes, they dazzle me.
But I shall always seek
What they keep hiding:
This game is final.

Poem

First it's a week, then a month, then a year.
I can tell myself there's nothing to fear –
That even a year is as nothing compared
To the length of a life. But empty time
Augments, has its own demands and rights.
The fear itself becomes my life unless
I leave some mark to prove I was here
Except these scabs I've worried off
The wound I won't allow to heal – but flaunt,
Preserve, admire, and call it art.

Grace-notes

My solemn simplicities, my vows,
My protestations. Tum-te-tum…
Self-accusations. I don't know how
To free myself, to overcome.
Except sometimes, a bird or a tree,
The light on the marsh – direct,
Without equivocation – speak
Of a power that seeks no effect
Outside itself, existing purely,
For which there are no synonyms.
It's a zone I approach unsurely,
That harsh place – where no hymning
Can drown the weak, explaining voice,
Nor grace-notes disguise the wrong choice.

Another Full Moon

(1976)

Vertical

Who told me my place?
It takes generations
To breed such a true believer,
Centuries to produce
Someone who instinctively knew
The only movement possible
Was up or down. No space
For me on the earth's surface:
Horizontal equates with delusive
When only the vertical
Remains open to my use. But
I am released by language,
I escape through speech:
Which has no dimensions,
Demands no local habitation
Or allegiance, which sets me free
From whomsover's definition:
Jew. Woman. Poet.

The Other

Whatever I find if I search will be wrong.
I must wait: sternest trial of all, to sit
Passive, receptive, and patient, empty
Of every demand and desire, until
That other, that being I never would have found
Though I spent my whole life in the quest, will step
From the shadows, approach like a wild, awkward child.

And this will be the longest task: to attend,
To open myself. To still my energy
Is harder than to use it in any cause.
Yet surely she will only be revealed
By pushing against the grain of my nature
That always yearns for choice. I feel it painful
And strong as a birth in which there is no pause.

I must hold myself back from every lure of action
To let her come closer, a wary smile on her face,
One arm lifted – to greet me or ward off attack
(I cannot decipher that uncertain gesture).
I must even control the pace of my breath
Until she has drawn her circle near enough
To capture the note of her faint reedy voice.

And then as in dreams, when a language unspoken
Since times before childhood is recalled
(When I was as timid as she, my forgotten sister –
Her presence my completion and reward),
I begin to understand, in fragments, the message
She waited so long to deliver. Loving her I shall learn
My own secret at last from the words of her song.

The Lace-wing

Does the lace-wing see me? I stare
Into its pin-point ruby eyes, head on,
At its bristly mouth-parts, my nose brushing
Antennae; the frail body and intricate
Veined wings an often-cited, not
Quite clinching, proof of God's existence.

When I look away the lace-wing turns
Abruptly, as if dismissed or freed.
Its shoulder-pivot swings a thread-leg forward.
It moves briskly across my paper,
Then disappears under a corner.

The intensity of our mutual
Examination exhausted me.
We almost exchanged identities.
Our pupils throbbed with the same shared
Awe, acknowledgement and curiosity.
We met beyond confine of size or species.

Next day, the lace-wing still is here.
It clings to the window-frame, drinking
Sunlight. It survives for its moment.
And what sustains our two existences
Remains as much a mystery as God.

The Usual Poem

It's hard to write when I feel happy,
To express that joy.
I lack the style and the vocabulary.

Easy to find rhymes for despair
And misery. It's this sense
Of well-being which leaves me unprepared.

I find myself encased by cowardice,
The fear that keeps the pupa
So long unmoving in its chrysalis.

But if, hoping to help the crumpled insect
Inside to free itself
Before due time, I crack the brittle shell,

The creature I thought to see, now injured
By my anxiety
And eagerness, no longer symbolises

What I want to say. My words are forced
To drag torn, useless wings
Rather than fly, certain and glorious.

And so, as though joy were inimical,
Thwarting my every effort,
The usual poem again gets written.

August Full Moon

Whichever I choose to look out from, here in my study,
Where the desk is placed in a corner between two windows,
I see her, the August full moon. Labouring towards
This completion, since yesterday she has freed herself,
Purged and dissolved the humours distorting her shape,
Making her swollen and clumsy, darkened from yellow
Of faded leather into the streaked, mottled red of an
Old woman's cheek. As if she had discharged her poisons
Into my veins, today I was almost demented,
Sodden, confused, barely awake or able to move
About the house and garden. But the moon,
Silver in a starless sky, windless night
After a day of stasis and sunshine, is disdainful
Of such effects on whoever is weak enough
To suffer this draining connection to her necessities:
I, who sit yawning and trembling in spite of the heat
Of a perfect evening, who will soon go, defeated, to bed,
To escape beyond dreams into emptiness
From this moment when the universe combines
In haughty balance against me, to wait until all the spheres
Lurch forward one notch and leave space again
For an opening that hope and change might stream through.

Another Full Moon

Another full moon. I knew without checking
The date or the almanac. Again I am
Tearful, uncertain, subdued and oppressed.
It becomes more an abasement each time
To acknowledge I still respond,
Anachronistic as an astrolabe,
Reliable as litmus paper.
No hope of escape, though I should
Much prefer not to be absolutely
In thrall to the rhythms of ocean and cosmos,

125

Such a solemn primitive,
A mantic pauper. With her roughened tongue,
The moon curdles my milk of human kindness.
Her maniac yellow eye glares
Through the curtain and follows every movement.
Her purpose is obscure, random, and cruel.
It is worse than being a prisoner, because
Between her appearances, I forget how
She rules me, how her gauntleted hand crushes
The back of my neck, forcing me lower,
Making me grovel, ridiculous and
Awful as a manticore.
I wonder if it must be true
That there will never be space for wit
Or humour in the universe
We share, and for all my days I shall bear
The scars of her torture, marked forever
As her creature and her fool.

Dinner-table Conversation

(for Robert Lowell)

I began to describe that female connivance
With the man who is duping you: amusement
Overruling outrage or self-protection;
Like recognising an art-form, appreciating
A fine performance, evaluating this
Particular one's potential for damage:
Entirely ignoring that it's you who will be
The material worked on, you who'll get hurt.

Women who feel such things, the man at my
Right side told me (after questioning closely,
To confirm he'd heard correctly), women
Who know these truths must relent, then accept
The role of Muse with its hampering duties.
I sensed more than a touch of malice in his
Assurance. It was judgement and dismissal:
No recognition, no inclusion.

But what I had been trying to explain, though
Not succeeding (he must have good reasons
For refusing to listen) was how awareness
Of this split is exactly the fault-line on which
I must build my own San Francisco: the place
Where hazard reigns and poetry begins.
Would I be less a woman or more a poet
Denying my own triumphs and defeats?

He would never surrender his right to be hurt.
He needed a Muse to hate. He would not even
Grant we shared a common dream.
I filled my glass. We shall soon be forced
Into the mud, consumed by the same worm.
Until that moment (may it long be deferred!),
I can still be as easily pleased by a man
As by the moon, a tree, a poem, or my dessert.

Last Days
(i.m. B.S.J.)

The confirmed suicide, calm and relaxed,
Reassures sometime-anxious friends.

They hope he's recovered, and he breathes deep
Like one escaped from the evil wood, from the need
To fight off every comer.

There the festooning snakes, fierce creatures
He wrestled with between clustering roots
And choking vines, now are flaccid
As cloth toys, punctured balloons, deflated tyres.
But Laocoön and his two sons together
Were never so assailed.

Like a firm machete cut, that gasping, joyous thrust
Through to the meadows of death.

He's there already. No need to hurry.
The decision made, he can linger a while
On the grass, in the sunshine. Nothing will hurt him.

Only that bruised fist of cloud, still
Almost hidden below the horizon,
That abrupt-rising flock of cawing birds,
The rusty lichen marking the eastern direction
Flaring suddenly into their vision
So the hedges seem wounded,
And one hot gust of wind, indicate
The lull before the storm's destruction.

The Spider and the Fly

Between an empty milk-bottle
On the top of the refrigerator,
And a corner of the cooker,
A small brown spider, overnight,
Has made – if one did not expect
Such miracles from spiders –
What otherwise would seem impossible:
An artefact, a construction
For survival, a web a hundred times
Bigger than itself, yet so transparent
I almost tore it. Only from one side
Were those fine guy-ropes visible.
In the centre, vibrating, balanced,
The spider was busy. It must not
Consider its life unusual:
To spin, and sit and wait for prey,
Such is the fate of spiders.
It expends more energy in a day
Than I shall, probably, in a decade.

The spider, in the middle of its web,
Symbolises the centred consciousness
Whose perfect actions flow, direct

Unmediated expressions
Of true need – or wisdom, which only acts
When the result is predictable.
Tangled in sticky filaments, a fly,
Dying, destroys the smothering web.
But the spider, pragmatic space-
Engineer, does not hesitate
Or wonder whether to begin again.
The necessary reconstructions,
Adjustments and repairs, are what
It lives for. How can a spider expect
More justice than a fly? My doubts
Are spun from just such questions.
I ponder the universe, while
The fly suffers its final agony.
Only the spider is not perplexed.

The End of July

I am languid
And the sky is clouded
And the sheep are louder –
Full moon tomorrow morning.

In every hedgerow
The flower-cups are crowded
With mating insects
Who will not separate

Although we lift them
Onto our finger-nails
For scrutiny, astonished
By such indifference.

Gnats halo us like spirits.
Somehow they make me think
Of my ancestors.
The full moon brings out ghosts.

Plaintive and angry
The newly-weaned lambs huddle
At each field's corner.
They must sense the thunder.

The trees' dense foliage
Hangs limp as costumes
Pressed close into a wardrobe –
Static phantoms.

Last night the moon looked almost red,
Engorged with power.
We wait, uneasy,
The approaching hour.

The Demonstration

Of course I'd throw my children from the sleigh –
Last, frantic bid to gain time. If only
The wolves hold off a while longer.
If only the horses are strong enough.
We race across the steppe,
Horizon dark as a Palekh box,
And the wolves' mouths red as inside the box.
When will their hunger be sated?
Are there enough children? Better, perhaps,
Not to survive such exposure of lust
To remain alive at any cost.

Nothing too precious or sacred to sacrifice.
I'll tell you all my secrets in desperation,
Secrets I drag into the gaudy light and betray
To evade the question, to guard my privacy –
(Such is the style of my conversation) –
If only you'll leave me alone.

I'll slip from my coat, leave my skin between your hands
Like a moulting snake. I'll breed another family
To feed the wolves again, veer back across
The snow and past the ermine-spotted spoor
To match your questions against my frankness,
To the place where you are waiting:

Where my bones will be broken and hammered and
Ground and carbonised, and that black power strewn
Over the bloody residue.
And then we'll rise, re-made, re-vivified,
Intact – my children and I – and the wolves
At the runners, whose hot breath fouls the sleigh
Where my children and I prepare once again
To enact the demonstration.

At the Horizon

The two sides of the road go straight on
Downhill past fields of yellow grain,
Green pastures, a barn door's glossy red.
The land undulates – rising regular
As the steady-mounting sun, or waves
Crisping against a shoreline's darkened edge.
But the road swerves neither right nor left.

Now, from this half-way pause for rest,
The air is so clear I can see as far ahead
As that place where elms and dust-white hedges
Meet. Their parallel lines converge
At the furthest point visible
– The always receding horizon –
Never to be reached before death.

Afterwards

I dreamed I walked into my own tomb
After the robbers, the grave-despoilers,
Had ransacked it through: to find coffin
Tumbled from its trestles, portraits of family
And friends, placed there for the dead
One's consolation, now broken mosaics,
Smearings of fard on fabrics woven
Thin as spider-tissue, the cloths
She used to wind around her body.
Trampled into shards, those fine jars
Of ointments she perfumed herself with.

I stood in the centre of the stone-paved chamber
But its real occupant was missing. I
Was only a dream figment, haunting
What it could not have effect on;
Ghost from a different dimension, less
Tangible than this monument
To a being more vivid – but gone.
Yet some essential part survived,
The pale observer I was, unsolaced
By everything I'd thought she lived for:
All lost pleasures here commemorated.

Souvenir

Was it another planet that swept by my own –
Some enormous body passing close enough
To make even the poles slip? Vibrations
Shuddered through every strata: distortion of aether,
Shifting of prairie and tundra, grinding of glaciers
Like stones in a quern. New heights, new depths,
The deepest, most intimate clefts and caches of glinting
Mineral fountaining upwards in jets of jewels
And fire; and rock worn smooth and bald and meek
By millennia's exposure, plunges into the healing
Renewal of burial, the relief of enclosure.

There was a lurch of seas, the waters braided:
One wall of stretched flakes, torn shapes of whales
And weed and foam a thousand miles high
Petrified an endless moment before strain
And torsion almost pulled the planet apart.
The mountains leapt, and sides of continents displaced
Collapsed or reared like wounded mastodons
With unchewed shoots still fresh between their teeth.
That fearful, high-pitched humming of movement,
As though a hive of giant bees was alarmed:
It was the crackling of stars, turning,
Attracted by some gigantic new magnet.

It seems aeons since then, when my life was wrenched
From its orbit. Everything but myself is altered.
The contours against the horizon are different,
The sun appears from an unfamiliar quarter,
The air I breathe has another density.
And I am left with hands still closed around
Those fragments I once clutched to save: all
That remains as souvenir of my first world.

The Fall

Once you start falling, you fall forever.
Once you let go, there's no hold anywhere.
Wherever your home was, having left it
There can be no other. As a meteor,
Brightness increasing with velocity,
Hurtling through space, need never intersect
Any planet's orbit, you will not find
A resting place – nor end your journeying
Until you've used up everything, consumed
Whatever feeds itself to you, is drawn
Into the plunging vortex of your fall:
Dark path you hope will lead furthest of all.

The Boat

Who is that person I see   distant   so busy
on the opposite shore   I should join her
she's waiting
a winter tree with scratching twigs
that won't let the wind be its master
she looks like me
but I'm drifting away   slipping   a boat
from its mooring   out   to the centre of the lake
where I'll float and sleep and dream
a black boat
in the heavy colourless silence   empty
simple   with no purpose   while light
withdraws below the water's surface
and the mountains concentrate themselves
fold into their centres
numbed with cold   lulled by monotony
as the black boat plunges through the one
sliver of red left   blood in mercury
from the already set sun
last trace of memory
to be eased away by water
before vanishing

Hair

We with the curly hair belong
To ocean, those whose tresses lie
Close to the skull, fall straight, are claimed
By all sweet waters, brooks and rivers.
Thus for our crown.

But body's growth
Affirms the spiral: torso and
Limbs attired in robe of such fine-
Woven mesh of undulation,
Whether conch-coiled or sparse as down.

The salty powers control. Dew-pools
And clouds submit at last to tides.
The moon throws shadows on your face
But glints triumphant on the three
Places that always taste of sea –
Looking into whose waves we drown.

Other Rooms

Afternoon, lying down, my eyes shut.
Winter afternoon, but the birds seem loud.
There's an air of spring, the days are lengthening.
I never remember, with my eyes closed,
Which room, or where it is. So many rooms.
So many sleepless nights, tired afternoons.
This feeling of weakness, of bleeding to death
Without pain or effort, while deep in the wet cold earth
Roots stretch and come to life again.
I know I shall get up when the lights come on and
Evening arrives. By then, I'll be certain where I am,
Wide awake, in control, with no thought for
The timid buds determined to survive
Through next month's frost, no lingering doubts
Nor memory of any other room.

My Thoughts

Volatile as incense smoke that swirls,
Corinthian, thickening the upper air
In my room and curdling beneath the ceiling,
Imbuing clothes, curtains, papers and furniture
With its scent of sweat and spices, hurting
My throat and eyes, giving me headache,
Finally making me dizzy; pervasive
As pigeons' murmuring under the window,

135

Circling between the clouds' marbled pillars,
Ravelling into the sky's enormity,
Then leading me to the verge, the edge
Of identity – my thoughts – like the plumed
Spiral of smoke, merge into the cosmos
Of odours, sunlight, and universal praise.

Burnt Paper

Papery eyelids, like curves of burnt paper
Which crumble the moment they're touched
But until then hold their form. Your eyelids
Are exactly the colour of burnt paper:
Gunmetal grey, dangerous shade, metallic
Glints in the creases around your eyes.

Eyelids like moth-wings, the same dusty,
Downy texture as a moth I saw once, with
A crest of hair fine as a sable paintbrush
And wings that seemed to be sheathed by scales,
A mosaic spangled with plaques of light:
Your eyelids, moving rapid as moth-wings or
Fragments of torn paper – love letters
Whirling in the updraft of a fire.

Traces

Street noises penetrate sealed windows
Like water leaks through porous earthenware
Or blood through bandages, tears through my fingers.

Smoke curls above the ashes in the grate
Where one blue envelope survives, and
Oily vapours linger in the drapery.

Nothing sufficiently impermeable.
I scrub my hands once more, but they retain
The smell of fire, the fish and vegetables

Habit made me prepare, then eat alone.
Traces of you – the cold side of the bed
I still avoid, fearing to meet your ghost –

Remain to torment and to disconcert.
And I remember every word you wrote
In all those letters I tore up and burned.

Waking

Sometimes one wakes, leaving the night world behind
As casually as though it could be approached
At any time, as unconcerned as if it need
Never be entered again. Dreams slide away
Like sea-water streams from the limbs of a swimmer
Coming up the beach, knees lifted high,
Clambering over invisible hurdles.

Almost black, the strands of weed that cling
To his arm, the sand-grains blocked by chevrons of hair
Down shin and thigh. The element has marked him
Intimately, everywhere. But he shakes it off,
Wipes salt from his eyes, like a sleeper surfacing,
Who does not remember the dangers: the slow sea worm,
Skin soft and rough as tripe, the wrecks and angel-fish,
The mermaids with their coral knives –
That splendour and turbulence to which, as sure
As tides flow back, he must return each night.

Appearance

Profiled, legs striding, arms held clear
Of his sides, mouth and eyes arched,
Pharaonic, head glistening
From sunlight or annointing –
A brief moment only I see him,
Superimposed against the trees
And sky at an angle which proves
His dimension is other than mine.

Here the day is cloudy, but his limbs
Gleamed, rounded by a stronger light.
Moving urgently, vanishing –
(For him the path continued) –
What pavement did he tread, that messenger?
Between whom was he travelling?
He will explain everything, later –
Reveal the purpose of appearances.
I wait our next appointment. I trust
In his return. I shall be grateful.

Pompeian Dreams

That lamp of pale brass,
Roughly shaped and finished,
Wick twisted from goats' wool
I pulled off the fence
Where it clung to the wire,
Filled with the olives'
Last pressings too rancid
For anything else –
Sluggishly burning. Even
Through sleep, its vapours
Trouble our nostrils.

We're resting on couches
In the stiff, ungainly postures
Of corpses caught by the lava.
And outside the house
Which stands near the edge
Of the cliff, dim moonlight
And vague shudders of summer
Lightning, sudden hiss
Of the sea, seem part of the dream:
A noontime darkened
By ashy eruption.

The screech of a Vespa,
Moan as its motor shifts gear,
Echoes through glinting
Labyrinths (in the cliff-caves,
The city buried by ash,
And our ears); another
Sound-effect to add
To the rush and stamping
Of bulls, the droning
Of insects, which populate
Our dull Pompeian dreams.

The Preserver

Don't meet it head on, avoid a confrontation.
Suck the belly in, up on your toes
Like a bull-fighter who tips himself back,
Sways sideways away from the charge.
Let that black bulk rush past, every particle
Of your brain alert, totally attentive
To its mass and path and destination.
Let the dusty pelt brush against your suit of light.
Only another learned in the art will appreciate
How close the horn came to your groin,
And your evasive movement, unflamboyant.

Most potent of all, the musty stench,
Odour of ancient sacrifice: temptation
To fall under the wheels of the Juggernaut.
But one moment's lapse of thought will leave you
At best a cripple. Let the dark horde
Meet those suicidal ecstatics, wreathed
In pale flowers, smiling with frightened blurred eyes,
Who cannot resist, and stumble toward it.
The old god needs his food – and his cunning priests
To soothe and groom him, pour lustrations,
Then lead him back to his herd and pastures.

Labyrinths to contain the Minotaur –
Or however you name that force
Which will crush you unless you use intelligence,
Ponder every detail of his strength
And your own weakness, devise a strategy,
A ritual to exhaust his energy,
A technique of survival which might become
An art. Then, perhaps, moon-faced,
The celestial bull will smile, manifest
His divine power which cures all evils:
Even Melancholy, Pessimism, Joylessness.

Realising My Solitude

Realising my solitude
From the sound of the wind,
I try to decipher some meaning
From the house's creaking, the hum
That underlines the silence
When the trees are still.
I'm translating sentences
From another language.
Nothing is direct. Everything
Signifies. But until I define the crime
How can I guess the motive,
Know who committed it –
Whether I am victim or criminal.

A noise outside intensifies
The doubt: has it yet been done?
If I am quiet, will it
Be easier to receive the message –
Perhaps this waiting is the act
Which will express my whole existence
(Never to be delivered)?

I listen. To the rain. Abrupt
Shudder of window-glass
When the gale snaps.
Hear my blood moving.
My breath, my sighs, whine
Of electricity
From the table-lamp,
Water in the radiators.
Everything is functioning.
But the code has not been cracked,
Nor judgement uttered if
This isolation is a punishment
Or fulfilment of my deepest wish.

Breath

Like a child who does not want to be born,
Who tries to back away from the light and
Pain and noise, the resistless pressure;
Or a sailor, drowning, yet fighting – flailing
And dangerous, though craving rescue;
Like a wild creature that has never
Been handled or caught, cannot be taught,
Who can only calm itself because
It will not be approached – impossible
To get too close – it darts away,
The whole process to begin again,
Over and over, again; I try
To breathe, not too slowly or quickly,
Breathe as I was breathing before
I became aware of my breath
And its fluttering impermanence.

My gasps become sobs, as though I mourned
The appalling fact I must accept,
Sole thought I strive to hold in my head:
That only this choking panic of air
Entering into and passing out
Through my nostrils, tethers me frailly
To life, separates me, absolutely, from
Death – as far as I can know – forever.

Glass-thoughts

Honesty, clarity, simplicity.
No hiding behind equivocations –
No dancing veils, false modesty.
Speak out in your own name.
The more revealed, the less unique
You'll see your anguish is.
The more you'll speak for everyone.

I prate of freedom, but what am I
That cannot be contained in the word 'fear'?
Hours awake, remembering.

What I have done (and left undone) through cowardice.
Recollect and contemplate. Without judgement.
This is what happened: clear neutral facts,
As clear as glass, and glass contracts, cracks mar
Windows which were never hit or jarred –
Thus self-esteem diminishes.

Glass, slow liquid, rigid and upright,
But unreliable as the citizen
Personifying those virtues:
Myself, behind the glass,
Reflecting shoddy dreams of triumph.
No matter how close I stand to another,
Glass separates, a formal boundary.

Are you encased as I am?
Do you yearn to break the glass but lack the courage,

Recoil if asked to damage
Even the wrought bars of your glass prison?
Are these your tears, vitrified?
Have you exuded
This curdled crystal
As scorn and envy?

Encased, immovable, no action possible,
You're forced to watch it all upon that screen:
Opaque now, though once it wavered like water
and seemed to restrain nothing
From flowing outwards or towards you.

Some influence from the past,
Generations of submission
Shocked by repeated uprooting, defeats me.
I construct these traps, dig my own pitfalls,
Arrange scenarios of humiliation.
In the battle I lose every advantage.
To gain a foothold in this territory
Means to surrender everything else.
I shrink from such finality.
My nature was formed to placate.

The glass is silvered by vanity,
Traps me in endless duplications of falseness.
Those actions are dimensionless, ghosts
Warped by the mirror, flattened by glass.

I will be neither judge nor warrior.
That is not me in the mirror.
It is a false exposure.
It has no depth.

The glass congeals into a crystal egg,
Gathers the waters:
Oil-fouled puddles, ocean's density, my tears.
I hold the egg to my eye.
It reverses everything,
Every failure and attempt.
Magnifies
Distorts
Enchants
Protects

My Position in the History of the Twentieth Century

Strange, how I've never lacked a certain confidence,
Been so dissatisfied with my face or body
That I couldn't cheer myself by posing at a mirror,
Sucking my cheeks in, raising eyebrows disdainfully.
Small, trim, not especially sturdy or slender,
Large-chested (though small breasted), rather
It's been a comfort to study the disparities between
Fineness and toughness, my own special markings.
I am not troubled that most people are taller:
Eyes always meet on the same level.

Lucky to live where it was not dangerous
To look like me (no need for a yellow star).
My good fortune took me far from the Holocaust –
Though it's easy to imagine how it feels
To read those scrawls on a wall, to be the African
From whose shocked, sick face I had to turn away
When I sensed how he hated me watching his pain,
Knowing we both knew he could not pretend
Those words did not stigmatise. His appearance
As much his expression and pride as mine is –
But I can still believe that white skin
Is not yet a primary signal to trigger hostility.

Because what I'm describing is privilege:
The being – soma and psyche – of one who expects
And depends on such luxuries as acknowledgement,
My self-image never subjected to a real test –
Not made anonymous, numbered, docketed,
Trapped and reduced until the one desire left
Was for a magic formula to make me vanish.
I flaunt my being manifest
To whoever wishes to read the signs,
And what seemed most private and unique in me
I find dependent on my place and time.

[*London, 1972*]

144

Bergamo Collage

Space packed with vanishing points –
angels and crucifixes,
angles and perpendiculars:
as if this place includes more than
the three dimensions,
as if the eras pressed,
contemporaneous and coexistent.

Another arch,
       another curve,
              another flight of stone
launched from the Celtic base, the citadel
besieged by Barbarossa.
Pale towers soar,
    air
    narrowing
    between,
compressed impossibly,
then surging out, released from time and piety,
from pride of weathering Venetian lions.

The pillars strain.
Roofs mount the sky.
The dome is buttressed down into earth's centre.
A green-winged angel lifts his arm
to indicate eternity
(wing and arm raised in the same perfect gesture),
or else, perhaps, that Christ
whose painted wounds congeal and fade
as his disjointed wooden body slackens,
darkens, seems more like the tortured Everyman
of sorrows those black-sprayed slogans
on the wall outside evoke –
more apposite for this particular moment
(space here so dense with symbols):
Mao; Lenin;
God's potent new names for men of faith
who will no longer be led
by what made all this live
and yet still holds each building upright.

Drunk Moon

New moon plunges into a deep well,
Topples over the parapet and vanishes.
A night so dark not even the moon could see
Where he was going. Like a drunk stumbling
Into a ditch, the moon lets go of the edge and
Plummets down the brick-lined sides: a steel ball
Shot through a pipe, a meteor racing away
From the telescope. The moon waning. The shock
Of his fall, the water's icy cold, will sober him up.
He'll have to climb out, find mossy hand-holds.
That's his face you see: clearer, larger, mounting –
The waxing moon, lurching across the always
Perfect circle of the well's opening. (Only
His clumsy movements make it seem to change shape,
Then his re-emergence blurs the rim completely.)
Full moon: those few short days of music, horseplay
And love for the toper until his next fall.

Moon

Moon, like a bruised rose-petal
Sinking into a small pool, like
A disk of metal, pendant
Of a Saxon necklace, fragile,
Almost corroded through
By time and soil's acids,
Earth's ceaseless tiny shifts
And movements; Moon, I look at you
And think of Japanese prints,
Of mist and sad cloistered ladies.
Moon, floating over the marshes
Like a fine slice of Prague ham,
Tender, pink, nearly translucent –
Oh angelic gluttony!
Old reliable Moon, who
Always makes me write poetry.
My sister Moon.

Words

Brute and hard in my mouth as
Rocks, words petrify. A flood
Of images and thought crashes
Against my teeth, bruises my
Tongue, suffocates, and leaves me
Dumb. Each time the force is
Dammed. That dream again.
Pressed close by a hostile crowd
I try to explain myself –
But cannot utter a sound.

I want to describe what I
See – there, before me, entire,
Like an ikon-stand. But no words
Come. I want them to share
My vision, take my gift. If
Only I could bring it alive
In their brains as urgently
As it glows in mine, clear
As though a genii unbound
Performed his miracle:

To show in the market-place,
Through the dust and confusion,
An object tangible as
A mountain piled from the stones
That choke my eloquence,
Or a statue that steps from
It marble husk like a rose
From its calyx: the argument
To amaze them, make them
Accept, and bow at its feet.

It's the need for patience and
Order, the stringing together
Of words like beads on Time's cord
Which dumbfounds me. Though saved
From my dream, I wake in tears.
Leaving my bed for my desk –

There at least I can try
To articulate and
Justify the grounds of my own
Defence – I write these words.

And the words end here: marks
On paper. I spread them out like
Opened bales of merchandise
For you to make your choice:
The ones to keep and remember.
Do they make you dream? Am I
Persuasive? Will you join me
In that endless game of chance
Whose instruments and prize
Are always poetry and words.

Sibyls and Others

(1980)

I. SIBYLS

A Sibyl

Her eyes have an indrawn look,
like a bird hatching its eggs.
To whose voice is she listening?
Anxious, the questioners, waiting
those words, but she seems relaxed
and calm, turning the leaves
of her book, does not even
glance down before her finger
points the message: this cave
familiar as a nest,
and she, its rightful tenant –
no longer forced to make
a choice between two worlds.

Aeneas' Meeting with the Sibyl

Hunched over rustling leaves spread out before her
on the stony ground, like a skinny gypsy
with a joint dripping ash in the corner of her mouth
quizzing the Tarot cards, pulling the shabby
shawl closer round elbows and shoulders, then squinting
shrewdly sideways up at a nervous client,
the Sibyl greeted Aeneas. 'Don't tell it from them,'
he pleaded. She was sitting cross-legged, right at the door
of her cave (Apollo! he thought, it's draughty here,
no wonder she looks so pinched and cold), and he'd heard
how often the wind would shuffle the leaves into total
confusion, which she didn't seem to notice or
amend. 'Don't show them to me. Say it in words.'

'You're all the same,' she grumbled. 'Always wanting
more than you pay for. Of course,' – tilting her head
sideways on that mole-strewn stringy neck
(he saw white hairs among her dusty curls)
an inappropriate cajoling smile
distorting her archaic features – 'if
you give me something extra, I'll do you a special.'
The tattered russet-purple layers of skin
and cloth wrapped around her body dispersed
an ancient odour of sweat or incense as her movements
stirred them. Through a hole in the skirt he glimpsed
a lean and sinewy thigh, and feet bound up in rags.
'Come inside, young man,' she ordered. 'We'll be private there.'

Remembering what came next: his search for the golden
bough, their descent into Hades, the twittering shades,
his painful meeting with Dido, the Sibyl's answer
to Palinurus, and then, at last, what he'd wanted:
embracing Anchises his father, and learning
the destiny of their descendants, the future
of Rome, Aeneas found it hard to reconcile
his first impressions with the awesome figure
who led him safely through the realm of death
and to the daylight world again. He looked
back from the shore to where she crouched outside
her cave, waiting for another questioner –
and saw she had assumed the same disguise.

A Desert Sibyl

A ranting middle-aged albino,
open-mouthed, eyes blurring, sightless:
that gaunt sharp-featured desert sibyl

who journeyed through the parching dunes
and past the heights of Mount Tibesti,
up from Lake Chad with her sacred ibis

intent that all should hear her message,
verses Tanit's power inspired:
warning for Dido, queen of Carthage.

The Cumaean Sibyl I

She was the one who, three by three,
burned her books of prophesy
when the asking price would not be met.
Like a wise old nurse who knows that children
rage and fret, but when night comes,
creep back into her arms, she watched
the flames, abstracted, stern, and calm.

Her face seemed veiled, the net of lines
a mask, a zone of darker air
penumbra of another atmosphere,
as though she stood before a fire
deep in her cave, brooding upon
time past and still to come, far from
this splendour and destruction.

Tarquinius Superbus gasped
and broke the silence. 'I'll pay your price.
More than my nurse or mother, Sibyl,
is your worth to me, your prophesies
and wisdom.' 'The same price as for all
the nine.' 'Agreed.' She raised her hand,
the fire died, the last three books were saved.

The Cumaean Sibyl II

Because she forgot to ask for youth
when Apollo gave her as many years
as grains of dust in her hands, this sibyl
personifies old age: and yet
those withered breasts can still let down
celestial milk to one who craves
redemption: a dry tree, not a green,
the emblem of salvation

From *The Sibylline Books*

(Book V. verses 512-530)

Threatening every star, I saw the sun's gleaming sword-blade,
the moon's rage between lighting flashes. The stars were at war:
God allowed the fight. For instead of the sun, flames
thrust from the east like searching beams of light, and stopped
the two-faced revolution of the moon's changes.

Lucifer fought hard, mounted on Leo's back.
Wily Capricorn attacked young Taurus; with murderous
razor horns, bull and goat bled out their future.
Orion smashed the Scales, Virgo and Gemini
invaded Mars. The bright Pleiades vanished. Draco
surrendered the Buckle and Belt, then Pisces overwhelmed
Leo – in dread of whom, Scorpio destroyed himself
with his poisoned tail. Armoured Cancer fled,
scuttling away from the whirling club of Orion, the hunter.
Sirius, dog-star, succumbed, vanquished by the sun's heat;
Aquarius consumed by ardent Lucifer.

Heaven itself was stirred at last to fiery wrath.
Horizon to zenith, the firmament shook, stunning the warriors,
plunging them headlong into Ocean's waters.
The hissing trail of their fall kindled the whole earth:
the sky remained starless, all constellations darkened.

The Hebrew Sibyl

I who was driven mad and cast out
from the high walls of Syrian Babylon,
I who announced the fire of God's anger,
who prophesy to those about to die
divine riddles
am still God's oracle.

Mortals in Hellas will claim me,
name me as from another city of birth –
Erythrae – one of the shameless.
Others will say I had an unknown father,
and my mother was Circe –
brand me a crazy impostor.

But when all has taken place,
when the walls collapse and the Tower crumbles –
that coming time, when knowledge is lost
and men no longer understand each other,
no one will call me insane –
but God's great sibyl.

Sibyl of the Waters

Noah's daughter
sibyl of the waters

first sibyl
the most ancient

with Shem, Ham and Japhet
saw her father naked

already she had prophesied
the flood

and understood
it was the nakedness of God.

Arms raised in invocation
officiating at the altar

where the Ark had grated
upon Ararat

she placed the burning brands
shielding her face –

ominous oracular gesture –
then crushed the dove to death

against her breast: a futile
propitiation.

The Delphic Sibyl

The tripod, the laurel leaves, the robe and style
of a virgin, though I was an honest widow of fifty:
because of my sober gaze and my docility,
the elders of Delphi chose me and taught me
what had to be done with the tripod and laurel leaves.
They offered a drink from the holy stream, showed me
the cleft in the rock where I must sit and breathe
mephitic fumes and chew the leaves until
my head began to swim and words came blurred.
Those gentlemen of Delphi's best, most ancient
families, our city's noble priests,
quite overwhelmed me. I was a simple woman,
obedient, eager to please, and honoured
by the role. And even had I wanted to,
been bribed to do, there was no chance
to slant the auguries. Petitioners
would proffer written questions first to them,
and their interpretation of my drugged
and mumbled ravings was determined
by Apollo's demands and the city's political needs.
I was an ideal oracle, they told me.
Thus I grew old, though monthly more confused,
appalled, exhausted, and in every way
the opposite of all I once assumed.

Destruction of a Sibyl

Right from the start, the Pythia was depressed.
Every omen came unfavourable.
He'd been on duty at the sanctuary, and
afterwards, telling his friend Plutarch
about the catastrophe, Nicander, one
of the priests at Delphi, could still remember her screams.

She'd gone into the proper trance, but how
reluctantly; at once began to speak
in a strange, hoarse voice. Whatever dumb and evil
spirit had possessed her would not reveal
its origin. No curse the priests pronounced could
banish it, protect her or themselves.

Like a ship on a stormy sea, foundering,
when bales of precious cargo are jettisoned
and the galley-slaves pull harder and faster because
of the lash, though their oars have splintered, she lurched
and shuddered, struggling to escape, tried to crawl
on bleeding hands and knees towards the door.

That cowardice could never be purged. No matter
how long they lived, the whole College of Priests
would not forget the shame. Everyone fled.
Contagion of fear: panic alone had ruled.
Apollo's priests abandoned their oracle,
and when they returned, found her broken and changed.

Python uncoiled himself, in all the glistening
length of his body, come back to remind them
of the ancient goddess, the Mother Apollo usurped.
It was She who had spoken and claimed the soul
of the Pythia to serve at Her altar and be
Her oracle forever in the underworld.

Herophile

Whenever she stopped at Delphi, Herophile,
the oldest sibyl, would stand on a special rock
and chant her oracle. Long before Helen
was born, she had foretold the girl would grow up
a trouble-maker, the bane of Europe and Asia.

Through forests and over mountains she wandered,
but two towns wrangled for the honour of her birth:
Marpessus the red (whose thirsty soil swallows
the rive Aidoneus), and Erythrae.

Sometimes the sibyl said her mother had been
a nymph, an immortal, at others named herself daughter
or bride to Apollo – Artemis, his sister and twin.

When Herophile died, her tomb was built by a stream
in Apollo's temple grove, and guarded by
a stony herm whose blankness seemed to mock
a life of traveller's alarms, poor food,
the sight of too much human misery,
hope and credulity and ceremony,
bad roads, virginity, and solitude.

Sibyl on the Run

Vague gaze from tired grey eyes
under the wide brim of her hat,
the fine-grained white skin of her face
mud-splashed, hair tangled, uncurling,

harried by wind and rain, she creeps
through the door of the smoky hut, and
quick as a snake, wary and furtive
as a forest animal, thrusts out

a scratched hand to take one of
the oat-cakes from the hearth, crumbles it
into her mouth, gulping with haste

looks round the silent circle of watchers
(no need to doubt, these were believers);
then reassured, straightens her back,
raises her chin, loosens her ragged cloak,
arrogant and proud; announces
herself: the wisest sibyl on earth.

Hallucinating Sibyl

As though burning upwards,
her waxy flesh become
candle to the flame of Apollo,
entirely possessed,
sibyl of Thrace,
sister of Pythagoras,
hallucinating sibyl.

Flakes of snow swirl and
drift though the cave mouth.
Gusts of wind
intensify the glow.
The brands throb
like the heart still beating between
the split ribcage of the sacrifice.

Entranced before the fire,
open-mouthed, throat and chest
reflecting light like a breast-plate,
naked shoulders shadowed
and glinting eyes rolled white
to see armies clashing,
phalanxes in the heavens

above the roof of the cave:
her mantic vision penetrates
through rocks, earth, roots
of winter-stripped trees,
the turbulent heavy sky
that shrouds the land
from the Euxine sea to the Hellespont.

Further back, beyond
the circle of light,
its range of noisome, pungent
fumes, stand priests
with the dagger and bowl for the blood
she drinks, the skins to clothe her
after she has prophesied.

Candle to the flame of Apollo
entirely possessed,
sibyl of Thrace,
sister of Pythagoras,
sibyl hallucinating –
but not yet begun
to use Apollo's words or speak with his voice.

The Cimmerian Sibyl

These habits come from the old place,
customs brought from home: almost
the only memories of endless
trees, a northern waste of cold
and dark beyond the Caucasus.

Because it was always so, here
on the shores of the Hellespont I still
must have my drum and lance, the three
mushrooms and sacred feathers, before
I rise to heaven and touch the stars.

Everything I know was taught
by the last sibyl able to recall
those days. Crippled, toothless, and blind,
she told me tales of how we fled
the Scythians, and ravaged Thrace.

I learned the steps of the magic dance
(my body burned in trance, the music's
beat made me gulp gallons of water
to quench such thirst); got by heart
the words that trap the reluctant god.

He slides under my skin as smoothly
as the blade of a knife in the hand of one
who slits the pelt and pours warm blood
from the throat of a perfect sacrifice.
Does god or sibyl then pronounce?

But now we are too near Greece, and priests
interpret my oracles, move
between me and the god, stifle my power,
altering the ritual;
fearful; changing the old ways.

Sick Sibyl

The ecstasy that drives salmon upstream
to spawn and die, eels across oceans,
seal to their breeding grounds, deer hundreds
of miles north (with the wolves who follow
to pick them off), geese winging south,
insects into fatal nuptial
flight, all united by
the spasm that verifies existence:
the ecstasy I never once
have felt, my ecstasy entirely
different, my ecstasy
a self-consuming sickness, an envy

of my questioners, who are one
with everything that lives and feels:
sustained, embraced and blinded by
the shimmering haze which only my
sick eyes can pierce to see the truth,
the future, and the end of love.

Blocked Sibyl

Sullen and stubborn, self-willed,
stupid, or just plain finished
as a sibyl – sometimes it happens
that way: one day, someone
who'd seemed absolutely right
for the job will dry up.
Hair messed, skin blotched,
eyes angrily or hopelessly
averted (but it's easy to tell
she's been crying), she won't answer
even the simple question:
What is it? from her apprentice-attendants,
much less pronounce. Maybe
she's sickened by laurel leaves, smoke
from the brazier, the sweet, foul stench
of anxiety. Better
be blind than always forced
to see those supplicating gestures.
Secretly, they've begun
to appal her – she's afraid that quite
soon she might break down,
weep or laugh with despair
at the most solemn moment. Finished
or freed: she knows as well
as they that she's useless now,
a blocked sibyl.

Rescue of the Sibyl

(for Françoise Claustre)

After our climb to that distant mountain plateau,
when at last we stood close to the chasm's dangerous edge,
and leaned across the shaky wooden railing
to fathom what lay hidden in its depths,
from that opening rose a smell as harsh as ashes
dowsed with water, a curling vapour dank
and raw as floats above a marshy waste.

An aged creature, her guardian, perhaps,
uncocked his rifle, began his tired patter.
'Those steps lead down to the quaking rocks. In the deepest
cave, our famous sibyl sits on her tripod,
chewing laurel leaves and prophesying.
I am the only one who can interpret
every word she speaks. For a fiver I'll take the lot.'

But we gave him money to go away instead,
and the other two unpacked their sensible macs
and brandy flasks for protection against the damp.
How thoughtless and deprived I felt, as well
as freezing cold. I hadn't prepared myself
at all for the expedition, hadn't even
formulated one serious question.

The sides of the cleft were slick and wet, they curved
away like vertigo. As though peering through drifting
cloud from a plane when a sudden wind clears the curdled
air, I saw something moving, a horrible dancing,
the stones were revolving, atoms of earth vibrating
and boiling. There were groans and flashes of lightning.
Then the fumes blew back, thicker than before.

The bravest of us moved towards the abyss.
With each rung trod, the turbulence retreated.
She drove it below, a sullen, defeated dragon.
The staircase lay exposed as a flimsy construction
and there, on the mud and grit at the bottom, stood smudge-pots
and clumsy machines to delude any watchers, convince them
the rocks had been quaking. Ashamed, we followed her steps.

That poor wretch, terrorised and abused,
stammered and rolled back her eyes when we finally found her.
It was months since she'd seen daylight or breathed fresh air.
Between her teeth were half-chewed laurel leaves, and her mouth
and chin were stained from their juice. Anxious and trembling,
like a hostage newly released from her ordeal,
she could not believe that rescue had come through a dream.

The Persian Sibyl

The Persian sibyl's powers augment with dusk.
She turns her book and face toward the shadow
and waits for revelation; prefers to guess,
not see, the written words – that gentle ageless
witch – and that you cannot read her expression.
The prophecies come clearer now; she makes
each phrase a merciful apocalypse.

The Sibyls in Amiens Cathedral

Thin-waisted Gothic sibyls
with pale calm faces
under wimples of clean Flanders linen,
holding your classical
attributes in elegant
fingers: the book,
the palm, the sword, the scroll,
images eaten
away and fading back
into the flaking
painted plaster and stone.

I can just distinguish which
is the Delphic one,
the Libyan, the Cumaean,
though your look and style
are those of later days,
Christian times,
your colours the gold and blue
of chapel banners,
soft madder-pink and red
of hawthorn flowers,
lush Somme-river green.

Your sister, the Tiburtine,
told Augustus
of Christ's coming, and so,
as oracles
of his triumph, on these cathedral
walls you stand
with the Prophets – proud pagan women,
half-forgotten:
like the message you brought once,
but long ago,
to troubled northern souls.

The Sibila

Sung at midnight on Christmas Eve by a young boy dressed in a rich, long robe and carrying a sword, in the Church of San Bartolomé and Nuestra Señora de Bonany, co-patrons of Soller de Mallorca, Islas Baleares, Spain.

The Day of Judgement comes
when there will be no Holy Service.
The Universal King of man,
God Eternal, then will judge us,
to everyone deliver justice.

Terrible fires will tear Heaven apart.
Lakes, springs, and rivers all aflame.
Even the fish will scream.

To the good He will say,
Come my blessed children
possess the Kingdom
which has been waiting
since the world was first created.

Humble Virgin, who this night gave birth
to infant Jesus, pray
He guard us from damnation's wrath.

With great severity and sternness
to the wicked He will say,
Go, evil ones, to everlasting torment
to the fire eternal,
to the Inferno and your Prince of Darkness.

The Libyan Sibyl

She casts away her clothes like soul's ascent
from the world of matter, shining arms upraised,

appears about to move with the ease of a dancer:
a hind setting its feet on the highest place.

Blinded by heavenly light, her eyes are closed.
What need of text – her message a psalm of praise?

It has come, the triumph of love above understanding:
ecstasy – eternal ardour – grace.

The Phrygian Sibyl

Speaking the language the first humans spoke
on that mountain plateau, homeland of Kybele,
Great Mother of the Gods, goddess
of caverns and wild beasts – words
only her eunuch-priests now
can understand – always, at the beginning
of spring, when the frenzy of lamentation
and blood-letting has changed to joy
at His rebirth, the Phrygian sibyl
blesses the whole earth – rivers,
herds of horses, flowering vines
and lovers – making the oldest promise
in the name of the Mother: eternal life.

The Shinto Sibyl

White snow settles on the sacred peak,
white clouds drift between the cedar boughs.
White bear and antelope, wild boar, run there.
White boulders mark the ever-trodden path.
White the robes the ancient pilgrims wear.
White the sunrise through the eastern door.

Long white hair hung down the sibyl's back,
white flowers from the branches of her crown.
White light reflected by her flashing glass,
white papers fluttered on the stick she bore.
White stone the pavement where the miko danced,
white drum she beat, and white her moving feet.
White sound I could not understand, her song.
Dead-white, but open-eyed, her face in trance.
White eagle-feathers left upon the shrine.
White bird that cried her message to me: 'Pure.'

NOTE: 'miko' – priestess, Sibyl.

The Tiburtine Sibyl

Albunea, nymph and sibyl of Tibur,
from your temple grove above the river's gorge
always you see the world through the spectral mist
of those plunging falls.
                The plain below spreads wide
and further west, upstream, like Hera's milk,
white water rises from a primal source.
Entering, at first, in spite of its warmth,
you shudder. Then, the sulphur bites, tormenting
as the centaur's poisoned shirt.
                With head rolled
backwards, sunken-eyed, you prophesy,
and all the richest senators of Rome,
the emperor himself, accept each word
of warning and advice as though the deified
Hercules spoke –
                whose voice comes forced
and husky from your throat as his was when
he climbed onto the funeral pyre; whose holy
rites you celebrate with mystery,
wild-olive fires, and serpent sacrifice:
his priestess, oracle, and virgin-bride.

The Oracle at Dodona

The oak is full of doves, they nest in clefts
among its naked boughs. This oak
is the oldest tree in the world. Homer wrote of it.
Here, Zeus rules with Dione and prophesies
through the throats of doves, doves they call oracles.
Three Doves: three women cloaked in furs,
whose calloused unwashed feet must never break
connection of their flesh from mother-earth.
Doves' voices speak gods' words. The women
stretch their vowels to sound like doves burbling.

Suddenly, the doves' murmuring
is drowned by the clangour of bronze rousing
the sanctuary – chains of a scourge in the hand
of a bronze statue, which every gust of wind
makes clash against a hollow gong and echo.
Someone has come to have his fate confirmed.

The stylos bit into the soft lead strip as he wrote
the question. The Doves approached. They stamped
their feet on the muddy grass. Doves in the trees,
reverberations of bronze, the women's song
and the oak-wood lots in the black, snake-painted jar,
agreed. 'Yes.' All would be as he wished.

A Young Sibyl

At first she appears
candid and chaste,
yet when she stands
in front of the altar, opens
her mouth, and the voices start
to speak through her throat
in that plangent blare,
everything is changed.
Does she draw down the power
or does the god ride her?

The sanctuary is dark
but her slender form
grows larger, seems
surrounded by a glare,
a holy nimbus.
The odour of stables
is stronger than incense,
and blurring all her phrases,
the snapping of reins
and champing of horses.

Ageless, sacred mare
who gallops unshod,
one of Apollo's steeds,
over past and future.
Those words have meant war.
Blameless though dangerous,
her gnomic speech
brings secrets back to light,
unriddles old mysteries
and knots new ones.

Introspection of a Sibyl

If only I could be aware of what is happening
in that void, that gap, that murky, fathomless cleft
where space and time must exist
between inspiration and the sound of my own voice:
the truth I never once have heard
a moment earlier than my listeners.

But I am no more conscious of the prophecies
than I can understand the language of birds.
A bird is singing now.
In spite of legend, like everyone else,
I wonder and guess at its message. My oracles
Come like birdsong – or how I imagine
they must begin to sing: by instinct,
neither needing nor able to think.

The most terrible phrases burst from my mouth.
My profession is to doom strangers.
Already, as a girl,
playing ball with my friends in the village square
or feeding my tame pigeon, I remember
being more appalled than my parents
by what I'd say: an unforgivable insult
dealt out in all innocence, or a blurted sentence
like a gift to confirm good fortune.

How I admire control, and yearn to achieve it.
I've become almost grateful to those who control me.
Before, I never knew when it would begin.
But the closed, startled expressions
on the faces of those standing round
– as though shutters crashed down –
meant again I'd defined or foretold,
unerringly exposed the poor secret
some old man kept hidden all his life:

with sight as sharp as an eagle
who spots the frightened creature
veering back and forth, exhausted,
across a rocky mountainside,
maddened by the shadow of its wings –
and heavier than every element,
surer than the laws of gravity,
swoops for the kill.

After a few times, you recognise
a universal wariness. It takes longer
to fear yourself, to accept the certainty
of never illuminating that blankness,
that vital hiatus when the demon or angel,
the god, perhaps, takes possession
and you don't exist
yet have the power of a god.

Panic of falling – said to be
the sole inborn fear of a human infant.
Deeper than fear, I've learned, lies the greatest pleasure:
nausea and exhilaration of plummeting free,
the glee of surrender to nullity,
temptation more primal
than any craving for security.

And the price for such knowledge? To have
absolutely no command over your life,
your words – no possibility
of calculated effects or tactics or policy.
But how useful you can be to others; and how lucky
if rather than burning or stoning, they protect you,
feed you, and let the simple folk praise you,
keep you safe as a caged bird,
and call you a sibyl.

II. OTHERS

Only the Magpie

Only the magpie among all its kind
had to be caught for the Ark, and ever since
bear Noah's curse. Yet beyond thought, more
acute than any thought, his rush of pale
and dark against the clouds and shooting twigs
evoke that time before the Fall when just
the wish to fly create wings and skill.

In paradise, fulfilment and desire
were close as white to yolk of an egg. Now,
desire destroyed by its pursuit, the bird of joy
cannot evade the hunter's net. Harsh
chatter of magpies out on the lawn. They pose
sidle and hop, pull worms, lift off, and never
wonder which pinion to use first.

Time's Metaphors

Four paw-marks filled with frozen water,
white brush-strokes drawn on a dark kimono
clutched against her haunches, bird-claw
hieroglyphs; the last surviving
haws and this spring's thrusting buds
enclosed by ice on the same twig.

Danger Areas

The landscape, hazed, recedes in layers,
pale heifers munching in the meadows,
hills crowned with castles as in fairy tales.

Those little touches so essential
to create the state of tension
that brings the picture into focus.

It must be strange. Deceptive comforts
of familiarity are not
effectual, are not allowed.

Otherwise, why does he seek
the dragon; why is she, so languid
at the window, hoping for catastrophe?

Romance, that necessary irritant,
becomes the only explanation
of sojourn in such danger-areas.

Driving Northward

There are stretches of road I remember,
autumn mist moving across a meadow,
driving northward, going home for the winter.

Such landscape is never spectacular.
A moment between dark trees and a river,
an outside curve, stones marking its contour,

and glowing with sunset, a segment
of the circling, luminous heavens.
Places where the unavoidable future

reveals itself: the panicked creature
that darts beneath the car's chassis
as we swerve around the next corner.

The Route Napoleon

Pollarded trees produce new growth:
this year's twigs and leaves displayed
as evidence. Trees marked by cryptic
streaks of paint, posters, reflector-disks
pressed into their trunks, wounds
roughly dressed with tar. Trees planted
to absorb the fumes of traffic, clothe
embankments and disguise the motorway.
Trees used; trees with the hopeless,
doomed servility of mutilated slaves
or trophy prisoners from some
forgotten war. Trees that can no
longer represent another realm
or further possibility,
but stand there, rooted, by the side
of the road, trapped as much as any
speeding driver or his passenger.

Trees

Trees, our mute companions,
looming through the winter mist
from the side of the road,
lit for a moment in passing
by the car's headlamps:
ash and oak, chestnut and yew;
witnesses, huge mild beings
who suffer the consequence
of sharing our planet and cannot
move away from any evil
we subject them to,
whose silent absolution hides
the scars of our sins, who always
forgive – yet still assume
the attributes of judges, not victims.

Deadheading the Roses

All day I clip the withered blossoms from the roses,
cut back till where at join of stem and leaf
I sense the chance of one more flower.

I work against maturity and the full cycle,
try to stop the dull hips from ripening
and using that energy

I want to move towards more buds and flowers,
repeat the same glory, achieve what yet
I know to be impossible:

rejuvenated immortelles; far easier
than to accept the pressure of further growth,
the destiny that hardens petals

into firm, streaked knobs of seed disdaining beauty
for the sake of the future: that power
the artless rose-bush manifests.

Because every rose on the trellis witnesses how
nothing can halt the closing of one phase
or shorten the interval between

fruition and death. While I tear my hands on thorns
in a losing fight against autumn, the same
wind parching the roses' leaves

is driving me nearer to my destination. Only
some miracle could force new flowering,
another scented season.

The New Tree

Planted a tree the afternoon before
what has become the first evening of autumn
(eucalyptus-spring in Australia),
wind dropped and clouds moved on, mid-August storms
seemingly gone. And now the moon, almost
at full, a thin-worn disk of beaten tawny
metal foil, or crumpled papery fallen
eucalyptus leaf, hovers above the hawthorn
and the bramble hedges, unkempt corner
of my northern garden, as I cross the lawn
to touch the newly planted tree, its short
rose-madder stems and glaucous foliage, once more,
and wonder if its roots can feel the draw
of the antipodes, the pull from that far shore;
confirm again that everything's in order,
and wish it well until tomorrow's dawn.

New Year in England

Red tiles on huddled village roofs
fusing into the smoky glow
the sun's last fanning rays illuminate.
The marshland and hills.
A further arch of winter blue
above the corded nap of new-ploughed fields.
That floating crimson lake of mist.
The clouds also demand their praise,
those purple banners. Yet something is lacking.

This calm afternoon
of early January, when all the world
still feels as if resting from festival,
needs more lauding, more gratitude,
than the empty road and separate houses,
heraldic television aerials,

the silhouetted tower of the vacant
church, seem able to express.
And I wait hopeful and uncertain
if fit words will come: the glory-song
to satisfy such daunting trust.

The First of October

At the turn of the seasons
that feeling, uneasy, uncertain –
blurred colours emerging
in spring's chill watery sunlight
as rain washes away the husk
of the whole winter's grime
from tree-trunks and buildings
– when the spirit is naked and cringing.

It's the same in October.
Rain also is working the changes
stripping the trees
mulching leaves into the gutter.
But sometimes, as the mud dissolves,
brings back a flash of summer's tones:
a leaf plaqued against the pavement
clear amber yellow and topaz brown.

The equinox.
Earth at midway point.
Any movement now must take us
further out or closer to the sun.
When the planet balances
perhaps it needs
and draws upon
even my equilibrium.

With David in the Nimrud Galleries

Once we passed under the archway into
the rooms of the Nimrud reliefs, the first thing
he asked about were the crabs – claws heraldically
uplifted between fish and floating horses,
soldiers' corpses tangled in their reins –
incised on the golden limestone tablets.

Further in, we followed Ashurbanipal
to the lion-garden, where the beasts were loosed
from cages to be shot (a rich man's safari),
then rode behind the troop to Marduk's temple
to make sacrifice. He noted how delicately
the shallow streams of blood from arrow-wounds
were graved down the lions' sides, like the river's waves,
and pointed out a gazelle turning to reassure her fawn,
and two birds fluttering above a palm.

His precise observations confirmed my pleasure.
I wondered about the craftsmen who did these carvings.
The columns of captives are endless: how they bind
the composition together. Such strong horizontals:
women, children. One too small to walk
into slavery straddles his father's shoulders.
On another tablet a group of prisoners
have abased themselves. So many battles: Thebes,
Tyre, the Elamite cities. Cunning use
of diagonals: lances, slanting siege ladders.
So many exiles. Centuries later, these
black streaks across a sinewy leg
or fierce helmeted head pitted and stained
by rain and erosion are the only signs left by nomads
who built their meagre fires and sheltered among
ghosts and jackals sharing the ruins of Nimrud.

All Assyria to be imagined
from these fragments. After millennia
of neglect, now they are treated as carefully
as premature babies. Every showcase of weapons,
vases, or jewellery with its own humidity
and temperature recorder. We could hear

the humming of machinery, concealed
neon-lighting and air-conditioning. Alone
in the gallery as scribes in a library,
I try to tell him what I remember. Politely,
he ignores the distraction, clearly more absorbed
and delighted by friezes of hunters and lions,
muscled priests with taloned feet and the heads
of vultures, banquets and triumphs: all
this precious detritus of Nimrud before his eyes.

Childhood

I see it like an illustration in a magazine:
the low and seemly blocks of middle-class apartment buildings,
with half-grown trees and sprinkled lawns between; colours
neither pale nor garish but chosen from the clear, most popular
and tasteful range: grass-green, sky-blue, an undemanding red, and
pointillistic touches from parked cars, fire-hydrants, freshly varnished
doors and window-frames. The streets do not run straight: the land
is hummocky, its dips and curves are on a human scale.

Here on the hill-crest where I stop to contemplate my whole
domain, I feel as powerful and joyful as the wind
that forms the clouds each moment into different shapes.
I wonder at the lives of such exemplary inhabitants,
confirm again that everything's in order, just as it should be
in Toytown; and only then I nod my head and check the straps
and buckles of my skates, let myself go, and swoop down, down,
past houses, families, up the opposite slope and into Heaven.

The Message

Hard to remember how long ago it started –
blankets drawn close round my shoulders, or in summer
only a sheet – dragging whichever near enough

to my short-sighted gaze to see the glistening fibres
silhouetted against an open door or window,
any source of light to define them standing upright
or angled, in regular series like letters. Eyes smarting,
I would stare for hours at the wispy lines:
that mysterious script, that wizard's calligraphy.

Sometimes I could disentangle single
words (mostly my own name), but never
the whole sentence potential in the fabric's
weave and texture, shadowy, waiting: marked
already on the sheep's back, grown with the cotton's
flowering, survived the washing, carding, spinning
and dyeing – every process in the chain of hazard
before it reached me, safe in my room, protected
by the wallpaper's pattern: those trellised roses
whose awful thorns baffled discovery.

No matter how I tried, though my brain felt
like a sponge being squeezed by large indifferent hands
and my eyes unfocused, it never showed clear.
Yet even now, when I wake at dawn, or nights
when the crumpled bedding is furrowed with lamplight,
if I twist my head or slide down the bed, the same
letters appear – unreadable, but insistent
to be read: that message I cannot decode.

A Child Crying

Gasps and sobs through the wall from the next flat:
a child's voice in dirge-like complaint whose words
I cannot make out but whose tone accords too well
with my mood – as though it were I in that room,
bitter and desolate, choked with grief,
oppressed by a world I cannot understand,
that withdraws and refuses to console me.

A child crying. We who can imagine
that to muffle the child to silence might be
kinder than to leave it in such distress
(at least would change our own distress), each time
are forced back to that old anguish – hours shut into
a bedroom, crouched behind a slammed door,
stifling in a wardrobe, throbbing temples
pressed against a bathtub; trapped horror
of the cot, suffocating blankets, the sickly
baby colours of their damp itching.

And when at last it has stopped, and the unknown child
is pacified, we are left exhausted and
ashamed as if after torture, capitulation,
and the final loss.

Almost-full Moon

First through one window,
then moving to the other,
she looks at me all evening,
sitting at my desk. But
I'm only one of the creatures
the almost-full moon watches.
There are so many rooms and houses,
so many open windows,
so much to see, such huge
responsibility.
She supervises moths,
moles and lizards, owls,
orchards, and empty beaches,
and wakeful lonely children
who stare up at the face
of the calm white mother,
till soothed, their heads roll sideways
on the pillow, into shadow
and they fall asleep.

That Smile

Sometimes I find myself looking at children
with that fond soft smile of older women
who've forgotten it all – which made me hate them
when I was yearning for confirmation
of my new maternal status, a decade ago.

But yesterday, though I should have known better
(or else why remember?) in a carriage
on the Northern Line with a distracted
mother and her two small boys, I felt
the same expression distort my features.

Sturdy, rosy, laughing, zipped into
anoraks, pressing their noses flat
against the windows, the naughty children
crawled across arm-rests and gabbled nonsense,
ignoring her restraints and protests.

Truer to their humanity than either
of us, they knew without having to learn
that for the short time given, whether
it ended at Edgware or in seventy years,
the only purpose of living is pleasure.

Maybe the smile that used to disconcert
had a different meaning. Those other women
might have been trying to reassure
and divert me, as I now wanted
to catch the mother's furious eye

and make her see her own two children
as emanations of wisdom and joy.
But even more, as empty station
platforms hurtled past, I wished
that she would turn to me and smile.

Unsuitable

When, instead of scrubbing their jeans, I'm rinsing
my smalls, it's not like doing housework (doesn't feel
right: neither justified nor sanctified)
no one to blame or accuse

When I open a box of matches and see one
is broken or shorter, or has a half-formed head,
it's that one I'll use

The tainted grapes on the bunch, those with a spot
of mould, softening away from the stem, I pick and eat
first, and the squashed tomato, blackening banana –
all the bletted fruit

Whatever is perfect, or beautiful or new,
I carefully save for a special occasion: a wardrobe full
of unworn, old-fashioned shoes

Waiting for something to happen (augmenting impatience)
I sense how the others avoid me, fearing a breakdown,
potential of chaos, shattering, splintering glass
as the genie gets loose

And the smile on my face, that calm of the over-cautious
to hide my resentment and envy, is like make-up
on a birthmark or a wound

Because I will not admit what I think, I have no
opinions; never admit who I am, have lost
my history; cannot admit what I want,
have forgotten how to choose

Until this huge discomfort constitutes
my whole existence: called to act a part
for which I'm completely unsuitable.

It Must

Friends, sisters, are you used to your face in the mirror?
Can you accept or even recognise it?
Don't be angry, answer me frankly, excuse
the question's crudity. I can't – no matter
how often I take the little square of glass
from my bag, or furtively glance into shop-windows,
the face reflected back is always a shock.

Those scars and wrinkles, the clumping of pigment
into moles, spots, faulty warty growths around
hairline and neck, the way skin's texture has changed
absolutely, become roughened and scaly,
coarse-grained, every pore visible, as though
the magnification were intensified: horrible.
These days, I prefer firmer flesh in close-up.

Younger, I remember staring, with a mixture
of attraction, repulsion, and pity, at the cheeks
of older women – the sort I chose for friends.
Did they need me as much as I idealised them?
There seemed something splendid and brave about such raddled
features, crusted and blurred with the same heavy make-up
I've taken to wearing – war-paint, if, as they say,
the real function of war-paint is to bolster
the uncertain warrior's spirit, more than
to undermine and terrify his opponent.

Now, I long to ask my friends these very
questions and compare reactions, blurt out
the taboo words. But we're so polite,
so lavish with compliments, tender, protective –
cherishing the common hurt: tenderness
of bruised flesh, darkness under the eyes
from held-back tears, watery blisters
on frost-touched fruit already decaying,
marked by death's irregularities.

Friends, tell me the truth. Do you also
sometimes feel a sudden jaunty indifference,
or even better, extraordinary moments
when you positively welcome the new face
that greets you from the mirror like a mother –
not your own mother, but that other
dream-figure of she-you-always-yearned-for.
Your face, if you try, can become hers. It must.

Anja's Poem

A friend told me
to keep all combings –
the loosened hairs
that fell into my lap,
onto my shoulders,
after shampooing –
and save them till I'm old
to flatter and augment
my thinning tresses.

I liked the thought.
It has become
a weekly usage,
almost my only form
of piety.
As I gather
the clean hairs, twist them
around my fingers, and
put them in the special
box behind the mirror
in a corner
of my dressing table,
I feel connected to
a host of women, ageing
or youthful, present, past

and future; part of a
continuity, that
basic history
indifferent
to boundaries, unmoved
by proclamations.

Like them, though old, I'll want
to look the best I can;
not to compete, or prove
I still can be a beauty,
but out of pride
and my own dignity,
in honour of
my family and
the peaceful, fruitful land.

And when I'm dead, I hope
my hair will be arranged
by careful women's hands
in memory of
its onetime glory;
that round my head they'll loop
the heavy rope
of all the hair I'll have
lived long enough to save –
as if a crown,
for my best ornament,
before they fold the cloth
over my face.

Divination by Hair

I

Every few days, looking into the mirror,
I find another dozen hairs turned white.
Though dubious about my purpose, almost
despising myself, I go on pulling them out.
She, the ideal I stubbornly adhere to,
would never search so urgently for their wiry
glint, crane her neck awkwardly
the better to ensure not one escapes
the tweezer, disdain pursuit of such
discoveries. White hairs are curlier
and vigorous, age and death becoming
more assertive the closer they approach.

I know it can be nothing but a losing
battle, paltry and ridiculous.
Sooner or later I'll have to choose
whether to be bald or white. I cannot continue
this depilation with impunity.
They'll never grow back as fast as vanity
can raze them. Like one enthralled (more
than mere scrutiny distorts my face),
hours at a time I stand in front of my mirror,
which long before now should have lost its power
and become a superseded altar, not
the secret place of panic, rage, and grief.

I'd prefer to be brave, to let my tresses fade
to mottled grey and white – but even the best
resolutions are hard to keep when every
day's attrition brings a new defeat.
If only it could happen overnight –
one morning I would wake transformed into
that dignified wise matron of my dreams,
matured at last to grace (though I make her sound
like the grandmother on a birthday card):
storms calmed, reefs passed, safe harbour now in sight.

II

Every day, new hairs faded.
Why don't I just accept it?
Why don't I dye them? What difference
would it make if I left them? Age
would not come sooner, nor my actions
avert dissolution and death.
Who do I think I'm fooling?
– No one except myself.
For who cares really whether
my hair is grey, white, or black?
Others, also, are doing their best
to conceal, refuse, forget.

III

Because death always seemed a mother –
or a grandmother, someone
familiar – now I come near
the time of greying hair, I fear
the mask more than the skull beneath.

IV

Silver hair is the warning sign.
To watch it spread is like catching fire.
I want to smother it, to hide
the mark that shows I'm next in line,
exposed, too near the danger-zone.
I feel death creeping up behind.
Those fading hairs and deepening lines
are the entangling net she throws.

V

Witch from an ancient forest-tale;
goddess; hag; Atropos-Fate;
Kali; crone. Can I placate
you better be careful hiding the blaze
you sear across my brow, or apeing
your style? Conquering queen, your embrace
in inexorable. Whether I hate
or deny or adore you, you will unmake
me, eternally, and create me again.

VI

        days   mirror

             dozen hairs   white

   dubious   purpose

despising

        ideal   stubbornly adhere

    urgently

                                  awkwardly

               not one escapes

       pursuit

discoveries

   vigorous   age and death

    assertive   approach.

                   losing

        battle   paltry   ridiculous

   choose

   bald or white

        impunity

               vanity

          enthralled

     scrutiny distorts

            my mirror

  lost its power

      a superseded altar

        panic, rage, and grief

        brave   tresses

  mottled grey and white   best

resolutions

   attrition   defeat   overnight

   transformed

dignified   dreams   grandmother

         grace

 far   calmed   passed harbour in sight

Satellite

Light streams into the room:
a presence behind the curtains
pushing against their edges
as palpable
and menacing and volatile as mercury.
Suspended in an empty sky,
above the black backdrop of pines,
that scalding glare,
flattening the lawn into a bald formality.
How could I forget the full moon?

Only this afternoon
impossible to stop the tears
forced from my eyes and down my face:
a water-mask
seen through the beaded curtain of a cataract.
Again and again I'm dragged off-course.
For days I could not wake – tonight,
quite lunatic,
I cannot sleep, but want to go outside, into
that light, and shriek at the moon.

I hope it will end soon.
And yet, if I withdraw beyond
her rule, through cowardice, or
she no longer
focuses her power and ceases to disturb,
how foiled and desolate I'll be:
a barren victory, gained
by banishment
from that world of extremity in which I've lived
as satellite to the moon.

Always Time

There's always time for making love or
writing poetry – the two
activities revealing certain
parallels. Whether those stories
one has often heard are judged
as more amazing or amusing,
it seems no situation's ever
been too complex or unlikely
or ridiculous to stop
determined people.

Words or phrases sometimes come
with that same urgency, and minutes
open up, allow the time
to seize or lure them (whichever technique
best achieves your purpose); tease them,
mouth them, use them every way
imagination leads, until
enough has passed between them and
yourself, and you feel sure there'll be
a further meeting.

Then, smoothing her hair and skirt,
straightening his tie, they go their separate
ways – return to where he was
before, to what she had been doing;
the prospect of a poem or
an assignation as secure
as such matters ever are –
only the time and place to be
arranged; minds already hard
at work and scheming.

Meeting

It would need witchcraft to see your face
of twenty years ago, and mine, revived,
confronted as if resurrected ghosts –

a banshee ceremony, screams and cries,
to call them back, those masks of flesh dissolved,
remade, and formed not by the grave but life.

What would the younger pair think of us now?
Might that half-wild girl still fall in love,
or you be charmed by what I have become?

Could who we were agree to such a future –
already our past, denied or mostly forgotten –
having our memories as foreknowledge?

How can there be a hope of recognition
when every cell has been renewed and altered,
the pattern coarsened through repetition?

Yet those four, meeting like strangers
outside time and matter's flux, accept
their actuality, and never question

the others' realness. Amazed and fascinated,
they wait to hear confirming words, or intercept
the one appropriate gesture of release.

Again

Suppose the prince who once had been a toad
changed back after a certain span of years.
Perhaps it always was intended.
Happily ever after only meant
a few decades, and this return to earlier
days inexorably programmed into
the experiment. The kindly fairy's
blessing lost its potency as princess
and her golden hero aged together.

Suppose one morning when he woke he felt
the clammy stricture web his toes and fingers,
his mouth begin to stretch into that
recollected lipless grin; and when she turned
to face him from her pillow, saw in her
contracting pupils the reflection of
cold warts and freckles surfacing like blisters
on his muddy skin. He dared not speak,
but waited, numb with hopelessness and dread.

Suppose that night she'd dreamed about the hour
her ball had rolled and splashed into the pool
and that foul toad had hopped towards her, croaked
his arrogant demand, and forced her will.
Yet afterwards, everything was perfect.
As though the time between had vanished, now
she smiled and clung to him, gazed deep into
unaltered eyes. Who could guess the coming
transformation? Let it all begin again.

Animal Tamer

You would have made a good animal tamer –
I can tell by the way you're taming the wild black cat
that appeared last week at the bottom of the garden.
Every morning she comes a little further.
You go outside with a half-filled saucer of milk
and put it down as if you didn't care,
but each day move it an inch nearer the door.

The black cat's glaring eyes have a baffled look.
There's something about you she cannot understand.
You've activated her curiosity.
But still she crouches watchful under the bushes
until you glance away and fuss with your pipe,
and then she dashes across and gulps and laps,
the hair round her neck bristling with suspicion,
peering up at you several times a minute,
relieved and yet puzzled by such indifference,
as though she missed the thrill of flight and escape.

Today, for the very first time, you turned and stared
at those yellow, survivor's eyes, and the cat stared back
a moment before she swerved and ran to safety.
But then she stopped, and doubled round and half
gave in, and soon, as I know well, you'll have
that cat, body pressed down on the earth and fur
electrified, stretching her limbs for mercy.

Going Back

There was only a six-year gap
between leaving and going back
yet they all looked like amateur actors.

Under eyebrows grown thicker –
surely they'd not been so wrinkled? –
eyes darted like confidence tricksters.

Clumsy, those lines on their faces.
And someone inexpert had shaken
talc over their heads. The make-up

was awful, but worse, their attempts
and behaviours as elders: gestures
compounded of pomp and burlesque.

They were children aping grown-ups:
subdued husband, bustling
wife, failure or success.

The first unguarded shock,
pity and horror
forced to stare into that mirror

when we met, after only six years.
But in less than an hour, all such fears
were blurred by laughter's easy tears.

The Function of Tears

The function of tears
must be to serve as language,
a message to others –
yet the bitterest weeping
takes place alone. The message
then for oneself, an urgent
attempt to reach
the shackled prisoner
in the deepest dungeon
far below the level
of the lake.

What do tears express
that words cannot do better?
Tears are the first language;
a glazed face and anguished
moans communicate
rage, pride, regret,
pleasure or frustration;
remorse and hatred:
almost every emotion
sufficiently intense,
before words can be formed.

Each of these feelings
in turn must colour
the soul of the prisoner
abandoned in her corner,
like the shifting greys
tinged by rainbow hues
of light filtered
through tears clogging
her lashes, jagged
prisms of memory
and hope in the gloom.

Such tears have little effect
on the silent warder
who checks the links
of her chain, brings bread
and drinking water
and sometimes even
changes the musty straw.
No one has ever seen
the warder cry –
not his wife or children,
not the torturer.

Perhaps the lake
was hollowed out by tears.
But until the castle
is assailed, besieged,
completely undermined,
with dungeons flooded,

crenellations tumbling,
and torturer, warder,
and prisoner are forced
to shout about the sound
of rushing water,

call to each other for rescue,
swim clear of the ruins,
embrace and cry with relief –
that lake, like the socket
of a giant eye drowned
by unimaginable
grief, will still stare
blindly up towards heaven
and go on weeping,
endlessly replenished
from a fountain of tears.

Suddenly

suddenly the mail stops
the car won't start
the telephone stays silent

and *suddenly* becomes
an indeterminate phase
with no foreseeable limit

someone suddenly dies
there's still a part of life
ahead for those left

to learn how to survive
until this stasis ends
suddenly more time

Grief

As poison may produce its antidote,
even grief be assuaged by itself,
(as every hope fades) – even grief abates.

That autonomic consequence,
its chemical results, which made
nerves wince, skin pale and flinch, brought sudden

sleep and agitated dreams,
oscillation through extremes,
a drench of tears unwilled as winter rain,

reaches saturation point.
The antidote, self-manufactured,
is elegant evidence of that fine system

of checks and balances which holds you
in the land of the living, impotent
as some laboratory monkey.

The purpose of the demonstration
proved: you don't succumb – immune
henceforth to this particular poison.

Not Well-mapped as Heaven

I know so many people who are dead.
The thought always insists on coming
in the present tense. How often they return,
old friends, when I am half-asleep, or seated
at my desk. Mostly their state was changed
by suicide or heart-attack; rare,
the lingering deaths. And yet, like friends in life,
we drift apart. I move into the ageing
they are spared. They won't grow old with me

– but that assertion doesn't mean I can
persuade myself to the belief that afterwards
those timeless dead and I shall meet again.
Nevertheless, that place they are, surely
has more expanse and depth than merely my own
memory: though not well-mapped as Heaven.

The Thorn

Is the thorn blunted, or the heart scar-hardened
and calloused?
                    Only the grating fall
of earth thrown from a spade, loosened
from the new-dug clay and knocking
against the wooden lid as if
I heard it from inside, can alert
and alarm, can awake –
                    as though it needs
almost the trump of doom to make
me see: frost-locked, soot-rinded tree
growing near the cemetery
wall, and balancing sure-footed
on its shaking branch, that bird's
wind-ruffled plumage; to make
me realise their hardihood
and valour.
          The bird's breast pressed upon
the thorn obeys the laws of life
and bleeds, the bird must sing its song
of faith and praise; and when spring comes,
even this thorn-tree will be capped with
flowers above the healing grave.

My Rings

On my right hand since then
I've always worn the ring
my father and I chose
for my twenty-first birthday present.
On my left, these months
since her death, my mother's ring:
the engagement ring he bought her
half a century ago
and gave to me,
after the funeral.

The only break in his grief,
those first mourning days,
was when he learned
the two of them would lie
together under the same slab.
Ten weeks later, throttled
to death by cancer, he followed.

If I forget...then let
the faded garnet oval
in its antique setting
tighten around that finger
like a garrotte: the diamond,
angular, stab sharp
up the arm and pierce my heart.

I spread my hands on the desk.
Prominent tendons and veins
on the back, like hers;
red worn skin of the palm
that chaps and splits
so easily, inherited
from my father. Even without
the rings, the flesh of my hands
is their memorial.
No need for anything
more formal. Not gold
nor platinum and precious stones
can serve as well
as these two orphaned hands.

Questions

How go on being angry with the dead,
remembering his mortuary face –
the chill when you bent and pressed your lips against
a substance no longer flesh: too cold, too dense;
the urge to take his body in your arms,
stretch out by his side – not believing any embrace
could warm him back to life, but simply a need
to lie with him there in the casket as though that
were your duty and pleasure. You wanted nothing else.

How go on being angry with the dead
when those last weeks of pain play themselves through,
over and over again – those sounds, those gestures.

The view from that room: luminous winter days.
The structure of a tree lit from every
angle. The setting sun sinking into
its cage of branches. After his death you lay down
on the bed to see exactly what he'd seen:
a glowing, endless sky, flushed and tender.

Yet unaffected by these memories,
still that anger. Is it merely anger
because he died – the rankling of guilt you share
with everyone alive toward their dead,
a ruse of the brain to survive the time of grief;
or is it a true and valid anger against
the ones who brought you into the world to die
but taught you nothing about how to die,
and leave you now, the questions unanswered.

Not Grief but Fear

It was less grief than fear
as I stood on the plastic grass
as the edge of your grave.
Fear of the grave –
the way the edging stopped
and the sides plunged
deeper than any hole
I'd ever peered into,
glistened and darkened downwards:
conglomerate of stones
and roots and spiders' nests –
a section through the foundations.

Fear, of course, for myself:
horror of suffocation
like that which comes at night
when the blankets press, crushing
the bones of my feet,
and the sheet across my mouth clings
like a membrane. Back into
the earth, dream of the time
before birth. Mother, you were too light
to bear the weight of my need.
My fear, entombed
with you, must resurrect.

Less grief than fear.
Now everything I do
though it seems in memory of you
is done to ward off the truth
of that death you've gone into
alone. Both fear and grief.
For though you loved me well,
your smoky torch glows faint
and only shows me pebbles dimly
glinting up ahead,
reflections from the clay,
but not the way.

Too Late

Maybe it happens one night, driving
through an unknown suburb, the realisation
that nothing is going to change, the time
will never come for explanation –

(those touching fantasies of shedding
your armour, final reconciliation,
and no further need for defences:
a childhood dream of smiles and embracing).

Until now, such hopes were what sustained.
But every crossroad and junction demand
an instant decision, with no one to praise
or help you find your way in the dark.

And stopping underneath a street-lamp
to consult the map again,
suddenly you're sure the meeting
though so longed-for, will not take place.

That night, lost, then arriving too late,
you understand why the others
(and you'd have done the same), could not wait.
They were gone. Now your turn has come.

Time Come

Hearing, 'His time had come,' do you think:
somewhere up there, archaic reassuring
plaster gods are smiling down,
leaning across a velvet padded rail:
the bar of heaven? Maybe their paint
is flaking, but behind them, the wheels and ratchets
turn, that giant, ramshackle mechanism:
diagram of ascendancies, cusps

and influence, the great computer
we're all plugged into, every last one
of the billions (more living now than ever
have lived before) – but the system can still
contain them, process the information
and spew out the numbers and codes of every
single one when his time has come.
Or, if that garish circus backcloth
were stripped down, and the empty blackness
of the space behind should be revealed –
satin sheen inside the devil's cloak
as the old gallant swirls it (if there were a devil);
a glassy void reflecting nothing
but your own image back, each time
further away and more and more ghostly;
that realm of accident where no gods punish,
supervise, or favour: a world
of isolated atomies,
insurance-agents calculating odds
against the chances – would you panic
and curse, or have you always known
the secret of the universe?

Terra Incognita

A day that makes me feel I've lived already
long enough, almost forever; with nothing
else especially to wait for; as though
I've had as much as anyone can have,
both good and bad: a day it would not even
matter if the coming few decades
(the most to hope for) were to be erased
from my allotted tally. Is this a fear
of what portends, or recognition of
a lucky fate?
                    What chafed, the bonds' constraint,
was my support. I never realised
the cords I strained to break were safety nets.

Failure can change into success of sorts,
perhaps. My perseverance led to just
this place. I must admit the paradox.

And yet I'm left in an absence of faith so
absolute that any suppositious future
mocks the prospect of change: awareness
which moves far beyond the spiralling,
recurrent plunge into despair – terra
incognita –
                    nor, on this calm, soft,
perfect autumn day, lets me forget
winter's worst storms still have to be faced.

That Coming Mystery

The longer you stare into its depths, the further
the fire recedes, the wider it spreads. Those knots
of heat, whirling eddies of light where the final
drops of sap lay hidden, untouched till now,
flare up, explode, as though a galaxy
were being born. Like staring into the eye
of a storm, when clouds are as turbulent as waves
beneath a cliff. If you look for too long at one
of these things it seems to surround you, and perhaps
for a moment you'll have the luck to become part of it,
to lose your separateness in the heart of whichever
element – in a water-bead, a flame,
the moving air, or rock and earth. What you watch
with such attentiveness is the breaking and re-creation
of matter's forms.... That coming mystery.

Fire

Fire, like all servants, must be watched
continually. Fire, the best servant,
therefore the most dangerous. Every
servant dreams to usurp his master –
moved by the same ferocity as fire
riots through tenements, incandescing
block after block of their pattern,
a chart lit up to demonstrate
the saturation bombing, (those who plot it
being fire's unwitting servants).

Once got loose, fire will eat metal
girders, cement structures, papery bark
of eucalyptus trees, household pets
or humans: consume anything. Because nothing
is alien to fire, as the perfect servant never
shows surprise at his master's demands. Contained,
fire can work miracles, but rampaging
free, reduces even his own hearth
to ashy desolation – then creeps back,
surly, to sit weeping in the ruins.

All Those Victorian Paintings

All those Victorian paintings, with camels,
and that eerie lavender light, just
after sunset, were absolutely right.
Not only Holman Hunt – yet goats
still scatter across the landscape like scraps
of burnt paper, or move down a hillside as though
a column of ants was approaching – but the other,
forgotten, painters (technique respectful
and serious as they once were):
ladies, cheeks flushed under plaited straw hats,
skirts dusty, with campstool, umbrella, and easel,

whose pictures of palm-trees and Arabs now stand
face to the wall in attics, or hang
in vicarage bedrooms; their bachelor cousins
and brothers, convalescents or artistic
consuls – saw the Holy Land
with a camera's focused accuracy:
triumph of objectivity
over believers' fervour.

Belief

It was trying not to wake up from a nightmare
of willed descent into the maelstrom
or, shrunk to the size of an atom,
forcing my way though
the shuttered iris of a kaleidoscope
into a glistening darkness of feathers
and suffocation, to learn what lay
behind that wall.

It was clinging to the top of the highest dizzying slide,
unable to let go, or,
petrified at the open door
of an aircraft, parachute pack on my back,
ripcord unfelt between paralysed fingers,
the roaring of wind, like sound come through ether,
a fading call.

Somewhere down there, hazed mountains in the distance,
the leathery saint sits in his cave,
wrestling with demons. Every attempt
takes place in a context of order and calm.
Hardest of all to give up the cold
excitement of hallucination:
a sword above the abyss which does not
ascend or fall.

Summer Storm

Only for some moments
the sky goes dark as night-time:
rain fuming up like smoke
from the tiled roofs opposite.
Sunshine, lightning, thunder-roar.

And cold air slides in, heavy,
across ledges of windows
there was no time to close:
a dense and chilly flood
that rises from the floor.

Already the storm is moving.
The separate drops
of water slowing in the gutter-
pipes drum their muffled
tattoo, after the downpour.

Midsummer Night

Midsummer night. Light never leaves the sky.
Dull as cooling coal, the hurt sun lingers.
Bituminous stones, their black surfaces
scratched with runes only spirits can read
rise out of the beaches: backs of whales seamed
by scars, or stars that mark the sky's old wounds –
evidence of violence, and its omen.

There are fires. From below the horizon flames
smudge the clouds with crimson reflections, bloody
the outline of dunes and boulders. Between
midnight and morning not one soul comes
to witness the sun lurch itself up
and begin its pained slow wheeling towards
the field of darkness, the opposite solstice.

Squirrel in Holland Park

An after-lunch walk: autumn's first flaccid, fallen leaves,
canopied trees which held off the raindrops and filtered the light.
Between trunks plaqued with moss the squirrels approached,
tails buoyant as brush-strokes, self-assured as spoilt children.

The most confident of all was blind on one side,
orb dull, shrunken, and white as the boiled eye of a fish.
With the other black, darting, totally alert eye
it judged the exact distance to reach the proffered nut.

Fingers and hair the same tarnished, chemical yellow as those
tense paws, when the man who was feeding it, clucking his tongue
and murmuring endearments, noticed me watching, with a confused
gesture he nodded and winced away, grasp tightening

on the crumpled paper bag. The squirrel stopped,
and turned its good side to judge another likely patron –
who pulled the collar closer round her throat, kept moving
down the avenue, feeling completely unwanted.

Hospital Flowers

Hospital flowers seem to last longer, or is it
only that they are kept longer, looked at
more often, share the same tainted yet
sustaining air until like us they are half-
drugged. Unless the nurses take them away,
day after day they wilt in regulation vases
or commandeered drinking glasses, reminders
of the friends who brought them and that fear
which, though omnipresent, looms clearer
here than in the world outside, the place
where flowers are forced for just this purpose.

Those fraying petals, having undergone
the entire process from glossy bud to
insect-like arrest, now resemble rare

aberrations waiting to be classified.
Tulip and iris, snowdrop and freesia succumb.
Carnations parch, anemones harden.
The delicate inner streakings fade, the scent
disperses. As though wincing under a probe,
narcissus, jonquil, and daffodil contract,
twisting around an invisible axis. Their trumpets
roll inward: visitors' crumpled sweet-papers.

Yellow and black of pollen powders my fingers
as I rearrange them, and the patterns of veins
marking their tissues, whose colours alter inevitably
as bruises, are like those on the limbs of flushed,
unconscious patients waiting to be wheeled back
to their darkened rooms. Yet though stem and
blossom may soften, fleshy leaves turn limp
and spongy, still they slope bravely as bullet-frayed
banners, torn trophy flags or yesterday's bunting
half-bleached by the rain, after celebrating
the same old local victory again.

Dreaming

Night after night in that place
I see myself from above,
hunched over an open
book – and watch words form,
the empty pages crawl
with an alphabet of worms.

Only by a tremendous
effort of will (almost
a miracle – as much as
must have been used to name
the world), can I create
the necessary words.

Fretful and restless as actors
paralysed on the screen
when the mechanism stops,

my characters wait, while speeches
and purposes are imagined.
Then the story continues.

The plots are complicated
and violent, histories
of the tribe. Like a weary
scribe who copies an unknown
script from a blurred and doubtful
source, I wake exhausted

by this obligation
to think each thought and write
each phrase before I read it,
for no reward – with nothing
ever understood or
learned, and the dream gone.

House-guest

Why is it that other peoples' beds always seem
too hard or too soft, and other peoples' food
always too salt or sweet; their houses too cold
or too hot – never familiar or comfortable?
Is it because as though one skin has gone
(brittle scarf-skin when a scald is finally healing:
the accident that happens away from home),
I am left exposed to every mood of doubt
concerning my validity, more dependent
on smells and textures and shadows and furniture
than the reassurance of words and friendship.

Yet how quickly we who at first are so unsure
establish new habits and territory, take over
a special corner and stake a claim. How soon
we feel part of the family – and how easily
are disconcerted by an intercepted
glance exchanged between our hosts at such
presumption of familiarity. Then

that skin crackles and splits, the blood beads out
on its shiny rawness, and we clutch at the nearest cloth
to wrap around the wound, even though it may be
an ancient silken robe, their most precious heirloom.

The Gambler

Everything gets thrown in, it's a gamble
for the highest stakes. As if you were a lord and could
dispose of standing timber, family plate, brooches,
horses, portraits, ropes of pearls, ancestral beds
and chairs, finally the house itself – focus
of your future hopes and earliest memories –
all goes under the hammer. The others may object,
but you're the heir. They're helpless. With your exorbitant
and reckless nature, to indulge a fraudulent
destructive passion, you seem set on ruination.

Or instead, look at it another way:
as if there's something that makes love and friendship,
every pleasure this world offers – wind and sunlight
on the water, music, books, and growing children,
even health – seem nothing by comparison.
For though you set these tangibilities against
the emptiness that gnaws your spirit, try to count
your blessings, still the need augments. The mysteries
and techniques of the style become your only chance
of satisfaction, the work which might authenticate.

Meanwhile, that trio: loneliness, despair, and boredom,
extend their territory and flaunt their winnings;
gains which must be countered, no matter what the price.
For in this gambling palace how decide if you
feel murderous or suicidal when the thousand
flashing crystals of the chandeliers dazzle your burning,
wincing eyes, and other eyes are challenging
and scornful; when this compulsion forces you to venture
heart and soul once more, and lures you always further
on towards perfection and away from life.

Meat

This subject might be better for a painter,
a moralising painter: the butcher's window
framing him – anachronistic whiskers,
ruddy face, white coat, striped apron, the sort
of tradesman one had thought no longer could
exist; and her – a proper Chelsea lady
of a certain age, hatted, necklaced,
mackintoshed, whose rouged and powdered cheeks
seem quite another substance than the flesh
of booted girls who stride along the pavement.

The gloomy afternoon accentuates
the disconcerting glitter of the shop:
refrigerator doors, refulgent tiles,
enamel trays displaying cutlets, kidneys,
liver, mince, scallops of veal, oxtails
and stewing steak – that close detail behind which
all the action will take place, and, as
a background (filling in for mountains, say,
or distant vista of a plain or lake),
hang carcasses made ghostly by their sheath
of creamy fat, and ghastly by the blood
congealing in their blackened, swollen veins.

He holds a tray of gobbets out for her
inspection almost deferentially,
as though the relics of a martyrdom,
some tortured part, and she bends forward, solemn,
thoughtful, curious. Two faces
from the crowd around the rack or headman's block.

I cannot hear, but guess he's vouching
for its authenticity: each animal
received an individual injection
of adrenalin, to tenderise the flesh
with fear and rage. She's pondering, her vacant
eye reflective as a sphere of gristle,
intent upon deciding what to choose.
And in that chrome and crimson antiseptic
antechamber to the slaughterhouse, they
seem the natural focus of the composition.

Aftermath

I

How many forms of life can clear a space
around themselves, create a desolation?
Only ourselves and some bacteria –
as one particular incident can cauterise
a zone of memory. Brain with its dying cells.
A whole epoch lost from the past, scar
seared on the mind, evasion, transference,
or pull-out – abandonment of a sector, then
re-grouping and counting survivors:
those cells, spores, memories lucky
to have been far enough from the centre.
There was no warning, no place in this scheme
for forethought or philosophy. And nerve-
connections are made by the same sort of chance
which sets spores floating onto the agar-plate,
or plots the next appearance of some new
mutation, the irresistible virus cutting its swathe
through a population, the forces which empty a city.
Streams of refugees push up roads,
across the countryside: microbes multiplying
in a Petri dish, organisms
liberated for new purposes
or circuits overloading, burnt out
by recollection's protective chemistry.

II

Before recovery, the entire
body – physical, political, or astral –
must descend to more primitive levels.

III

Like a shaman, whose blood is drained away
and set in pans to cool like curds or gelatine,
whose every bone is disarticulated,
moans and raves to know himself lower than hell,
further than heaven, more helpless than in the
torturer's cave, the courtyard of the Comneni,
the plague-house or the kidnapper's hovel,

yet trusts in his re-integration; or an astronaut,
months out in space, feeling his identity
stretched like his trajectory across
the constellations, must never doubt he will
arrive – the sufferer can only wait
for resolution and eventual peace.

IV

Whatever its scope, the disaster, private
or global, reaches equilibrium.
Veterans of epidemic, madness,
and war, find their way back home
with faulty limbs and half-gone memory.
And in neglected fields, self-sown, old
strains of wheat, emmer and spelt, with sparse
bristling heads, show tall against the sky.

The King Must Die

King of this once-splendid country
now falling apart
beneath the blows of my most favoured subjects –
I know how he must feel, that wounded activist
hidden in a mountain village or
a room behind a garage in the suburbs.

This city, the capital,
stained by blood and noisy with explosions,
has been my heart and brain;
that mountain range the spine to hold me upright,
the river my bloodstream –
rocks and earth and sky as intimate
and vital as my own body.

Somewhere near the palace, in one of those ministries
whose flags are shredded with bullets, windows shattered,
walls plastered with proclamations,
the sons of murdered deputies
argue with their followers.

If this country is my body,
are they the cells that multiply with jungle energy,
or my true doctors?

I have become just one more man amazed
and helpless as he learns the process of decay:
a miner coughing his lungs out (we are rich in metals),
a forester who watches his leg mortify
where the saw slipped – or a woman after days of labour,
who feels the child refuse, her last blood pour away.

Like them, and my son's friends
(they tell me he has disappeared),
I know that I am dying with the country
I still love and call myself,
yet have no power or wish to save.

The New Science of Strong Materials
(With acknowledgement to Professor J.E. Gordon, and the 2nd edition of his book,
The New Science of Strong Materials, *Penguin, 1976)*

Plastic flow or brittle cracking:
whatever the material,
always the inescapable
potentiality within the structure
of either form of fracture:

these two failure mechanisms
are in competition for
all inadequate and earthly matter.
If it yields, the fabric's ductile.
Brittle, if at first it cracks.

Trying to visualise the three-
dimensional reality
of imperfection, dislocation's
vortex, the maelstrom of shearing, I can
only guess the faultlessness

and ease with which the rows of atoms
can reject the slightest deviation,
yet not acknowledge or accept even
a modicum of individual
involvement or decision.

They barely need do more than shuffle
one small fraction of an Ångström
in position, and quite soon
the incomplete half sheet of atoms
has been edged outside. The others

have combined, closed ranks. Stresses
and strains, pressure and tension: the language
not only of engineering. Though
the combinations seem almost endless,
the basic elements are few,

their governing rules the same: just different
ways of dealing with dislocation
and stopping fracture, rare
recorded attempts and even at times
success at cohesion, bonding, and union.

Usually Dry-eyed

'Do you cry easily?' At times. Always
at what is called the cheapest sentiment.
Especially when lovers are reunited,
brothers reconciled, son safe and well
at home with his mother, husband and wife
smiling together. Those are the basic tales.

I'm moved to tears also when the hero wins through
and the siege is lifted, the message delivered, the years
of work rewarded – whenever modest virtue
is recognised. They are tears of pleasure
at the closing of the circle, when Heaven sinks
to earth and existence becomes ordered, just, and perfect.

And tears are brought to my eyes by any report
of natural disaster: when rains fail or fish
move away; devastation destroying the labour of hundreds:
sharp-tipped heel crushing the ants' nest.

But tears are not appropriate nor adequate
response to the arrogance of cruelty.
Tears make one impotent. Anger is needed. Anger,
the activist. And anger must stay dry-eyed.

To Somehow Manage a Poem

There's a patched-up, incongruous neatness about his appearance
like an orphan child who's just had his collar buttoned and straightened
and a careless flannel rubbed across his face

Or the photo sent of a hostage, yesterday's newspaper
propped against his chest to prove he's still alive

Or that figure in the witness box, so pale and thin, who
whatever the consequence cannot control his grin –
happy to be out of the cellars, to see
other people after months of one ranting inquisitor –
though his smile reveals the missing teeth; soon
he'll start to say everything he was told, he'll reiterate

And the hostage's wary muffled voice, scratchily taped,
left at the pre-arranged place, will accuse all his colleagues

And the child will stumble over his age
and name, but somehow manage a poem.

The Dancing Floor

Is this the thread? Have I found Ariadne?
can my luck hold and let me reach
the centre, meet and kill the monster,

Ariadne's slobbering half-brother,
or will the Minotaur trample me down
in the stench and dark of the labyrinth?

Such precedents. She betrayed her father:
but that was not enough to hold
Theseus. He abandoned her.

Then he forgot to change the sail
to white from black – in his turn caused
a father's grief and death. Where

to end the tale? Before Phaedra
and Hippolytus or after?
One action leads inexorably

to the next: victims of the gods,
their own passions, or types of cunning
and vainglorious will? I do not know

if Ariadne died at Naxos,
or married Dionysius and thus
escaped the family drama – nor why

I must accept the risk, and trust
this clue will lead me straight into
the maze's core, the sacred dancing-floor

where Ariadne, Theseus, Minotaur,
triumphant in their unity,
wait to welcome a new partner.

Poems from Chapbooks

(1973 & 1983)

Today

Will this be   really   my only life
– between past and future –
Recurrences, anticipation,
Whether neutral or foreboding (dear God,
How far must one go back cast oneself forward?)
The arc can be extended
As recklessly as energy and bravery and curiosity
Support the traveller.

Yesterday you left. Tomorrow, Friday,
Today I cannot bear the sound of wind, the bleating sheep,
        the birds.
I flee into the past or future – anywhere but here.
No memory could be as painful as the feel
Of time   wrenching its barbed way through me   moment
        after moment
No hope as pitiful.
My heart beats protest at its passage.
The present, now, is dragged, bleeding, away,
But I sit here forcing myself to know it.

A Midland Goddess

Across a field of royal cabbages
Half-rotting, I see a big girl laughing,
a freckled midland goddess, carolled
by a copse of raucous birds.

She husks dock stems of their flat seeds,
Tears yellow petals from brown-eyed daisies,
Despoils bright autumn hips and haws,
Falls back on tousled rose-bay and rusty fern;

Then strips the ragged brambles of their fruit
Which stain her mouth the same dark hue
As that stiff mud which clogs her shoes
And soils the dangling lace beneath her skirt.

Moon Landing

They float
In amniotic fluid
Drift dreamily across
The screen
      Padded and helmeted
      As if descending
      Into caves
Weightlessness
Must bring back memories
Remind the body
Of that paradisic state
Perhaps even pre-uterine
The moon
Attracts their ship
A destination
History ordains
The first bright planet seen
And pointed at –
That yolkless egg
They smile, encapsulate
Instinctual as cells
In spite of all machinery
      As self-contained
      As angels dancing on a pin
      Or embryo
      Flexing its limbs
      Exploring how much space remains
      Within the cave
      Where food and air are fed
      Into its veins
Their womb
The universe

The Atlantic Beaches

Lost among dunes.

Those distant figures –
Are they birds or
White-robed women?

A scorpion
Buries itself.

Above the surf
Bladders of weed
Shine three-dimensional.

Pink haze of noon,
Tepid green water.

Menace of solitude.

Fragments of a Dream

In the kingdom of the dead, south
Of the river, warehouses line
Wide streets, the sky is dull, a girl
Runs nowhere. From the other pavement
A white-haired man calls out, his voice
Is urgent and surprised. He knows
Her name. 'So you are here?' he says,
Affectionate, regretful.

Outside the city wall lies sand.
The plough is old and wooden, and
To use it futile. The sterile
Grains will take no furrow, but slide
Back down into the hollow. This might
Be hell, condemned to work such land.

CLIMATES (1983)

With woodcuts by Ki Batei (1734-1810), one of the Japanese scholar-painters of the 'literati' movement. These artists stressed the kinship between painting, calligraphy and poetry. Ki Batei's master was Yosa Buson, the 'second Pillar of Haiku' after Matsuo Bashō.

Further...Closer

First day of the second half of another year.
Again the evenings will be shorter, mornings later,
the centre of the solar system further away.

This fear of being exiled further from the source,
trapped in the desolation of my own centre,
where frozen winter will be autumn's only harvest.

What could be further than my soul from any centre
of light and warmth and energy? If the sun is a jewel
in its creator's crown, his face is turned away.

But what horror, if he should swerve round and fix his gaze
on me. Nothing I was or thought could endure those eyes
as they came closer, and cauterised my darkest centre.

And yet, I still keep moving closer to the furnace-
centre, that jewelled horror now as cool as water,
where he reigns, lord of all knowledge, where night and day

have the same length, winter and summer eternally stopped
at Heaven's equinoctial centre, closer towards
the promised revelation of his other face.

While Summer Runs Its Course

Somewhere a few miles south or north
the sun is shining. Or closer still,
straight up, above the cloud, a brilliant
azure summer sky, unlike
this pallid swathing around the grey
church tower, asserts the actual season.
But here, a milky hush obscures
the day, and birds behave as though
it's almost twilight, not late morning.

Today this muffled noon conforms
well with my mood – it seems to promise
change (the birdsong strengthens, blueness
curdles, shadows harden) yet
everything remains potential.
Later, if the local pattern
holds, the sky will clear and colours
throb and deepen into glory
just before the sunset chorus.

Or the day might end in storm,
piling clouds above the trees
that form a curtain closing in
the garden, and the birds go silent –
which would answer to another
aspect of my need: a sudden
rain to filter through the rocks
and roots and graves, be purified
into the universal water.

This year, while summer runs its course
and I attempt the furthest zones –
expose myself once more to all
those different climates of the past –
I expect to alter as often
as the weather. And if the sun and rain
again produce their normal
miracle, the harvest – perhaps
I too shall come to that reward.

The Distant View

Summer rain
streaming down the windowpane
is the sound of the wind,
and shaking trees,
heavy with their fullest leaves,
are the shape of the wind.

Ten years looking at the same scene,
the same tower, the same steeple.
Either the church is slowly sinking,
or the trees are growing taller.

Always the birdsong. The first
sound at dawn: pigeons
in the chimney, with the changeless message
of another morning.
And only the heaviest rainstorm
can drown for a moment
their mechanical calling.

Flaunting its burden of foliage
every branch and twig moves
in a different direction: thousands
of despairing gestures – an outdated syle.
Inside the house, the silence,
except for wind, rain, birds,
makes such extravagant
expressiveness even less viable.

Then, between showers, the flat grey sky
is stretched apart, coagulates
to cloud. The horizon returns. The trees
are calmer. Soon the sun will be setting.
Birds begin to celebrate
that blue and crimson certainty.
Everything looks smaller, clearer,
further away, and quickly, before
I lose the distant view and rain
comes down again I close the curtains.

Like shadows on the lawn –

sentences form in my head,
float in and out of my mind.
The thinner the cloud and stronger
the source of light, the firmer
the outline: a tentative smile
spreading across an unknown
face. The pale sky moves
above the empty garden,
and moods and memories
as seeming-motiveless
as this uncertain weather
follow each other, colour
my thoughts, then fade before
expressed by tears or words
or action. But that stranger,
with features so familiar
I might be looking in
a mirror, could determine
my future if I will
accept what she bestows,
and every shadow harden
wane and disappear
when noonday sunlight burns
away the morning haze.

Another Variation

Motor mowers, shrieking children,
and the slamming of car doors.
Sunday dinner smells. Summer
in the village. Soon the bells
will start. A stranger still, tonight
I shan't go to the pub, but stay
here in my room. Then, the only

sound, after everyone
has gone back home and dogs have stopped
their barking, will be my own pen scratching,
matches striking, papers torn
perhaps as I reject another
variation of this poem.

Angel from the North

Now, between July and autumn,
August makes its own season.
The clouds seem higher, piled in sharper
whites and darker greys, the sky
already colder – arctic tones
above the glowing apple trees,
laden with a better crop
than these ten years I've lived here.
Next month such rain would strip the leaves,
every morning raise another ring
of tawny mushrooms and mournful flocks
of martins gathering for their long journey
south. Today, the lawn shows only greener
and more livid when the storm stops,
and still the sun strikes hot before
a further bank of cloud blots out the light,
moving like an angel from the north:
whose fiery sword of frost will bring
the apples down to rot among
the sodden leaves and faded grass –
and mark the garden like the first-born.

Vanguards

Autumn starts with drizzle and the smell
of burning stubble. Though I shut all windows,
acrid smoke permeates the house.

That sound is not artillery nor rain,
but straw's dry crackle. Only from the attic
am I high enough above the garden trees

to see those black paths streaked across pale fields
where ash becomes the final harvest
and birds rise in alarm. Later, at twilight,

the distant glow, orange and red, with its nimbus
of white, could be a battle-ground,
and every separate fire a gutted tank –

vanguards threatening a long campaign
of skirmishes, encirclement, and siege-
famine, as winter closes in.

An Unmarked Ship

An unmarked ship, entering
the harbour of an undefended
town: autumn bears down on the land.
Driven by a north-west wind,
banks of cloud are the weight of sail
carried by its towering masts,

and that relentless grinding back
and forth of harvesting machines
across the fields becomes the distant
shouts for help and last attempts
of the inhabitants to save
themselves before the rapine starts.

Red Sky at Night...

Clouds in horizontal bars
lit gold beneath, shaded mauve
above, with flame and scarlet centres.

Puce and dove become a pure
blue sky that deepens, heightens. Red
brick house, red roof-tiles, rose-hips

and crimson autumn leaves. And all of it
my delight, though I am more
one of the hungry flock than a shepherd.

Anticipated

This month I've watched the moon through every change
from thinnest crescent into ripeness, from August
languor into clear September. Unseen
between two darknesses, full moon will be
tomorrow morning, just before noon. Tomorrow
night, hours after the unmarked climax,
her strength already waning, will be too late.
Tonight her energies are at their height.

Full moon used to awe me, craze me – now
I feel equal to her power. This
moment perhaps I too have reached an acme,
and the over-arching sky, the garden trees
with their rustlings and shadows, their nightingale-language,
are satellites circling around the centre
everything on earth anticipates
and this one night allows me to become.

To Break This Silence

Wind and trees and birds, this vague and always
changing weather: how they cut me off
from him with whom I share my house and life,
and I am altered by the seasons' power.

Hours each day together. Yet not enough
to counterweigh the glamour I succumb to,
those hours spent staring at the fire. It seems
that nothing happens but the rain and sunset,

night-mist curling through the hedges. The habit
of our mutual isolation forces me
to seek the most persuasive words to break
this silence: the key and explanation why

the radiance of a sphere of light against
the clouded autumn sky, swathing the moon
like fruit around its stone, confirms that we
have come to be the other's space and climate.

Fifteen to Infinity

(1983)

Passenger

Not watching trains pass and dreaming of when
I would become that traveller, glimpsed
inside the carriage flashing past a watching
dreaming child, but being the passenger

staring out at tall apartment blocks
whose stark forms cut against the setting sun
and bars of livid cloud, balconies crowded
with ladders, boxes, washing, dead pot-plants,

into lighted, steamy windows where women
are cooking and men just home from work, shoes
kicked off and sleeves rolled up, are smoking, stretched
exhausted in their sagging, half-bought chairs,

under viaducts where children busy
with private games and errands wheel and call
like birds at dusk: all that urban glamour
of anonymity which makes me suffer

such nostalgia for a life rejected
and denied, makes me want to leave the train,
walk down the street back to my neighbourhood
of launderettes, newsagents, grocery shops,

become again that watching dreaming girl
and this time live it out – one moment only
was enough before a yawning tunnel-
mouth obscured us both, left her behind.

Stubborn

My Stone-Age self still scorns
attempts to prove us more
than upright animals
whose powerful skeletons
and sinewy muscled limbs
were made to be exhausted
by decades of labour
not subdued by thought,

despises still those dreamers
who forget, poets
who ignore, heroes
who defy mortality
while risking every failure,
spirits unsatisfied
by merely their own
bodily survival.

I know her awful strength.
I know how panic, envy,
self-defence, combine
with her tormented rage
because they will deny
her argument that nothing
but the body's pleasure,
use, and comfort, matter.

Guarding her cave and fire
and implements, stubborn
in her ignorance,
deaf to all refutation,
I know she must insist
until the hour of death
she cannot feel the pain
that shapes and haunts me.

Here

Here, like a rebel queen
exiled to the borderlands,
the only role I can assume
is Patience, the only gesture,
to fold my hands and smooth
my robe, to be the seemly one,

the only precept, always
to know the truth, even if forced
to silence, never to deny
my unrepentant nature.
I am my own tamer.
This life is the instrument.

And yet the iron hand wears
such a velvet glove,
and dreams and memories
of prelapsarian happiness –
simple actions which, when
first performed, lacked that content –

return to slow my steps
as I climb up and down between
the parlour and the kitchen
to fill my watering-can again
and give the plants their ration,
make me question that self-image.

Some power, created by
an altered vision, moving
to a different rhythm,
annihilates the past, revealing
space enough for another
universe. And there,

where needs and wishes synchronise,
where truth is changed and laws
revised, the capital has fallen
to a friendly tribe,
and I can leave this exile
when I choose – or rule from here.

Outside the Mansion

As though we stood with noses pressed against the glass
of a windowpane, outside a mansion, dazzled
by the glowing lamps, the music and the circling dancers:

festivity, ceremony, celebration –
all equally alien to my sort of person.
Such a failing passes down the generations.

It could well be a fairy story, half-remembered.
I've often wondered if some godmother uninvited
to the party, vengeful, cast her mournful spell.

So profoundly known, the joyless spite spoilers
use to ease such pain; envy and disappointment
proudly claim choice of the unavoidable.

Stronger than the doubt of being right or wrong,
that denial is our sole tradition. We watch
the windows darken as the curtain slides across.

Author! Author!

What I am working at and want to perfect –
my project – is the story of myself: to have it
clear in my head, events consecutive,
to understand what happened and why it happened.

I wander through department stores and parks,
beyond the local streets, seem to be doing nothing;
then an overheard phrase or the way light slants
from the clouds, unravels the hardest puzzle.

It takes all my time, uses so much energy.
How can I live, here and now, when the past
is being unwound from its great spindle, and tangles
forgotten motives around the present? Rather

than set the record straight, further knowledge
complicates. I cannot stop the action
to make a judgement, or hope for better.
Every gesture casts a longer shadow

into the future, each word shifts the balance.
I see myself as one more character
in this extravagant scenario,
the story not yet finished. And who's the author?

The Journey

Head against the glass, eyes close
to the train window, everything that grows
along the siding blurs and streaks: a green
and brown and yellow diagram of speed.

Not until I urge my gaze backwards
down the line can I distinguish saplings,
plumy grasses, flowering weeds and briars
sown there haphazard. Lifting my eyes higher,

one pigeon, pale against thunder-clouds,
spot-lit by a fitful summer sun,
rises above a formal wood, dense
trees all the same size, as though planted together.

Softened by the mirror of a tunnel,
my reflected face stared out, much younger,
superimposed like an old photograph.
If I sat opposite, one glance

comparing the two would be enough to inform
myself of every change that time has wrought.
Suddenly, I learned I was not other,
earlier, than what I have become

but only now am forced to recognise.
Wings beating it further up the sky,
to a bird's eye, the whole route is visible.
The nature of the country makes no difference,

nor the hastening traveller's confusion
(journey unended, memories unproved)
between conflicting versions of the legend
uniting images and questions

concerning fate and chance and fortune. Dazzle
of sunlight, then shadow, blinding me in the carriage.
A horse alone in a meadow, the level crossing.
A steeple. The first houses. The train is stopping.

Launching

Autumn. Early morning.
A bench near the pond in Kensington
Gardens. This park is where
I've watched the seasons change
for twenty years. Under
my feet, yellow and crimson
leaves, colours as pure
as though with death their poisons
were purged; but further away,
against an empty sky,
the rusty foliage
of a shrubbery like a head
of hennaed greying hair.

Through the playground railings
the swings and slide and sandbox
I feared and hated. No one
told me how short such moments
were, nor taught the art
of living in the present.
There seemed so many dream-
scenarios. Now,
the only roles left: leathery
tourist, plastic-bag crazy,
literary lady or
admirer of grandchildren's
model racing yachts.

Spring and summer passed,
winter marking its own
bright blaze on what will not
endure, the balance shifts
from hope to human nature,
and the last self manifests,
poised for survival. But meanwhile
come days like this, when nothing
yet seems crucial, blue
and gold and calm, with time
to feed the ducks and learn
about finality, all
the different styles of launching.

After Fifteen
(to David)

First there were close-ups: fallen petals,
patterned bark, fungus on stones,
a baby's pram: garden scenes.
The playground where, laughing and rosy-
cheeked, you waddled after pigeons
in your padded snow-suit; I,

another discontented mother
by the sandbox. All photographs
which seemed to need between three
and six feet. Then the focus shifted,
lengthened, changed. Now, Sunday
morning in the square, six feet tall,
you stand against the peeling
plane-trunk, look up through its leafless
twigs and branches, camera aimed
at pallid winter clouds. 'Fifteen
to infinity?' you ask, to confirm
the setting. Yes. You have grown
to become the photographer, and time
expands around you like the dizzying
crown of the tree and sky above:
fifteen to infinity.

Love-feast

Sulphur-yellow mushrooms like unlaid, unshelled eggs
inside a chicken's stomach when my mother cleaned it.
This morning, mushrooms on the lawn made me remember.

Bright as dew on the grass and silver with air-bubbles,
a stream of water splashed from the dull brass tap against
the side of the sink and her red-chilled fingers when she
opened the carcass and laughed to show me how some were almost
ready – yolks only needing their coating of lime and mucus,
while others were still half formed, small as pearls or seeds.

Always, once the chicken was plucked and quartered and boiling
my mother would take those eggs, marked with twisting coils
of crimson threads like bloodshot eyes, and the liver put aside
on the draining-board in a chipped old china saucer, and fry them
with an onion to make our private treat. In the steamy
kitchen, the two of us would eat, and love each other.

Handbag

My mother's old leather handbag,
crowded with letters she carried
all through the war. The smell
of my mother's handbag: mints
and lipstick and Coty powder.
The look of those letters, softened
and worn at the edges, opened,
read, and refolded so often.
Letters from my father. Odour
of leather and powder, which ever
since then has meant womanliness,
and love, and anguish, and war.

War Time

'Stand here in front of me,' my mother said,
and pushed me forward in the downtown office
doorway. 'Hide me.' Behind my back she fumbled
with a sagging stocking and broken garter.

That garter: salmon-pink elastic crinkled
at the edges, half-perished, stretched too often,
it had lost the rubber button. Her stockings were
always too long. Something else to blame her for.

Her flushed face. My stern eye. Of course
I noticed: the folded rayon top exposed
an inch or two of thigh – soft white flesh,
neglected, puckered with cold. Another torment.

Her round felt hat, pierced by a tarnished arrow
glinting in the drafty corner, bent low
as my ten-year-old shoulder, and the safety pin
held between her lips seemed further off

than that umbrella-tip or those galoshes
of passers too distracted to ignore us.
No peacetime knowledge would assuage the future
we determined, one rainy winter morning.

Or Her Soft Breast

I could not get to sleep last night,
burning on the slow fire
of self-despite,

twisting on the spit that's thrust and
turned in such cruel manner
by my own hand,

until those earthy clinging arms
lifted out of the dark
to hold me fast

and drag me back to the same place
I thought I had escaped,
to see her face

as close as when I knew it first:
smiling, tender, perfect.
My fetters burst,

but the puzzle and the meaning
of my sudden freedom –
her touch on me,

soothing and cool, as though I sank
into a pool and drank
there, thankful –

was it a dream of love, or death?
The grave, where I now slept,
or her soft breast?

Lost Drawing

Bare winter trees in silhouette
against a clear cold turquoise sky
just after sunset: during the war,
at my aunt's house in Virginia, I tried
to draw them – trees like these in England
which she never saw – and now,
trees in my garden make me feel
the first true pang of grief since her death.

Between the washtubs and store-cupboards filled
with pickled peaches and grape jam, crouched
into a broken wicker chair,
I peered up through the basement window.
Sketchpad on my lap, with brushes and
bottles of black ink, blue ink, and water,
I wanted to convey the thickness
of their trunks, the mystery
of how a branch puts out a hundred
twigs, the depth and power of evening.

I heard her cross the porch, the kitchen
floorboards creak. As it grew darker,
that halo of light, outlining
all the finest intersections,
faded. Night absorbed the trees
the house the woman and the girl
into itself, kept every aspect
of that time alive, to give
me back today the memory
of my dead aunt and my lost drawing.

Crystal Pleating

(for A.G.)

Crystal pleating around the neck and shoulders
of that flamboyant crêpe dress I only wore once –
I remember the two of us shopping for it. Since then,
pushed into the back of the wardrobe, covered
with a dusty plastic, I've watched it fade
the way black dyestuffs do, to grey and copper-
purple, except those jetty streaks in folds
and hem. If mine now seems a witch's costume,
the queenly robe of silver-white you chose
must be all tarnished, should any part remain.
What a pair we looked. I knew how much
you needed me for a foil: the negative
of such a vivid presence – and I was glad
to serve your purpose. But my regards was not
enough, nor what you wanted. And though the dress
would be quite perfect for a mourning garment,
I have not dared to put it on again.

The Storm

Harry, I know how much you would have enjoyed it.
I can see your mouth's ironic curve as the heavens
opened. The umbrella over my head was almost
useless – rain and hail at the same slant
as your amused imagined gaze darkened
the side of my coat and trousers. Hard to resist
the thought that while we hurried back to the car
as soon as we could to wait it out, cold and
distracted, someone up there was paying attention,
taking notice. The sky had been clear
enough as we drove through the cemetery
gates into those horizontal acres
ignored behind the bonfire sites and tool-sheds
of suburban gardens, then parked and walked
between memorial stones to our appointment.

A spare man in a mac held the casket
chest-high as he approached. I stretched
a finger to touch a corner. The brass plate,
engraved with your full name, flashed paler
in the altering light as cloud thickened.

Cut into the piece of ground that was
the grave of both our parents – a square hole,
its soil piled nearby. A superstitious
qualm made me look down: too shallow
to disturb them. It must have been the very
moment the sexton stooped to put your ashes
there – where I hoped you'd want to be:
with them – that the storm broke. Instead of a struggle
with grief, we were fighting the weather, reduced
to the ludicrous; instead of prayer, a dry
shelter was what seemed most important. Water
running across my hands, inside my sleeves,
I took the spade and being chief mourner,
made the first movement to bury you. Harry,
I think you would have found the symbolism
too facile and pompous, and your sense
of humour stopped you taking it seriously –
though certainly delighted by the conceit
of Nature aghast and weeping at your interment,
my poor brother, her true and faithful poet.

In Memoriam H.P.F.

God, the dead, and Donna Elvira
all inhabit the same realm:
the great democracy of imagination.

Every paradise and underworld
beyond a blue horizon –
Sheol or Elysium –
is a beautiful product of mental function:
conjuration, prayer, and purpose.

I shall not meet my dead again
as I remember them
alive, except in dreams or poems.
Your death was the final proof
I needed to confirm that knowledge.

As Though She Were a Sister

As though she were an older or a younger
sister, whom I might bully, flout, ignore
or use, my dealings were not serious
enough. How could I think she was my sister?
What insolence – and luck, to dodge her well-
deserved rebuke. For she, more like a mother
(I the disrespectful child who shouts
and flails and pulls away) till now has not
abandoned or betrayed me. I must have seemed
ridiculous or worse to all who watched,
and most to those who recognised the Muse.

Spring in Ladbroke Square

Embers still coated with ash,
these February buds – while others
already show the glowing nub
of life, each one Dionysus'
cone-tipped staff; and the first raw leaves
unhusked seem frail red curds and fibres
of flesh clinging to the twigs, as though
bacchantes had been here last night
to carry out spring's sacrifice,
and thrown the torn and bloody shreds
of Orpheus' limbs into the branches.

Marvellous Toys

(with acknowledgements to Marcel Detienne & Jean-Pierre Vernant)

How was Dionysus captured by the Titans?
With marvellous toys: a cone, emblem of the goddess,
a pierced stone that roared like a bull,
a tuft of wool, like those his killers used
to daub on gypsum and disguise themselves,

a knucklebone to grant divinatory
powers, a golden apple as his passport
to Elysium, and a round mirror
to see his ghostly other image – what child,
no matter how divine, could resist?

Who wanted Dionysus' death? Hera,
furious, had plotted to destroy him
in Semele's womb. Her malign advice
ignored, next she goaded Zeus to launch
a thunderbolt against the moony girl –

but the six-month child was sewn into his father's
thigh, for when the time arrived he must
be born. Yet wherever the boy was kept,
Hera's vengeful eyes pierced his disguise.
She sent her hit-men, the seven simple Titans.

What did the murderers do to Dionysus?
They cut his body into seven parts
which first they boiled and then they barbecued
(the ritual procedure) – but the heart
was put aside, to be saved by Athene, his sister.

Why did Dionysus triumph? From
his beating heart, the vital central organ,
he was resurrected to defeat the Titans
(whose blood and ashes formed the human race),
to open the cycle of death and generation

and, horned like a goat or stag or ram, raging
over the mountains with his pack of Maenads and Satyrs
brandishing cone-tipped ivy-twined spears and tearing
apart whatever the met, to bring drunkenness
and madness: those marvellous toys of paradise.

Titian's *Venus and Adonis*

He with that calculating look,
sated, half-rueful, of the local heart-breaker –
mustachioed garage-mechanic – and she,
the blacksmith's wife from further down
the square, mortified yet pleading:
why should he want to leave
all that lavish flesh and golden hair?

Even Cupid is asleep, drugged
by her perfumes and odours, his quiver of arrows
abandoned – but the dogs turn back to their master
and pull at their leashes, as though they sniffed
the waiting boar – and the plume in Adonis's
jaunty cap, stirred by the autumn
wind (perfect hunting weather,
sun pouring through thunder-clouds)
is equally restless. Nothing will thwart him.
Her insistence seems futile, his young
arrogance triumphant: and yet
her power has never failed before.

Susannah and the Elders

Sometimes she's painted clothed, but most
prefer her naked; she's shown at various
ages: a sturdy angry girl
able to fight back – then more
submissive; flesh to eye and handle
by merchants choosing cattle, or ancients
hoping to regain their youth.

Often the elders are timid, crouch
under balustrades, hide in the bushes,
peer around statuary. But when the maidservants
leave her alone in the garden, bolder,
the turbanned, scrawny-necked fools
creep to the foreground, pluck at her towels
and drapery, grimace encouragement.

Yet no matter how passive she seems –
or complacent, frightened, even peacefully
unaware of their presence, always
she inhabits a separate universe,
realm of the indifferent good:
purified with living waters,
a talisman of flesh and blood.

The Noonday Devil

Demon of accidie, the noonday devil.
How well I know his power – he, who besieges
the soul, slackens the hands and will, holds the sun
still, and makes each hour as long as fifty.

A bowl of lukewarm milk where flies settle:
my mind, subjected to these restless thoughts,
this weary languor – until I hate my work,
my room, my friends, myself, and my ambitions.

Under his torpid spell my life seems endless:
fallow earth and unused rusty plough,
a waterless cloud that never lets down rain,
a tree too often transplanted whose roots have withered.

Some days I can muster all my strength
for combat, others, just endure his torments.
But I have lost my hope in prayers and tears,
my appetite for anguish. He always wins.

Ulysses, Troilus and Cressida

Each infidelity left Ulysses
more uneasy. (What was Penelope doing?)
He knew that every woman was a whore –
why else were they here? – while warriors
were enemies only when they fought.

A guest at Menelaus' camp, that boy,
Troilus, brother of Hector (what joy to meet him
on the battlefield!) was being fooled.
It made him furious. His first look
at Cressida enough to guess the truth:
a daughter of the game. No doubt about
his duty. In spite of worldly wisdom, talk
of enterprise and reason, on one well-worn
subject Thersites was no fouler. She
personified expediency: a born
survivor – he understood and loathed the type.

It's called a tragedy, though none of these three
dies. And yet if every change brings death
nearer, to tear the scales from Troilus' eyes
was almost murder; while Cressida resigned herself
to the fortunes of war, and Ulysses sailed home.

The Song of Matho-Talen

(the last voluntary victim)

Like priestesses in megalithic
times, ancient village mothers
still Death's celebrants and agents

take the consecrated hammer
from Carnac chapel from Morbihan
and raise it in your freckled hands

to crack my skull release me from
life's burden and death's terror,
in honour of the trinity you serve

be kind as to your favoured youngest
son or each dead Pope whose head
is tapped three times with a silver mallet

then lay me near the Seven Sleepers'
stone to let my spirit turn
the wind and bring good fishing weather.

Miriam's Well

(from Talmudic sources)

On Sabbath evening, Miriam's Well,
and all its healing miracles –
that holy liquid which for her sake
saved the children of Israel, followed
them through the desert forty years –
moves from well to river, from river
to stream to well.
                    After her death
the flowing rock of Miriam's Well
sank in the sea, to rise again each

Sabbath and work its wonders. Miriam
died by a kiss from God. The Angel
of Death could not take her, nor worms
touch her body. When you draw the bucket
from Miriam's Well, if you want to hear
her prophesy, remember to fill
your mouth with water.

Archive Film Material

At first it seemed a bank of swaying flowers
windblown beside a railway track, but then
I saw it was the turning heads of men
unloaded from the cattle trucks at Auschwitz.

The Mount of Olives

Eternity has staked its claim
to the hills around Jerusalem.
The dead have prime territory,
every slope a cemetery,
caves, crypts and catacombs
like ancient ovens hollowed
under olive groves and churches.

Cars and buses grind their way
below the Walls and up the valley.
Today, you are the only ones
who want to have the door into
the Sanctuary of Ascension
opened, the boy there told us. How
can I make a living without tourists?

Sitting on a rock beside
the Tomb of the Prophets, two men,
deaf and dumb, talk with their hands.
If across the Kidron Brook
the Golden Gate unlocked to let
Messiah through, and the resurrected
sang his praises, would they notice?

But still the dead ones sleep like babies
undisturbed by bombs, while above them –
rosy as bakers, stern as Crusaders,
watchful as soldiers, pale as Hassids,
silent as angels – spirits hover,
and Eternity settles deeper
into the land around Jerusalem.

Leonard Baskin's Death Drawings

I *Death the Gladiator*

He looks like the oldest gladiator left,
the only survivor from seasons of murderous games;
a pensioned-off mercenary from the border
campaigns, veteran of every atrocity.

Under the arena – those passageways
as complicated as the convolutions
of a brain exposed by primitive trepanning,
that warren of storerooms and cellars where
animals and slaves, weapons and chariots, are kept,
their walls of kidney-coloured brick rotten
with sweat of fear and pain – lies his kingdom:
trainer of the Colosseum's favourites.

II *Death's Labours*

Sated and exhausted Death,
head bent forward, heavy jaw
and scabbed bald cranium
a schoolroom globe marked with
only the largest seas and continents.

Sagging dugs, bursting thighs,
belly like a pregnancy
(womb which holds a universe
of irredeemable flesh),
he's glutted, stupefied.
Sick from over-eating
that eternal harvest of corpses,
he gags and vomits; gorged
beyond endurance, lowers himself
back as though onto a close-stool.

Eyes sunk deep in their sockets
(candles guttering out, choked by matter)
teeth worn down by endless grinding
of bones, nose corroded like an old
syphilitic's. But lax across
one knee, the bruised meaty hand
of a labourer. Death works hard.

III *Death's Cloak*

His fuscous wings could be a cloak
of ruffled feathers, incrustations
on an insect's carapace:

the chrysalis that broke to show
his arrogant incarnation
his evil glutted baby face

his hairless massive torso:
the god whose cruel dilacerations,
limb from limb, no one escapes

as though for sport he thus torments
worms impaled upon his beak
summer insects in his busy hands.

IV *Death With No Wings*

It is the death you saw:
the tense hands of a wrestler
reaching out, the taut forearms
of a weightlifter, a prizefighter,
a porter from the meat market.

Nostrils like nares in a skull,
mouth a wound's torn lips,
tiny ears and eyes, head sunk
between the slab-slopes of his shoulders,
no neck. Great belly
and heraldic genitals.
Flesh pink-raw and hairless.

It is the death that comes with no pity
to thrust you into the charnel pit.
Death with no wings.

V *This Meat*

This meat browning for our meal –
these charred woody fibres where
the seared surface seals and darkens,
clings to the pan, is what must have stuck
to the bars of St Lawrence's grille
or the iron beds of Phnom Penh.
The sound flesh gave as the heat took
was unheard then through cries of pain.
Here in my kitchen, I cannot ignore it.
This meat is the same stuff I am made from.
This meat I cook now for our meal.

Trompe l'Oeil

(at the Villa Farnesina)

A blank niche in a wall
that you walk towards
with a vase in your hand
to place on the painted pedestal.
Fragments of broken glass
bent stems
fallen petals
and on the floor a pool of water.
Yourself putting them there.

The Angel

Sometimes the boulder is rolled away,
but I cannot move it when
I want to. An angel must. Shall
I ever see the angel's face,
or will there always only be
that molten glow outlining every
separate hair and feathered quill,
the sudden wind and odour, sunlight,
music, the pain of my bruised shoulders.

Silk Kimonos

Jade green and pale gold
under dark autumn cloud, worn flimsy
by rain and frost and wind – the planes'
leaves shift across their boughs
and the closed fronts of houses like silk
kimonos over dancers' limbs.

Sediments

The moment the door closed your smile fell
like cigar-ash onto the carpet, leaving as little trace,
and once again alone, off-guard, worn out
by the party you had to work so hard at,

all that's left to do now is rinse out
the glasses and raise the window to air the place,
watch the brake-lights interweave their pattern
up the boulevard and throw the butts out,
pull the heavy curtains to, then undress
and slowly clean the makeup from your face
while your brain keeps circling round that print-out
of what you meant but never got to say,

until the bath filled with its scented comfort,
and afterwards (the naked footstep marked
so clearly in the talcum powder spilled out
across the floor is like a castaway's)
you take the silver pill-box from your handbag
and wide-awake though tired enough to pass out,
lie down on the bed and feel the swirling
sediment dissolving in your veins.

The Prism

Braided like those plaits of multi-
coloured threads my mother kept
in her workbox (beige, flesh, and fawn
for mending stockings, primary tones
to match our play-clothes, grey and black
for Daddy's business suits), or Medusa-
coils of telephone wires, vivid as
internal organs exposed in their packed
logic under the pavement, nestling
in the gritty London clay,
associations fray into messages:

codes to unravel, cords to follow
out of prison, poems which make
no concession, but magnify
the truth of every note and colour,
indifferent whether they blind or deafen
or ravish or are ignored; the blueprint
of a shelter against the glare
– and the waterfall to build it near –
the perfect place to sit and hear
that choir of hymning voices, and watch
the prism of the rainbow spray.

Red Message

Stern ancestors, with features as intricate
as Japanese print-makers' seals or circuits
of transistor-cells. Wherever you lived,
flesh and bone of the clan became that place;
lives gone into the earth like water
poured for ritual, or dark ash strewn
from a sacrifice. Programmed by return
and repetition, watching the changing pattern
of smoke and sparks and leaves made time
another code to break: a white cataract
crashing over the head, or flames transmitting
their red message from the funeral pyre.

Entries

Like notes of music black against the stave,
the look of words and letters in purposeful
groupings, printed or written, seems to convey
meanings more definite than their overt
message – even when understood.

But, thorns on the knotted stems of briars
thick as the hundred-year growth around the sleeping
princess, or a spider-web's decoration
(dried-up flies like November blackberries,
legs contracted in death), how well they hide it.

Dark beetles, swimmers with glistening backs,
etching their hieroglyphs between worm-casts and pebbles,
bird-claw cuneiform and rabbit-tracks
across dawn's snowfall, runic silhouettes
of trees upon the sunset-streaked horizon,
the icicles' oghamic alphabet,

each mark, spoor, trace, or vestige left,
every shadow that stirs the wheatfield
as if a god strode there, are the imaginings
and melody of energies beyond
control until expressed: entries
in the dictionary of another language.

Observations of the Tower Block

During the day the building becomes a gigantic machine
collecting data from the whole district. At night,
a Cunard liner with every cabin occupied,
rigging decorated for the final gala.

Different patterns of lights. No matter how late
I go to bed or early I wake, there are always lights burning.
Nights of insomnia, when I look out the window,
someone else in that building is also not sleeping.

The lights glow pink and yellow, green and orange.
Is it from coloured bulbs, or filtered through curtains?
Who are the people who live in those apartments?

Illuminated lift-shafts, halls and balconies.
Is it the grid of the structure determines their lives?
My sightings are too irregular to grasp a pattern or meaning.

Spring in the City

Petals from the trees
along the street
revolve and fall.
Complex currents
lift them up toward
the boughs from which
their flight was launched.

All the space between
the rows of houses
in swirling movement
like sand in a rock-pool
as the sea sluices through
raising fine clouds
that blur its clearness.

Gutters choked with blossom
pavements patterned
the wind-blown hair of girls
tangled with blossom
a swarm of insects
aquarium of fishes
snowflakes in a storm.

Shaken by the breeze
and cornering cars
reaffirming the spiral
of the galaxies
the air today seems thick
with stardust and we
are breathing stars.

Spring Light

These first few days after the clocks change
and darkness comes an hour later
(the start of Summer Time)

seem to hurt most, deal the cruellest blow.
The weather gets colder. Winter won't go,
puts up one last fight.

While sunshine at an unfamiliar angle
through the window shows a haggard
face with harsh new lines,

and restless during lengthened afternoons
you're forced to realise how soon
the reckoning arrives.

Every year, spring's return brings
it nearer, marks it clearer with
that unrelenting light.

Calcutta

Carts loaded with sacks and planks
moving into the pre-dawn city.
One man in front between the shafts,
two pushing from the back.

Knees drawn up to the chin,
rickshaw men asleep
on the poles of their vehicles.
Black crows roosting.

A five A.M. sweeper,
stiff-legged, stooping
at an empty crossing
by the silent kiosks.

The gaunt fronts of hospitals,
their windows bright
as strings of coloured lights cascading
down this wedding pavilion.

And now the hired car goes past
another drug-store, another clinic,
the Panacea Laboratory,
another sweet-shop.

Dark brick obelisks and pyramids
along the ruined paths:
'... guide on, young men, the bark
that's freighted with your country's doom,' –

Derozio's memorial,
and Rose Aylmer dead
in the Park Street cemetery.
Blood and marigolds at the Kalighat.

Give that girl thirty pice
because she's singing.
But don't look at the leper's
blunted fingers.

In the Tibetan Restaurant, drinking gin,
middle-class intellectuals
to whom the greatest insult
is to be accused of pity,

and out at Dum Dum airport,
rising above the burning cow-dung pall
that blurs the skyline, another tourist
who can't take any more.

Valleys and Mountains

What I know are valleys
between the mountains
have buried beneath them
the crests of other mountains,

and I can see through depths
of stormy ocean
the drowned empires
there before the ocean,

trace the cool fern's pattern
in burning coal,
ancient sunlit jungles
become black coal,

and proving every tale
concerning love's
transforming powers,
surely this must be love.

Passions

Let's not mention love. It's like a glowing
stove to someone covered with burns already.
And hate is that dark cave whose depths conceal
a reeking oubliette where rivals groan.
One glimpse enough to turn your head
and make you lose your balance, envy will have you
spiralling from the top of the cliff, down
onto the breakers. Anger is the sea.
Gasping and buffeted, no matter how
you struggle or plead for mercy, you drown. But pride
can clothe those shattered bones with perfect skin,
and breathe into the lover's mouth her song.

Natural History

– then you captured my distracted spirit,
called it down from where it danced and hovered
over our heads, brought me back to myself,
trammelled by your gross and loving grasp,
into the realm of our own natural history –

into that garden where the flowers strain
on bristling stems toward the sun and arch
their petals wider, and the snail's slime-trail
stops at a broken shell as the harsh triumphant
beak stabs over and over through its pulpy heart,

where sounds and smells and colours, taste and touch
of hair and flesh, glistenings, swollen
heats and tension, matter's prodigal
and irresistible excess, all
transform the butterfly into a rutting primate.

The Music

I sit alone in my room
on a cold summer afternoon
upstairs from where you in your room
are playing the gramophone.
Though you don't know it, I open
my own door wide enough
to share the sound of the music.

Another floor up, in the attic,
two adolescent lovers
play a childhood game, just
rediscovered. Laughs, and the rattle
of dice, drift down from above.

Barely more than their age,
hidden on the steps below
the next-door villa, whose stones
still held the heat of day,
my head on your shoulder,
we listened to someone
playing the same tune.

That night, we hurried home
to our new games – perhaps
your memories are the same?
Or else, I have to wonder
why you chose the music.

Death's Love-bite

A slow-motion explosion is what my mouth's become,
front teeth thrusting forward at impossible angles.
Incisors once in satisfactory alignment
cruelly slice through lips and tongue, and molars
grind each other into powder. Though it took almost
thirty years for them to drift so far apart, the pace
accelerates. My mouth contains meteors
and molecules, the splintered bones of mastodons,
galaxies and Magellanic clouds; feels like
a photograph of particles halted in
a cyclotron and magnified a thousand powers,
a microscopic re-enactment of the planet's
coming total fracture, elements dispersing
out in space. That's the truth I clench between
my jaws, behind my face. And all the technical
ingenuity called upon to solve
this dental problem won't heal Death's love-bite.

Acrobatic Full Moon

A fat but agile acrobat
from a Chinese circus, the moon contracts
and elongates, then flattens out
again, making jokes with the clouds.
Or is it more a double-jointed
golden cat glimpsed between
gloomy jungle ferns, an orange
segment, an apricot-coloured egg yolk
slithering across the oily
surface of a frying pan?

Watching it pretend to be
a car's headlamp, the smiling face
of a Michelin-man, cloth cap worn
at a rakish angle, I almost thought
that flower-pot of geraniums

nodding their heads in the pre-dawn wind
further down the empty street
was someone else still awake
leaning out to contemplate
the antic moon's variations.

Now at five o'clock this morning
standing in the same corner
to brew myself a cup of coffee
where every evening, cooking dinner,
I look westward through the window
towards the sunset, I can see
the full moon slide behind the trees
and blocks of flats, to vanish as
the room lights up behind my back –
heralding the next act.

Products of the Pig

Once upon a time and long ago
when I lived in Majorca,
they fattened pigs with over-ripe figs
before their slaughter. (They were delicious.)
This autumn, visiting
a London garden, I saw a fig tree,
branches leaden, leaves already fallen,
with small hard withered green fruits
that never had enough sun to ripen
stuck against the naked twigs:
like scabs, I thought at first, or little
pig-snouts. But then somehow they looked
so harmless – and jaunty –
surviving in England.

The Power Source

In this part of the country
all through July, sometimes
round the clock, after
the first crop's cut and stacked,
the rape-seed brought inside
that new blue corrugated
plastic barn behind the
churchyard, the driers keep blowing.
Industrial farming. Often
annoying, ignored, it fades
into the background: one more factor
in the ambient pattern of sound.

I can let it lower my guard
and mood – becoming sulky,
agitated – or get me
high on the idea of progress:
a theme to brood on. Either
way, stimulated or
nerve-wracked, I find the summer
different than before
I noticed the strain of trying
to be a nature poet
these unbucolic days.
The power source has shifted.

When it stops, though other
motors seem much louder:
passing tourist traffic,
helicopters spraying,
tractors (drivers earphoned
to muffle their own noise),
the vital note is missing.
I wait its starting-up,
knowing I'll be uneasy
in the interval
between now and the August
combine-harvesters.

The Circle

We did not meet that often: once
or twice a year for drinks, or walking
to the store we'd stop and talk –
she the village dowager,
I the foreigner who'd stayed
a while but then decamped, become
one of the weekend people. Always
I admired that upright stance,
gallant style, and undiminished
presence. She still could play the perfect
diplomatic hostess: draw me out
about the house, the garden, children,
and not touch on the personal.

But the last time – I was crossing
the far orchard, taking a short-cut
to the river – she called me over
to join her and the dogs. I noticed
something different. Those fine
eyes never were so bright before
nor cheeks so gaunt and flushed,
hair disordered, gestures bewildered.
I started to say the usual things
about the weather and crops but
almost peremptorily, was
interrupted and asked, 'Tell me,
please – do you enjoy fairy stories?'

It was the end of summer. I
remember watchful apple-pickers
as we paced back and forth between
the trees and she described the pleasure
of rediscovering old tales;
how, disconcerted, I tried to believe
that like a circle closing, connection
had been made between her past
and present. Months later, a bitter
April day, I heard the news.
The circle was a fairy-ring,
as false as fairy gold, and nurses
guard her from worse bewitchment.

Judgement at Marble Arch

Office girls doing their lunchtime shopping.
Bewildered blond families up from the provinces.
Africans, Arabs, Italians and Spaniards.
Cut-price teeshirts, blue jeans and haversacks.
Oily exhaust fumes and noisy rock music.
Hot August sunshine, then the first autumn shower.

Just past Lyon's Corner House,
near Marble Arch Underground station,
I heard a low but penetrating moan
by my right shoulder, and turned to confront
a tangle of greying hair not quite concealing
eyes squeezed shut and open mouth (saliva
stretched in threads between the drawn-back lips)
of a woman – about my size and age – wailing
her distress. Her naked goatish legs
in heavy shoes kept stumbling forward,
somehow avoiding all obstructions.
The large red plastic bag in her dirty hands
was held as though at any moment she
would cover her head to hide from the assault
of sound and sight, or use it to vomit in.

Someone else had noticed: our glances intersected.
Both relieved from having to make a decision,
but wondering whether – the other a witness –
we were now committed to action, as well as pity
and horror. Slowly, through the midday throng
we followed after, murmuring our uncertainty.
Whenever I got close enough to hear,
she was still mouthing her fear and curses.
The woman with me seemed as nervous.
'I'm frightened,' I confessed. 'Me too.'
Bright brown eyes stared back, grateful.

At Edgware Road a man reached out
to touch her arm. She had become visible.
The circle of watchers broadened.
She flinched and dropped,

then stretched the plastic bag across her face
as though it were a magic hood,
the fluttering red wings of a wounded bird,
a shaman's regalia with its tawdry glamour.
'Where's a policeman?' my companion murmured.
I had to get away. 'I'll try to find one.'

In another story I'd take her home and nurse her,
heal her, be a holy martyr. But
I didn't want to; nor did I want to hand her over.
When I returned from where I'd stood
around the corner in a hotel entrance,
the crowd had scattered. 'She crossed the road.'
The voice had changed – perplexed, almost indignant.
'There might have been an accident.'
'Maybe she's been like this for years,' I mumbled,
ashamed of myself. 'So many sick people in the cities…'
For the first time we had to deal with each other,
(if we talked longer, might be forced
to make a further judgement), so said goodbye
and went back to our separate errands.

The Barrier

Up ahead, a tangle of rocks and earth
and caught twigs half damming a river
of rapid water under heavy branches.

The flow is almost halted: that steady movement
which unimpeded scoured the stream-bed deeper
and polished every stone, now baulked, reverses.

Behind the barrier, the new pool
slowly fills with dead fish and leaves.
The simpler life-forms take possession. Will

the next storm wash it clear, the stream run smooth
and vivid from its source; will the current
turn and broaden, then reach the ocean?

271

Difficult Reward

The future is timid and wayward
and wants to be courted, will not
respond to threats or coaxing,
and hears excuses only
when she feels secure.

Doubt, uproar, jeers,
vengeful faces roughened
by angry tears, the harsh
odours of self-importance,
are what alarm her most.

Nothing you do will lure her
from the corner where
she waits like a nun of a closed
order, or a gifted young
dancer, altogether

the creature of her vocation,
with those limits and strengths.
Trying to reassure her,
find new alibis
and organise the proof

of your enthralment and
devotion, seems totally useless –
though it teaches how
to calm your spirit, move
beyond the problem's overt

cause and one solution –
until the future, soothed now,
starts to plot another
outcome to the story:
your difficult reward.

The Knot

(1990)

The Knot

One of them showed me how to split a reed
and plait it into a holder for my hammock.
'When you know you've got to get away,' she said,
'use this piece of cloth, faded red, and knot
it tight at either end. Find somewhere far
from the children and dogs and vague old people,
the women thumping grain, those noisy men
around the smoky fire. Loop it under a branch
or over a beam in one of the empty huts
at the edge of the clearing. Then crawl inside,
when you need to be alone to hear the story,
the story you tell yourself all day but sometimes
cannot hear.' And sometimes, there in my hammock,
words would come and cluster together like wasps
between the poles and matting of the roof
as black as rotting fruit or drying membrane,
a blossom of words in a dusty ray of light.
Words would form a knot and start a story.

The European Story

I

A story? There's not enough action –
just an endless loping
through the cobwebbed aisles and arches
of a Gothic forest unreeling
like a painted backcloth. Then he stumbles,
and the heart in the cup of his bloodied palm
bounces into the ferns.

Red-cheeked, raw-boned, black-mustachioed,
a puppet escaped from its master, a soldier
on the run, he served the story's purpose –
did the murder, cut her open.

Now he doesn't matter.
The heart becomes the drama's centre.
Its voice calls out: 'My son, my son,
have you hurt yourself? My dear, don't fall!'

II

My mother might have told that story.
Cave-crone guarding the fire spark
as safe inside its ball of clay and moss
as an infant lapped by womb-water,
she handed on the ancient curse
(the lesson I refused to learn),
mother-tongue mumbling heart-words.

Last breath from an open mouth,
moisture beads the fluttering threads
spiders wove between the branches
and makes a nimbus of splintered light
through tear-clogged lashes, a pearl-encrusted
iconostasis of wonderworkers
to prove Death weaker than mother-love,
and reconcile rebellious daughters.

III

I was born in a smothering caul,
a veiled woman. My first cry was a protest.
I feared the antlered maskers' shadows,
the rooting goddess who eats her farrow,
the touch of Balder's frost-burned mistletoe.
In dreams I was the puppet-killer,
her defender, with sword and dagger sharper
than the Angel's, armour brighter than Joan's.

I have danced as either partner
been tormented and tormentor
but could not find the right disguise
to fool her – neither child nor mother
with my child. Oh what grief, never
to hear that special note in her voice:
'My son, my son, have you hurt yourself?'
You want to plunge the knife in your own heart.

IV

Cast your bread on the waters.
But the Old Man of the Sea
rises up and straddles your shoulders
tightens his grip on your windpipe.
There's salt in your mouth.
He's wet and cold and heavy.
You stagger and almost drown.

Then up from the ground between your feet
another one comes
and splits you open
thrusts his hand in the shambles
wrenches out your heart.
When he stumbles and drops it, the heart
cries out, 'My dear, don't fall!'

V

A fish appears with a ring in its mouth
and three questions. An old woman
asks for shelter. If you pass the test
each wish is granted until the last

unless it is
to break the mould,
open out a parchment scroll,
cherubim and gargoyles
twining down the margins
throstles perched on gilded letters
leafy plants and scaly dragons,
and let the variations flourish;
to change the definitions
of feminine and masculine,
son & mother, love & duty,
and that final one, 'The End':
tell the story different every time.

VI

Change the heart into a ticking bomb,
the soldier to a girl – a terrorist,
the very last Crusader,
sure that a dark annunciation chose her

to save the Holy Places of the planet
by casual explosion.
That moves the story on.

Her ideas and actions must be examined
as carefully as a bomb's fuse and circuit,
with the tender skill a surgeon uses
cutting live flesh to open up a heart.
She has been formed by what the story means.
It started in Europe. It spread like radiation.
There's no immunity to images.

On the Theme of Artifice

'Himself, maybe, the irreducible X
at the bottom of imagined artifice.'

What does Wallace Stevens mean? I've pondered
those lines, tried to decide if the imagined

always must be artificial – mind's
construction upon, and against, Nature, which he

projects into a pineapple that looms
gigantic as the jar in Tennessee.

*

It seems a form of magic: the poet artful
enough to draw the essence of reality

like a shawl, cobweb fine, through a golden ring,
or coax from the constraining bottle, a genie

who surges like a mushroom cloud. The same
thought that split the atom, had to imagine

its irreducible nucleus
and the artifice of Time and Space, first.

*

At the bottom of imagined artifice,
rather than familiar gods and demons

or current versions of total destruction, he
himself is dreaming pineapples and jars.

The Yellow Plate

(i.m. Assia Guttman)

A painted plate, yellow-glazed below
the shallow curve of its white porcelain rim,
> (yellow I'm always drawn to:
> the saffron robe of a mendicant
> or the silk curtains a friend bought in Burma,
> mine now, because she's dead),
is the yellow road of the sun –
that bright furrow ploughed between the stars.

Underneath is the painter's complex square mark,
lacquer red, and round scarlet stickers reading:
'Chia ching' and 'Seventeen ninety six to
Eighteen twenty'. On the front, twelve creatures.

It took a long time to see
they were the Chinese zodiac,
animal, bird, and reptile, real
or imagined (the one in the center
is a dragon, not a crocodile),
that give names to the hours of the day
and the little twelve-day cycle,
the months of the year and the sixty years
I guess was the expected life span
of those hunters and shepherds.
> When she died, my friend was younger.

Tradition has it that Tajao, a minister
of Emperor Hwang-ti, circa
Two six nine seven BC, invented them.

So little has changed since, the same
names are still used (though I can't compute
what our year is by that calendar,
nor my own sign), and I sensed before
I knew what they meant and were.

The colours are green and red and yellow:
jade, cinnabar and sulfur,
the drawn line blackish sepia.
A pale wash of pink fills
the bodies of the wrinkle-snouted pig
and the rat, whose ideograph is 'water'.
Too anxious for the luxury
of variation, the rabbit is pure white.

Cloudy patterns blotch the horse,
whose mane and tail fall fine and soft
as new-washed hair, and the bristling dog,
like shadow dappling windblown corn.
Flamey stripes unite the horned sheep and
the thoughtful tiger biting a raised paw.
Dragon and serpent are scaled, chequered
and barred, their dangerous twirling tongues
high-voltage warnings.

The hen looks fierce as a cock, crested
and hook-clawed, not domestic
and submissive like the ox
with a rope through its round nostril.
The monkey has delicate hands, subtle
lips and watchful eyes – a courtier
wondering if he's telling the right story.

Everything about the plate – all
the moods and colors, characters and patterns –
    she was like all of it,
      as beautiful.

Flower Feet

(silk shoes in the Whitworth Museum, Manchester)

Real women's feet wore these objects
that look like toys or spectacle cases stitched
from bands of coral, jade, and apricot silk
embroidered with twined sprays of flowers.
Those hearts, tongues, crescents and disks, leather
shapes an inch across, are the soles of shoes
no wider or longer than the span of my ankle.

If the feet had been cut off and the raw stumps
thrust inside the openings, surely
it could not have hurt more than broken toes, twisted
back and bandaged tight. An old woman,
leaning on a cane outside her door
in a Chinese village, smiled to tell how
she fought and cried, how when she stood on points
of pain that gnawed like fire, nurse and mother
praised her tottering walk on flower feet.
Her friends nodded, glad the times had changed.
Otherwise, they would have crippled their daughters.

Poppies

A bed of them
looks like a dressing room
backstage after the chorus changed costume,

ruffled heaps
of papery orange petticoats
and slick pink satin bodices.

Every petal's base
is marked with the same
confident black smear as a painted eyelid

and the frill
of jostling purple anthers
sifts a powdery kohl that clogs the lashes

shading watchful glances
from dilating pupils, as though
all the dancers swallowed belladonna.

The pleated velvet star
at the center of each flower
is the top of a box filled with jet beads.

The hard green buds
are their husbands' fists, the silver-
bristled leaves are their admirers' beards.

Flies

November sun as warm as a Levantine
winter made me push my window up
this morning, brought back donkey-drivers' calls,
the look and smell of bakers' stalls and offal
butchers. Flies were everywhere.

But the shudder of glass (fear a splintering shard
might pierce me) from the frame carelessly jammed askew,
as heavy lorries brake and lower gear
to take the corner for a shortcut to the A40,
changed those images to Home County:
a pan of clarifying sugar syrup
on the Aga wrinkling as it starts to boil
(the crab-apple jelly-bag dripping draws flies
to the kitchen), or the irritable twitch
of a horse's flank to shift the biting flies.

The noise I heard could have been
the drone of a distant combine harvester,
a helicopter spraying, or closer still,
here in town, a treadle-machine next door
(that new family must be tailors) and their
muffled hullabaloo through the party wall (they're
killing each other: the flies are driving them crazy).

So I went to put the window down, to stop
the thrumming and its associations, and found
summer's last fly, trapped by the double-glazing.

Early Rivers

This jar of rosy-purple jam is labelled
Early Rivers, August '84 –
the date I made it, the name the farmer gave
those plums, smooth as onyx eggs, but warmer.

The dimpled groove, bloom-dusted, down each fruit
pouted at the touch of my knife, yielding
the stone I put inside a cotton sock
(relict of a worn-out pair – every
boiling dyed it darker crimson – from one
plum-season to the next I saved it), then pushed
the lumpy tied-up bag into the center
of the pulpy amber halves and melting sugar
in the preserving kettle, and let the mixture
ooze its pectins, odours, juices, flavours,

until the chemistry of time and fire
produced this sharpness, sweetness, that I'm eating
now, straight from the jar, smearing my mouth,
digging the spoon in deeper, seeking a taste
undiluted even by nostalgia.

August

August is like a woman who's already thinking
that she'll soon be forty. There's something old-fashioned
about her, emanating a womanly odour
of sachets. You can tell that she's been badly treated
by men. Her daughter has left home. She's probably
divorced. She's the manageress of a dress shop.

One might talk of her carriage: she seems to be wearing
a corset. She's quite large and very white skinned.
Her hair is set, her face is powdered matt, and her
thin and rather mournful little mouth with lips
firmly closed on each other except when she bites
them, is carefully painted and always looks wet.

August is the month when everything stops growing.
She feels she stopped growing a long time ago; although
she wouldn't put it like that. She doesn't believe in
too much introspection. Dignified and solitary,
she walks through the park after work, under
the heavy, dusty, dying green of August trees.

The Neville Brothers
(at Vanderbilt University, Nashville, Tennessee, Spring 1985)

As soon as he walked on stage, I saw
that the lead singer was Lord Krishna
wearing a sleeveless red teeshirt, jeans
and high heels. He was gorgeous. In the dim
blue exit lights of the auditorium,
adoring him, we were all milkmaids.

I'd bought pictures of faces like his, full-cheeked,
almond-eyed, from Bombay street vendors.
Just this side of fat, those shoulders
and pectorals for the moment are perfect.
A lush male torso slowly swayed
as nervous legs pranced and pawed like a horse.

Amplified drumbeats were driving them wild.
How often before he had watched tranced
devotees or dawn dancers wanting
more and stronger, like the audience now.
But this was a concert on campus, not
the Juggernaut temple, or a bar in New Orleans.

NOTE: The Neville Brothers, a New Orleans rhythm and blues group.
Krishna grew up among a troupe of milkmaids who were entranced by the sound of his flute.
He is worshipped in the form of the Juggernaut at the temple at Puri on the Bay of Bengal.

Rock Island

(to the hunters)

Deep pools in the stone bed of the river.
A dry pavement between tumbled rocks
and boulders. Jade yellow of flowing water.
The wide valley closed by limestone bluffs.
Soft tones of blue sky and white clouds.
Bright greenness of new leaves and buds.

The pale fungus, the litter of bark and branches
from fallen, broken trees along the hill.
Confusion of greyness against earth's redness.
I pulled a mushroom, tall and bullet-like
with a gun-metal glint, and turned it over.
The gills looked inky, sooty, dangerous.

Possum or raccoon, the dark-furred creature
that ignored my nearness? It emanated
misery, a concentration of pain
and stillness I could not understand until
I watched those dead back legs slowly dragged
across the field's rough grass into a ditch.

In Tuscaloosa –

– a puppy trotted down from a verandah
past the yard-sprinkler, and led me to
the corner of an avenue
where oaks were swagged with mauve wisteria.

Breathless and excited as an orphan
I watched a misty nimbus form
around the streetlamps and glowing from
windows of houses where I knew no one.

Out on the Porch

Who expects the whole bus-queue
she passes while shopping,
like a chorus of gossiping aunts and neighbors
or the row of sunflowers, obediently heliotropic,
shading the porch where they sit and watch her,
to forget everything else, wishing her luck?

Whose neck stiffens and spine arches
trying to do what they want (she can't be
that much younger, yet still feels débutante),
desperate for approval.
It makes her eyes itch with exasperation –
like saying a poem for the aunts and neighbors

then later, from an upstairs window, hearing
that tolerant laughter out on the porch
over clinking teacups and impatient slaps
at mosquitoes as they change the subject.
Who insisted? Who arranged it?
Thank God when the bus comes.

Off the Interstate

Following instructions
we stopped at every viewpoint
around the Painted Desert.
Mineral deposits
streaked like bird-droppings
over faded purples,
bled-out pinks and reds.
It looked like a crater filled
with cooling clinker under
rain-clouds that might have been
smoke from its last eruption.

At the Petrified Forest
an elderly man in the car-park
started to talk about Jesus,
and the Day of Judgement
which was coming soon.
He wouldn't leave us alone.
Not even a downpour enough
to deter him. I kept busy
with my camera while he
invoked the Four Horsemen
to a mystified Japanese girl.

Hard to find the motel
Rosemary recommended.
We had to double back
to the last exit, where streamers
fluttered over gas-pumps.
Turning from the highway
toward the horizon – the sky
was perfectly clear now, golden
with sunset – there seemed nothing else
but the wind and rolling Coke cans
between me and the North Pole.

Rand McNally

The route, if it wasn't through mountains
in northern lands broken by glaciers, kept
to the contours, crossing plaited water-courses
split by sandbanks and bushy islands.

Furrow-puddles glinted and swirled
as we hit the boggy bottom land of Arkansas.
Dappled horses turned toward the car
from a blue pond in a broad meadow.

Flickering under-leaves of tamarisk,
cottonwood, wild olive and willow
carried the Rio Grande past Albuquerque.
Pine reflections snagged in Taos gorge.

The current of the Little Colorado
was terracotta like dissolving pottery.
The Missouri near Omaha and the Mississippi
at Rock Island bracketed Iowa.

I saw the tarred beaches of Lake Eirie,
muddy Susquehannah's meandering valley.
Woods now instead of forests,
the planet growing its green fur.

Not compass circles, but stains from coffee cups.
My Rand McNally Atlas falls loose from its staples.

Between the Canyons

(the Navajo Sibyl)

On the rim of the canyon, between
the canyons, rifts and gashes
in the earth's carcass (tarry scabs
of broken badlands, clotted red
of its inner body), a storm woke you
at three a.m. in the motel near
the clinic for alcoholics. Full moon
thunder flash and lightning strobe.

Sluggish green and seeming-harmless
at the lowest level sliced through aeons
the river had pulverised boulders
polished the cliff face blocking caves
where buried gods spit out
Time's soporific layer-cake
and shrug their painted shoulders. Earthy
patterns ripple as they move closer.

Magnetic, cosmic, geological
the energy was actual
demanded absolute homage.
You were its chosen medium
and focus: a substance tested
to the limit of endurance, flattened
against the planet's raw surface
like a fly on a windscreen.

Survival of the Cult

Osiris's head is buried like seed-corn
at Abydos. His temple is built west
of the river, near the edge of the desert.
He was called 'Chief of the Westerners'.

Over his recumbent body
on the sanctuary frieze, Isis hovers.
Wing over wing, through fanning sun rays,
above the palm trees, two kites glide.

The covered well and stone seats
at the side of the road are plastered blue,
red-striped. Old men lounge there,
and watch the women fill their pails.

'The Mother of Pots': a grey field
of shattered votive jars that pilgrims
left since Pharoahs' time, stretches
between the temple and the village.

Some houses are decorated
with holy words and drawings of boats,
planes and the black rock of the Kaaba.
A man who lives there journeyed to Mecca.

And on every painted wall, holding
his crook and flail – still the protector –
corn-crowned and mummy-linen robed,
Lord Osiris stays part of the picture.

Bouzigues

There's a place on the road
coming down from the hills
where rows of oyster frames unfurl
on an indigo sea,
like a pattern of bamboo fans
or blocks of pale embroidery
on a geisha's kimono –
whose knees and shoulders
press against the border
of the wood engraving
tight as Alice's
when she started growing.

The high-piled mass
of the dead volcano cone
is her oiled and twisted hair
fighting free from its combs
to tangle in the shell-
encrusted poles. Her eyes
look crazed. A small tooth shows
between pursed lips, and one breast's
tip in the oyster scent
of watered silk's loosened folds.
Her mood is storm clouds
over the lagoon.

NOTE: Bouziges – a French village on the Bassin de Thau, south of Montpellier, famous for
its oysters. The lagoon is closed at either end by the extinct volcanic cones of Sète and Agde.

The Garden

Christmas Day (which was sunny and calm, not one
cloud in the sky) we planted thirty-five fir trees
as a wall between ourselves and the next-door neighbor.
We'd been shocked to see their large pink house,
so gaunt and high, after summer's green enclosure,
once the chestnut and acacia leaves had fallen.

Some firs have blue-tinged foliage, others look golden.
We didn't notice, or choose them especially,
but it seemed a happy omen. Variation is promised,
a flicker between the primary colours
that combine to make green, like vivid brushstrokes
in the dense impasto of a painting. Today,

the fourth of January, weather still fine,
we bought three-metre bamboo stakes, cut them in half
and hammered them into the earth, to hold the trees
firm against the north wind – Tramontana it's called –
and help them survive the hardest part of winter.
They'll be alive next time we come, I hope.

The garden was neglected for decades. Under the brambles
we found a half-dead box hedge, stone-bordered flowerbeds,
roses and fruit trees gone wild. Ivy smothered
the lilacs and lapped the steps, twisted around
the rusty wire-mesh fence, and wove a net
that had to be unravelled strand by strand.

Planting and clearing, not wanting to change things much,
we are taking possession – and being possessed.
What could be more demanding than a garden?
'Don't start work on the garden!' friends warned, 'or
you'll never get away.' But we bought the house because
of the garden. We are putting down roots in the garden.

Blossom and Technology

I wasn't sure what to expect,
after flying for eighteen hours
over the Pole. Japan
was contradictory images:
stone and technology,
crowds and cherry blossom.

I came too late for the blossom,
the one sight I did expect,
as if technology
could slow seasons and hours
until certain images
confirmed: this is Japan.

Some things were strange in Japan:
not the imitation blossom,
but those plastic images
of meals you might expect
in restaurants. The hours
to make them, the technology!

An older technology
had created another Japan
where no count was taken of hours
spent training flowers to blossom
in a place you wouldn't expect,
or painting a screen with their images.

I wanted to keep those images.
My camera – technology
of the sort I came to expect
from anything bought in Japan –
was aimed at every blossom
and stone as it changed with the hours.

I stood and watched for hours
near the temple images
people's faces blossom:
prayer's technology

must be what fuels Japan,
which is not what you'd expect,

nor expect that so few hours
in Japan could reconcile images
of blossom and technology.

The Japanese Bath

I feared my heart would stop: the depth and heat
of water in the wooden tub, the thought
that even if I called you would not hear
from where you sat, beyond the anteroom,
silk-kimono'd by the painted screen.
I stretched my legs out, saw my body small
as a court lady of Kyoto, green
as moss around a temple garden pool
carp-filled, and how the same droplets of steam
frosting my hair beaded the darkened walls.
The silent isolation made me feel:
to come this far and drown could be my doom.
Then I stood up, showered off the dream
and ghosts with cold water, calm now, released.

Japanese Syllabics

When the tea-master's disciples praised
Kobori Enshu's beautiful scrolls
and plates, saying that no one could help
but admire them, he sorrowfully
answered: 'This only proves how common-
place I am.' His dissatisfaction
at their response quite opposite to
my constant need for reassurance,
my placatory smile – the nodding
head-piece of a jointed wooden doll,
agreeing, agreeing.

                    Legend tells
how he built the Katsura villa
on the following conditions: no
limits on money or manpower
or time, and no one to disturb his
conception of temples and gardens
and pavilions by seeing the work
until finished. He was so secure
in his judgement, knew what he wanted.

Each gesture and implement exact,
the simple tea ceremony is
a junction of choices, decisions;
its purpose (or am I imposing
an alien system of values
and totally misunderstanding?)
to enact and confirm the balance
calmness and grace I yearn for and lack.

Yet even such a grand tea-master
could doubt his purity of motive,
lament a lack of courage, wonder
whether his most precious treasure had
been chosen more to please others than
because it was to his own taste.

                    Now
I'll show you my favourite puppet:
black brows, white face, and fluttering sleeves.
Her expression is so subtly drawn,
the painted features almost change with
my opinions. But when she's being
praised, or when I'm confident enough
to stop equivocating, then how
balanced, graceful, calm we both can seem.

NOTE: Kobori Enshu (1576-1647) built the Katsura Rikyu in Kyoto
for Toyotomi Hideyoshi, exacting the three famous conditions.

Incense

A dull shine like black ice:
the bronze urn at the top of the stone steps,
its incised pattern the same pale colour
as the ash that fills it – from how many
millions of burned-out incense sticks?

Shiomi told me I could light one
if I wished. I watched the other mourners
pass their hands through the swirling smoke,
smooth it over their heads and waft
it down the fronts of their kimonos.

The red tips of the incense sticks
pulse and glow in the shadow of cedar
pillars and temple roof-tiles as I bend
close, murmuring prayers and names,
half a world from where they lay,

yet certain they were here with me,
supportive spirits among this strangeness.
The shrine doors swing shut in the wind
and the incense billows. Three women
laugh as though it means good luck.

Keeper

Mother's fur coats,
silver teapot and velvet
boxes of broken earrings.

Aunt Ann's crackle-glass lamp
with its patterned parchment shade,
her mahogany bookcase.

Daddy's volumes of Jewish Thoughts,
A Hermit in the Himalayas,
those plaid plus-fours.

A faded suitcase, corded,
the sort a schoolboy uses,
full of Harry's notebooks.

Albums of glossy photos.
The last smile dimmed,
since I heard about Cousin Fanny.

I see the family face
break through the surface
of Grandpa's speckled mirror

and hardly recognise myself.
Every object
claims me as its keeper,

souvenirs of joy
and anger I'm not sure whether
I want to cherish or destroy.

Learning About Him

A sheep bleated, and sounded
exactly like someone imitating a sheep,
which made me think of my father –

the sort of thing he'd do,
suddenly start to clown and act crazy, or like
a warning cough of static

from the jelly-mould
Art Deco shape of the big valve radio,
its glowing amber dial

showing places he'd been to.
I'd twiddle the knobs and move the needle through
London, Bombay, Rio.

'Look after my Feigele,'
(the Yiddish name meant little bird) her dying
mother said to the lodger,

my father, so they got married.
I heard the story after his funeral
and finally understood

why I was born in New York.
I'd recognised another melancholic
early on, but not

that auto-didact hunger
for self-improvement he dissembled (as though
it would be shameful if

any of us knew), until
clearing his room, choosing which books to keep,
I found old favourites.

I hate to read books marked
with comments in the margins, underlinings,
but these were different.

I was learning about him.
For instance, how he'd saved what seemed every
postcard I'd mailed home –

grudgingly dutiful –
and pasted them in scrapbooks, tracing my routes
red and his bright blue.

We'd almost meshed the globe.
I wonder if his restlessness was soothed
by mine, or irritated?

Dear father, now your crazy
daughter's weeping sounds like bleating
or a faulty radio.

'Softly Awakes My Heart...'

Saint-Saëns' aria
chosen by a man in Saudi Arabia
for his daughter in Ghana
(that version on His Master's Voice):
a Sunday morning World Service broadcast.

It brings a complex recall
of dusty velvet armchairs
a pile of records and the old victrola
net curtains faded and crisp
from sunlight through the dining room French window.

The mezzo-soprano
would smooth your mouth and eyes.
Your whole body calm except for
one hand turning on its wrist, accompanying.
I preferred a harsher music then.

Those Photographs

Always the rowdy one, pushing
toward the centre, the one demanding
absolute attention, who had to be
Daddy's little darling:
the beam in my eye still only lets me
notice how hard the others are trying.

Those photographs. I'm sure we sent him
hundreds, during the war. The reason
I'm standing so close to my mother
near the porch steps, like a sapling
not yet grown free of its root-stock,
is to keep my balance and seem the taller.

Don't laugh at that dress: gauzy muslin,
green-checked, was my version of
a dryad's costume. Barefoot, I'm squinting
because I took my glasses off
and held them awkwardly behind
my back, to look older, and glamorous.

She looks what she'd been born as:
a shrewd, ironic Jewish peasant, who knew
competing daughters are best ignored.
Her indifference drove me quite berserk.
For years I fought it. But she slept
at concerts, and in museums her shoes hurt.

Sweet smile and strong jaw of an ogre,
I think she was my feminine ideal;
as every hero had to be my father's
opposite, in honour of that taboo.
She made me a shape-shifter: all
things to all men. Except hers.

Towards My Waiting Mother

The animal decency of my father's death.
With vacant bright gaze that could not be
deflected understood or met, like a forest
creature who crawls into a hollow tree
or ditch when its time has come, he curved around
the smallest possible space in the hospital bed.

He didn't talk much – none of the stories
I'd hoped at last to hear, which only now
I realise that I expected (still
the child demanding his attention). Instead,
how simple everything seemed as he moved further
away from me, towards my waiting mother.

Station Road

Fond memories of the garden shed
behind our ground floor flat in Station Road.

Daddy talked about the Oxford Group
and Chamberlain. Hateful Grandpa said:
'Be good, sweet maid, and let who will be clever.'
I thought up riddles to confound him
and shouted all the facts I'd read.

Mother pushed me into bed with shoes on
and tied a rag around my neck
when the school inspector called. 'She has a fever.'
I've forgotten why she kept me home
but not my admiration for her lawless style.

Privacy in the high-ceilinged toilet:
pressing fists against my eyes I saw
kaleidoscopes and arabesques.

After ballet class, walking to the shop
which sold black liquorice straps
and envelopes of Japanese paper flowers
that unfolded and blossomed in a glass of water,
we sang, 'Under the spreading chestnut tree,
it's time to join the A.R.P.'

My brother slept in a deep square pram
under a tree in the front garden.
I stooped to peer beneath the hood.
The blank, glistening white ellipses
of his eyes rolled back
behind half-shut, delicate, violet-webbed lids
were another sign the war was coming closer.

That was when I wanted to be Tarzan,
teased and nagged till Mother bought
two lengths of cloth so I could cut brown spots
and stitch them to the tan, to make a leopard skin.

My friends from the house around the corner
could only wear one-colour costumes
and had to obey, whatever I ordered.

I can remember how I lured
my eager victims between the spider-webs
upended broken chairs and rusting
earth-caked forks and spades; how,
among the dust-motes of teatime sunlight
and moulting plumes of last year's pampas
grass that made us sneeze, we tried out
faulty versions of being grown-up – as if
the future wouldn't offer time enough.

My Fuchsia

My fuchsia is a middle-aged woman
who's had fourteen children, and though
she could do it again, she's rather tired.
All through the summer, new blooms.
I'm amazed. But the purple and crimson
have paled. Some leaves are yellowed or withering.
These buds look weaker and smaller,
like menopause babies. 'Yet still
she's a gallant fine creature performing her function'.

– That's how they talk about women,
and I heard myself using the same sort
of language. Disgraceful.
Then I understood my love for August:
its exhausted fertility
after glut and harvest.

*

Out in the garden, playing
at being a peasant forced
to slave until dark with a child on my back
and probably pregnant, I remember
wondering if I'd ever manage

the rites of passage from girl
to woman: fear and fascination
hard to choose between.

*

Thirty years later, I pick the crumpled flowers
off the fuchsia plant and water it, as if
before the shrine of two unknown grandmothers –
and my mother, who was a fourteenth child.

The Crescent

My stick of lipsalve is worn away
into the same curved crescent
that was the first thing I noticed
about my mother's lipstick.
It marked the pressure of her existence
upon the world of matter.

Imagine the grim fixity
of my stare, watching her smear
the vivid grease across her lips
from a tube shiny as a bullet.
The way she smoothed it
with the tip of a little finger
(the tinge it left, even after
washing her hands, explained
the name 'pinky') and her pointed tongue
licking out like a kitten's,
fascinated, irritated.

It was part of the mystery
of brassières and compacts and handbags
that meant being grown-up. I thought
my own heels would have to grow
a sort of spur to squeeze right down
the narrow hollow inside high-heels.

Now I am calmer and no longer
paint my lips except with this,
pale as a koshered carcass
drained of blood in salty water
or a memorial candle,
wax congealed down one side,
as though it stood in the wind
that blows from the past, flame
reflected like a crescent
moon against a cloud,
in the pool of molten light.

I carry the sign of the moon
and my mother, a talisman
in a small plastic tube
in my handbag, a holy relic
melted by believers'
kisses; and every time
I smooth my lips with the unguent
I feel them pout and widen
in the eternal smile
of her survival through me,
feel her mouth on mine.

The Fabric

My mother's glee, ripping half-rotten cloth
fibres weakened by countless washings
towels twisted and wrung out too often
unravelling cuffs and collars
laddered stockings
pyjamas split at the crotch.
How can I forget her expression.
Her hands are white with tension.

After thirty or forty years
mending the linen caring for things
what release what freedom
to wrench the weave tear the weft and warp

into smaller and smaller pieces
until totally useless.
Something always goes wrong enough
not to be mended except by death.

The snap as each strand parts
is harsh as the rattle of gunfire
but the strips are too narrow for bandages.
Fragments of lint swirl in the air
swarming locusts dust-motes in sunlight
drift of duckweed on the water's surface.
Her laughter is a thread in the fabric
that nets the furthest stars.

A Discussion with Patrick Kavanagh

about his poem 'Intimate Parnassus'

I could sit here for hours, twisting my rings,
dazed by the light and colour a diamond flashes,
without a thought in my head. An image which must
include everything that went to form me:
the universal gases, ultra violet
infra red, the seams of giant ferns
compressed to carbon. My mother's photo album.

'…to be / Passive, observing with a steady eye'
is the poet's purpose, you wrote, praising
a god-like detachment (another world entirely,
but who would want to argue?) Trying to calm
my frantic heart with such-like axioms
I would guess is not exactly what
you meant, but still the only path I know

apart from total recall: the paraphernalia
of personality – too much baggage
there for transmutation. Staring
in the crystal ball of my mother's diamond ring
doesn't serve to clarify connections
fused by violent words and acts. The conflict
between poetry and contemplation.

To be passive, observing with a steady eye
(the only duty I acknowledge) needs
a cool ironic style I've not yet managed.
And pondering one's destiny is suspect
from whatever viewpoint, even Parnassus;
forces the language to defensive postures.
My mother's ringless hands keep turning the pages.

Like Manet's *Olympe*

Like Manet's Olympe, naked in the afternoon heat
and manilla-shaded light, my aunt lay
on the green watered-silk of her bedspread. Smooth hair,
proud head, short but shapely legs and
high breasts were so much the same as the painting
I had just fallen in love with, that I faltered, still
half in the doorway, almost afraid to enter.

Through one moted beam that cut across the room
between us, I saw her reflection, pale as an ocean
creature, floating deep in the dressing-table mirror
over splinters of sun from the jumble of bottles
and jars – stern eyes seeming to draw me closer.

But this was a small house in Virginia, not
the Paris of artists. In spite of leather-bound volumes
of Schopenhauer and Baudelaire and Saturday
opera broadcasts, her aesthetic was helpless
against suburban power. The loneliness
and vanity and fearfulness which kept her
from dalliance, made me the only possible
audience, and her adoring victim.

About art and beauty, loneliness and
fearfulness and vanity, how much she taught me.

Ovid Among the Scythians

(after Delacroix)

Marshy banks of the Danube, reeds and bushes
and muddy crescents of horses' hooves. Their
clothes are earth-coloured, his dark blue.

He feels the autumn starting – that sky, those clouds,
the way the wind is moving them. The mountains
roll back, uncharted as far as China.

Ovid is writing another letter to Rome –
a gentle puzzlement to his watchers, which weapons
and dogs don't quite shield them from.

He wonders whether a linen toga, his scrolls
and pens, and their unknowing admiration,
can be protection against such sadness,

if he can metamorphose Chaos to Order,
exile to Fate, the amorous summer weasel
into the noble winter ermine.

Unique Forms

Umberto Boccioni, what you did
with metal – this striding concept,
a Proteus of the four dimensions
to celebrate the sequent moment,
objectify dynamic movement –
I want to do with words.

Is it streaming from the past or future,
the force that defines and deforms
this science-fiction Crusader battling
forward through its turbulence? (Spurs,
trappings and helmets. Fluttering banners.
Then trenches, searchlights, bombs.)

I note the dates. Pure sensation
speed and violence now are standard fashion,
that fierce manifesto just another
historical relic. But your shape-shifter
still maintains unique forms
of continuity in time and space.

Umberto Boccioni, 1882-1916
Marinetti's Futurist Manifesto, 1909
'Unique Forms of Continuity in Time and Space', 1913

Driving I

Umber, amber, ochre. Viridian and sepia.
A Victorian painting: 'After the Storm'.
The branches seem wrenched by a torturing bully.

Tested and found wanting: a character corroded
by putting money on the wrong horse.
Faster, faster.

The purpose of writing notes
is that the words are not spoken: a system
which would be shattered by articulation.

Sounds heard with the inner ear
surface as slowly
as other disturbances you learn to ignore.

Clay-smeared discs of sawn tree-trunks
like split stones or stained amoebas,
annular pools in the fields like the roots of clouds.

The one who gets blamed
always has the power.
Driving is the metaphor.

Driving II

Each species is allotted its number of heartbeats.
A mouse has the same life span as myself or a whale
but lives it more quickly, at a different tempo.

The fluttering heat of a heart or a forest.
How many leaves to a kilometre?
I want to be astonished, but it happens less often.

Such solid coils of steam and smoke extruded from
the tall cone-chimneys of a power station,
like chalky turds defying the laws of gravity.

Trees and cars and clouds blur in the speed. I have seen
almost enough for a whole life – endless renewal
and repetition. The planet belongs to the trees.

Driving III

Village after village, evidence
filters from the back of the café
louder than the lotto numbers –
people laughing, dogs barking.

A frieze of bright brown chickens
with scarlet combs
that strut and scratch below the hedge,
running interference.

Iron body oozing rust
into the wooden cross,
roadside crucifixes
transubstantiate to brioche.

Behind the garage, a car jacked up
at the inspection pit
like a woman with her legs
in obstetrical stirrups.

The museums of Europe
are textbooks for martyrs.
The river barges inspire noyades.
Two people dragging each other down.

The Dead Sea

Nights I don't sleep, however I lie,
every limb and organ aches
and though I stretch further up
the pillows, throw the blanket back,
I still can't breathe and the dark vibrates

its molecules into a form
pressing me close from mouth to hip,
stifled under an embrace more
urgent than any human lover's,
when I become his favourite

to float with him upon a sea
of melted bones and curdled clouds
and phosphorescent glass towards
a hidden shore we never reach
through waters where we cannot drown.

The Planetarium

It makes a difference
whether the earth is at its winter
nearness to, or summer
distance from, the sun.

A few hundred miles change climate
and terrain from ice
to jungle, north to south,
every fact of life.

Which seems strange, compared
to the vastness of space
(my first visit
to the Planetarium

fixed an image of blackness
struggling against
a fragile net of light)
yet comforting, because

a millimetre's alteration
in the angle at
the corner of your mouth
can have the same importance.

Rosebay Willow-herb

Rosebay willow-herb in clumps
among the brambles,
as bushy as my hair was then,
thirty years back.

We'd walked across the stubbled fields
looking for somewhere
to lie, while a combine harvester
working nearby
returned and retreated, louder and softer.
Off the path
a bale of straw's dusty chaff
served well enough.

Our parched hands and mouths, deprived
too long of what
they wanted: a touch as irritating
and electric
as rosebay down on skin and cloth,
urgently clung.

Our starved eyes craved colours
in close-up: fleshy
pinks and purples like the willow-herb
flowers that clustered
at the ditch's hidden edge
and challenged the sunset.

When we stood up, my hair was full
of fluffy down
and straw. I had to comb it out
before we parted.

I remember the stripped pallor
of flat fields
under a glowing sky, the shadow
of dark-leaved trees
along the hedge, as if a small
enamelled picture,
an amulet to guard me till
our next meeting.

And I know why, every August
since, my hair
feels tangled with rosebay willow-herb.

String

Unknotting the string you tied
my fingers make the same movements
but in the opposite order
undoing what you did

while smoothness sheathes my skin
with its electric aura
as if our hands entangled
space and time

and the rough twine recalls
your morning face,
tales of knots impossible
to loose – how they were untied.

Cartography

(for Alan)

            In every room you've had
I've lain back on the bed
            or in a chair and while
you've fondled and caressed me
            over your shoulder
eyes narrowing with pleasure
            before they open wide
I've stared at shapes and patterns
            symbols for swamp and heath-land
highways' venous systems
            concentric irregular
contour lines that tilt
            lake to valley to mountain
aniline intensities
            of mineral strata
deepening oceanic tints
            the Irriwaddy Delta
Spitzbergen   Deception Island

imagining the planet's
surface folds and hollows
    swelling smoothness
the secrets of its massive body.
    Who's been the navigator
who the cartographer?

High Pressure Zone

Smoke from the bonfires and fireworks of Guy Fawkes night
combined with a high pressure zone and a clear calm sky
doesn't seem to add up to much, and yet was enough
to cover the whole country next morning with fog.

Your changes of mood, or mine, consume days
as the foulness bounces back and forth like claps of thunder
between curdling clouds. You say: 'You get rid of your hurt
by passing it on to me.' I think you do the same.

It's something like: 'For want of a nail the battle was lost'.
Every thing affects everything else, and the truisms
become truer. We walked to the square to watch the fires.
When I saw the children waving sparklers to make patterns
against the dark, I knew that we were in the last part
of our lives. But if nothing ends, how can we two die?

Sister, Sister

'Sister, sister, I am sick.
Come and give me meat and drink.
Let me eat from your hand.'

        *

Amnon lay on his bed, moaning
with lust and vexation, knowing
that Tamar was still a virgin

by the special colour of her dress.
(Such was the custom for a princess.)
'Come closer, sister, you

yourself shall be my meat and drink.'
Her ran his tongue around her wrist.
She could not make him stop.

'The sweetest food is your hair and flesh.'
First he wheedled, then he threatened,
She argued, 'Do not force me.'

Those words meant less to him than the insects'
drone outside the curtained window
or incense fumes trapped

between the roof-beams, and he was stronger.
Afterwards, he could no longer
bear that tragic face,

called a servant to bolt the door
and keep the woman out. She tore
the bodice of her dress

(lost, the right to wear it now)
daubed with ashes head and brow,
hurt more by his hatred

than her ravishment. What
did Tamar do when Absolom,
two years later, killed him?

The story leaves her desolate,
but doesn't tell. One has to guess.
I imagine Tamar

in her chamber, burning incense
and remembering. The insects'
whining seems a song:

'Sister, sister, I am sick.
Come and give me meat and drink.
Let me eat from your hand.'

Cup and Sword

The cup has to be stone,
cup-holes
in the lower face of the protecting boulder
dripping stone-milk.

Which means that the sword
is Excalibur –
King Arthur's slashing sword –
hard-belly, the voracious one.

Those bodies in bloody armour
were knights-errant
who fought to hold their cavern,
keep the cup hidden.

Something that started a long time ago
can still nourish –
like a Grail story –
though the cup is empty, the sword broken.

Evil Enters

Evil enters when there is no answer
so don't ask any questions.
You want to know too much.

For instance, are those half-seen figures
moving up and down a ladder
angels, demons, snakes,
or other souls in the same dull torment?
The Sphinx and Oedipus?
You'd wrestle hard, and all night through,
just for the company and some response.

Before dawn broke, surely
there'd be a gasp or groan you could interpret
as a revelation,
a whole theology – and you its prophet –
whatever best diverts your rage and grief.

Evil enters when there is no answer
so don't ask any questions.
But you can't make yourself stop.

A Room

That room is too dark for me.
There are things in that room I don't want to see.
That door has been closed for a long time.

The most I can do at first
is change the wooden panels for glass.
The black ovals of my spectacles
flash blue when my head is raised, and white
shapes of clouds move across them.

Light dissolves the door frame
to a glowing margin, but the paths
I've walked in every mood and season
show clear as through the rifling
of a telescope: memory's target.

Trees form the walls of a green room.
Between the restless branches, sunlight
glazes rose windows.

The Restlessness of Sunset

I pull the curtains to
open them again
get up from my desk
sit down stand up again

to go to the window
and watch the changes
of cloud and colour
every moment changing

and every afternoon
as dusk begins
I can't stay still
or close myself in

until the sun has gone
behind the trees below the line
of the horizon
until the sky

has dulled and darkened
enough to let
the evening start and soothe
the restlessness of sunset.

The Limitations of Tiredness

The fierce hiss of sap in a burning log
is the same sound sleep makes as it withdraws
from me when I lie down these winter afternoons.
At first my hands relax and warmth spreads
through limbs which suddenly seem larger.
The blue and brown of moving skies and
surging water as the tide pulls out
across the sandflats concentrate between
my brows into a point of light I stare at
while the noise gets louder. I never know
why it stops, why, with a heart-lurch and a deep-
drawn breath of alarm I turn back to the room
and fire and desk and wake to a stormy dusk:
the limitations of tiredness.

That Presence

Like a painter stepping backward from the easel
straightening up from the worktable
with a loaded brush, to see exactly where
another touch of red is wanted, like
a carpet weaver wondering if the time
has come to change the pattern, a sculptor
hesitating before the first decisive cut,
I ponder a poem, repeating every word,
trying to hear where a note needs altering,
testing by breath and sense and luck –

like staring at the surface of a mirror
through soundless levels between glass and silver
into the pupils of that reflected presence
over my shoulder advancing from its depths.

Autumn Garden Poem

I want to know the name of those leaves,
pale and felted one side
smooth and green

the other, like strips of paper torn
from an endless scroll and strewn
across the lawn.

*

Two Japanese ladies, leaning
fondly as lovers: a willow's
ragged sleeves

brushing the grass. The jade-blue discs
silvered by dew and frost
from a eucalyptus

bush are their broken necklaces.
Spiders' webs have tangled
their ragged tresses.

*

I can show you rosebay and golden
rod, moulting thistles
and rusty clover.

But what are those pallid flowers called
that open in sunlight, and close
when the evening falls?

The Wittersham Sibyl

The pattern of dew on spiders' webs
and how it hung like crystal beads,
every hole the birds had torn –
pucker-edged and starfish-shaped
for frost and rain to work upon –
through fallen apples lacquer-bright
among the swathes of dripping fern,

these, and the angles the rising wind
bent from the pampas' papery leaves
and straw-pale peeling stems, the way
the shattered-topaz acorn husks
livid toadstools and rusty moss
reclaimed the lawn, she knew must be
messages from the god.

The Same Power

Lush chill of spring in Holland Park.
Dark glassy flesh of the bluebells, hoarse
cry of a peacock strutting his courtship cope
against a wind which flattens it out behind
and ripples the quills like waves on a squally sea.
Striped bark of birch trees' pale trunks
as sharp a white as opening hawthorn flowers.
Vivid rainclouds scudding across the sky.

Which all must be attended to now,
not half-ignored, only recalled later (perhaps) –
that common regret for not having been alert
enough to recognise the one moment
when beauty, truth, life and death became
the same Power: evoked not described.

The Same Ease

Walking in the square, through the damp and misty still-mild air
    of a late October Sunday morning.
Only at the second circuit do I meet another person: a young family,
    parents and children,
but otherwise the paths are empty – and the tennis court, the sandpit
    and climbing frame, seven acres
(do I remember the size correctly?) of grass and flowers, shrubs and trees:
    the delicious colours of the leaves
and their softened texture like the gloves and handbag from the wardrobe
    of an ageing elegant woman;
the last few roses, gnarled buds scentless this late in the year; some stalky
    toadstools: as if all for my sole pleasure.
Suddenly I think it's raining – not that I feel the drops, but because of
    the sound – and watch a shower
of leaves detach from their branch with the same ease, the moment come
    to let go, that I hope for.

The Novelty

Winter's charcoal structures and autumn's flaring challenge
after summer fattens spring's sketchy foliage:
like a million gas-jets,
crocuses ignite beneath the warming boughs.

Meadows flushing green for what seems just a day
before their tawny paleness is stacked away as harvest,
ponds sink low and hedges wither.
Lambs becoming sheep, and babies, parents.

Then months of frost and clouded skies until the change
from open fires to windows; and as the sun approaches
the extreme of solstice,
the novelty of watching it all start again.

In Drummond's Room

(William Drummond of Hawthornden, 1585-1649)

This morning, after
lighting the fire, I looked
from the deep window of Drummond's room

over the glen
toward cloud so dark that the black
horizon-trees blurred against them.

Only the flames were bright,
burning under the pilgrims'
scallop-shells carved on the mantel.

Then the wind veered,
the wood smoked, and the tall yew
whose needled boughs

fill the other window
soughed, louder than
the logs' seething, and through the glass

splinters of colour –
the red excited push
of growth, the yellow of last year's leaves

that strengthens green,
patches of blue, sun and shadow –
signalled a new front

of weather moving in.
For an hour or so at noon
the sky was clear. But I prefer

to stay in here
and build the fire up, squeeze
the bellows, watch exactly how

sparks jump and
the cinders shimmer, how
the branches turn and lift at the same

agitated angle
as the sudden-falling slant
of whirling snow that will not settle

and the calm curve
of the sunset rainbow
above the swollen river,

to disentangle
the single pattern through each
recurrence and renewal since

he stared into the fire
and from the windows, to see
and feel and think what I do now.

The Poet –

    sits at her desk, watching an insect
moving its antennae in time
with Mozart. A quiet evening in August,

invoking the melancholy pleasure
of aimless thought. Knowing that what
goes unrecorded is written on water.
The ripples disperse, as is their nature.

But beyond the roofs, the crescent
moon and stars seem points and markers
of a limitless expansion.

Later, she might wonder whether
something precious was squandered, ointments
poured extravagantly out
(almost swooning from the odours).

The torment starts whose cure is nothing less
than pen and ink and paper –
    and the entire universe.

This Time of Year

(1993)

I.

This Time of Year

Parked cars on the street have pale leaves
plaqued to their roofs and windscreens
after the storm, and the same sodden
mosaic is pressed into the pavement
(the pattern fallen cloth-scraps mark
on a tailor's floor). This time of year
the last leaves on the trees are stained
with the watered colours of Mother's chiffon,
crêpe and sharkskin pre-war frocks.

This time of year, my mnemonic
for the date of Daddy's birthday was:
If the eleventh is Armistice Day,
it's the seventh; an association
hard to detach from such concepts as Father,
and God and birth and death et cetera,
when my father had gone to the war.
Nightly, in the double bed,
Mother and I read *Mother India*
together, enthralled by the gory details,
and tried to imagine him there.

They always happened in November,
several consecutive Novembers
(he must have come home then – Mother's
mouth would soften in remembrance):
our worst battles. To break his hold
and her power. There was much
damage. A normal adolescence.
This time of year, between the dates
of their deaths, with a swirl of brittle leaves,
foggy muslin veils and ice-blue glitter
(does it come too late, that promise?)
the forgotten returns. As if
for some purpose. Stronger than ever.

The Coptic Wedding

Decades go by, yet I keep mouthing
the same stupid lines.
I notice a bird in the park and can't
remember its name,
but wonder again, for the umpteenth time.

Young women behave
as if they have been taught to believe
a show of ignorance
charms every admirer. From someone
my age, that's tedious.

Where lay the harm
in my Mother's reiterations
and nervous denials –
except to herself? My impatience
when she insisted
she'd never been there, heard of or done it,
whatever was mentioned,
like a child who always gets blamed,
still makes me ashamed.
She seemed afraid of everything.

Being stupid – or becoming like her –
was my worst fear
as a girl. When I forget, now,
what something's called,
it can conjure her up from the ground.

Celebration noise,
ullulation and the throb of drumming
across the formal paths
and flowerbeds, drew every Sunday-
morning stroller
toward its source: a Coptic wedding,
a dancing circle
of white-robed men and henna-footed girls
around a couple
with solemn faces topped by golden crowns.

Our hunger for ceremony matched;
side by side we watched.
Neither of us would rest until
old promises were kept,
neglected rituals performed.

Far from her own ancestors
was how she must have felt, uprooted
as that groom and bride.
Recognising a chaffinch, I knew it.
All of us spun out of orbit.

Lineage

When my eyes were sore or tired or itched,
clenching her hands in a loose fist,
my mother would rub her wedding ring,
carefully, along the closed lids,
sure the touch of gold was curative.

She also believe in hot water
with lemon, first thing in the morning
and, at any time of day, drank awful-
tasting infusions and pot-liquors
to purify her blood. She warmed
a spoonful of sweet almond oil to pour
into my aching ear, wrapped torn
old woollen vests around my throat,
and blistered my chest with a poultice
if I came down with a cold.

Remedies and simples from the old
country, still useful in the city,
were passed from mother to daughter
and not yet scorned. We rarely saw
a doctor. When I was little
it seemed normal to be sickly
for half of the year. I never told her
that I was proud she was a witch.

Choosing

How I yearned for a velvet dress
with a shirred waist and lace collar
like all my friends, but couldn't choose
which colour – dull green or
dark red. It seemed a contest
between the nursery horrors
of a fairy-story forest
and the scary glamour
of portentous tomorrows – crazy
guesses and conjurations based on
grown-ups' talk, books and movies.

There is a photo of me
in a garment almost the pattern
of that ideal model.
Above the collar, a self-conscious
face, tormented by the problem
of choice (and every other),
which from the vantage of the present
moment, still makes me want
to laugh or weep or fight.
So was it red, green or blue
I chose? I – or my mother.

Nails and Spiders and Jacks

First, four flat-headed shiny tacks
had to be hammered into the top
of an empty wooden spool, after
the last span of thread was unreeled, measured
the full stretch of my mother's arm,
and pushed through the eye of a needle.
Then I'd untangle ends of crochet
skeins and darning wool from her workbox
and take one of her crimped and coppery
hairpins – which was just the right tool
for looping yarn up and over the tacks
and through the bobbin's hollow centre.
As long as I went on making the same
movements (like a spider extruding its silk)
the motley cord kept growing.
Later, I'd coil it into a doily
or a tea-cosy – something I thought
was pretty – to give her for a present.

And there was jacks: a game we played
with small glittering silvery objects –
each like six nails joined together
into a three-dimensional Greek cross,
a dice-chassis, a tank-trap,
or a nervous spider signalling
his mating intentions – that had to be tossed
in the air from the back of the hand and land
on your open palm while trying to catch
a rubber ball before it stopped bouncing.
I almost choked from the excitement.

The jack's six arms had clubbed tips
like the four nails in the wooden bobbin.
Remembering one brings back the other –
a connection that seems more important
than the shape of nails and jacks. Perhaps
it was a diagram of how
a message travelled from deep in the brain

through fibres finer than gossamer silk
until it reached my body's furthest limits.
Those childhood speculations.

Crosses and nails. Sixes and fours.
Trap-door spiders and private pleasures.
The game can be played with stones, shards,
dibs or jacks. Check-stones were buried
in Roman tombs and Celtic barrows,
where primitive looms are also found.
Angels and devils gamble for your soul,
they say, with ball and knucklebones –
and not only if you're Christian.
But I didn't know any of this,
polishing my skills at jacks
or musing over my French knitting.
I might have been thinking, though, about space
and pattern and number, female spiders
eating their husbands, shiny metallic
broad-headed nails and blunt-tipped jacks.

The X-Ray Machine

Ten years old, I loved to look through
the periscope of the x-ray machine
in the shoestore where, even the sunniest
day, neon flickered. Metal edges
and nylon carpet sparked with static.
Those sharp white lines I saw were tacks
someone had hammered into the soles
of lace-up winter oxfords or summer
sandals. Those chalky shapes, denser
than the blur of flesh (a popsicle
of sweet red water frozen around
a wooden stick) were bones, the structure
that held me up and would survive me.
It gratified, more than it frightened
me, contemplating the future.

Tosca

Above the walnut cabinet where
Uncle Roscoe kept pistols and bullets,
moulds and targets and tins of pellets,
dust motes drifted through a shaft of sunlight
while my Aunt Ann and I listened
to *Tosca* broadcast from the Met.

I know it was summer, because
that glittering swirl blurred
the linoleum's pattern: the carpets
had been rolled, and stored until winter.

But which pattern was it, which room –
before or after our move –
am I remembering, where we sat
between the radio and the cabinet,
which sunny Saturday afternoon,
during the war, assembles
around me as I listen to *Tosca*
now, in a half-dismantled apartment
the day before a new departure.

I have heard *Tosca* so often,
I think I know each motif
by heart. The grand themes of my life
must have been already waiting
in the wings, incarnated as
the jealous woman artist,
Scarpia's potent menace. Those two
make the couple. Cavaradossi's
revolutionary fervour can
never deflect their trajectory
of mutual destruction.

Uncle Roscoe's guns and bullets
somehow stay connected to the story,
but he was gentle, indifferent
to the passions of the music –

and the wife he had chosen:
that thwarted fantasist of every
métier and alternative.

So much talent misdirected
into trimming hats and bottling fruit.
She taught me to listen to opera,
to believe I was an artist,
to read Baudelaire and to iron a shirt
as well as a Parisian laundress.

Tosca is telling the whole world
how she has lived only for art, and I
an in another place and apartment,
writing my notes, watching dust motes drift
in the sunlight, about to move on.

Aunt Ann's floral-patterned linoleum
on one or other living room floor
crumbled decades ago. Each house
was gone when I tried to find it,
the gardens asphalted over.
I never learned what happened to her
walnut cabinet, or Uncle Roscoe's
collection of guns, after they died.

II.

Mottoes

If you run with the hare
and hunt with the hounds
you fall between two stools.
No changing horses in mid-stream.
Where you make your bed
you have to lie,
among roses and thorns. Really,
it's like the boy who cried, 'Wolf!'
when he saw a lost dog from the pack.
In the land of the blind
the one-eyed man...
so don't try,
we all know how it ends.

Out to Lunch

Always on the look-out
for God's talent scout –
eyes sliding up and down and round

Pushy and anxious
as an out-of-work actress
(imagining he might be Dracula)

Always on the look-out
for God's talent scout –
outright smile, worn-out teeth, outsize mouth

Just sanguine enough
to out-class the others
(but ugh, love – not from the jugular)

Always on the look-out
for God's talent scout
who's gone to ground

or somewhere out of town
with the Count.
(He's out of this world!)

A Couple

As smug as death,
Daphne and Dorian Gray,
eternal honeymooners,
plunge into another tango.

To be forever young
seemed the best gift
to ask of the Devil.
Since then, they must have danced
ten times around the world.

Like melting sugar skulls
at a Todos Santos picnic
in Mexico City,
or a gallant hussar's
fancy epaulettes,

those perched smiles
above each other's shoulder,
mimicking a lust that bores them.
Mais toujours la politesse.

Warped Toward the North

Warped toward the North,
magnet pulsing at the polar core
with the hot glint and dull throb of a brazier

or a lit-up liner freighted
with wordless dancers, sequins swaying
on the hems of their skirts, and their tuxedoed partners

the moment before the boilers burst
and orchestra, passengers and sailors
were plunged through fire and steam and frothing water.

The bald white brow
of a whale or a god, arms as soft
as snowdrifts, or Death's cradle, but strong enough

to save me from the devastation,
are attributes of my Angel.
His song so beautiful that I forget the South.

The Author

[he speaks:]

I feel no need for what is called real
life – enough in my writing. (Which shows
such wisdom, warmth and worldly nous,
they say, one might easily think
I'd gone everywhere, done everything,
been a slave, an explorer, a diplomat,
even a tree or a bird or a horse.)

I stay at home each day, sit
at my desk most of the night, with no
desire for anyone except
the characters who move between
the page and my imagination.

There was a time I had to smile,
adapt, and learn it all, observe
the faces, attend the conversation.
But I've almost forgotten the hard facts.
Or I confuse them with the fictions.

There used to be friends. Now they don't seem
necessary. So much happened,
I could think about it forever.
I run the action through again
and listen to those voices from the past.
There is always something new
to alter. And my dreams get better.

My Lucky Star

Just to imagine the smell of his quarters,
the state of his linen and wardrobe,
makes one nauseous (you were supposed
to love him, warts and all):
that arrogant and alcoholic
clerkish solipsistic charmer
who cannot manage to keep even
his manuscripts in order.

Always in the background (in spite of or
because of? an unresolved, almost
Pavlovian misogyny)
is that essential dual support-system:
a 'woman of the people' who sometimes
lets him fuck her, and the other,
upper-class, innocent whose stern
profile he worships from a distance.

The history of European culture
confirms the same pattern
from the Tagus to the Urals.

(I'm talking about the only model
of "artist" on offer: those daunting groupy-
hagiographies I read, as a girl.)
But I recovered, apostate:
thank my lucky star.

A Village Story

Under the canopy of plane trees
shading the plaza in full summer,
young girls of the village,
     the butterfly sleeves and wide stiff skirts
     of their starched cotton dresses
     (pink, blue, green, white and yellow
     pale virginal colours)
     speckled by disks of sunlight
     filtered through the branches,
are standing in small groups
with hands or arms linked together,
shocked into silence –
to watch an act of public penance.

               On her knees
               in the square
        near the fountain and church
          in front of the café
        the place where it happened.

The daughter-in-law, pallid and swollen-eyed,
serving drinks to the tourists,
looks stupid with shame,
like someone beaten half-conscious.
But those discoloured patches of skin on her face
are not bruises. She is pregnant.

Her husband moves between the bar
and the café's open door
as if treading water.
His head is in another element.

The body –
    'strong as a bull, tall as a fishing-boat's mast',
    covered with black hair
    that sprouts below the cuffs, curls above the neck,
    of a perfectly-pressed white shirt –
was the cause of the problem.
The expression on his small-featured face
is haughty, reproving, and frightened.
His eyes will not focus.
He has poured out the cognacs and coffees,
mixed the *horchatas*, so often
it has become automatic

        In the square
      near the fountain and church
       in front of the café
    the sinner, the mother, the mother-in-law,
      the woman disgraced,
        on her knees
     making public repentance,
a deep-breasted vigorous matron
like a Mediterranean goddess
almost as tall, surely as strong, as her son.

Since the time of the troubles, the old man
has stayed on their farm in the hills
with his books and his guns.
His wife and son have always run the café
where they, the other children
and the young wife, live upstairs.

       Public repentance.
     On her knees in the square.
    Hands upraised and head thrown back,
      glinting eyes and open mouth,
     like every holy picture on the altar.
     Doing what the priest told her
after the door was forced
the sheet torn off
the two of them caught
in her wide matrimonial bed,
where he might have been conceived,
and where she gave birth.

Whatever his penance, it was endured in private.
The couple brazened it out, bringing vermouth and ice cream
in stoical silence. The others went somewhere else
for the rest of the season, as if into hiding.

That winter, once the grandchild had been born,
she came down from the farm
wearing black, a widow, prouder than ever.
The young girls could not stop watching and talking.
The young men adored her.

A Saga

Coldness scents the path.
Cold ores salt the caves and cliffs.
Stars sift light
through the black veil night wears,
and the sea nudges against earth's rocky breasts.

On the weed-strewn beach
below the walls of the castle keep
she gathers bands of purple kelp
curled tight as a whip
and watches the horizon change:
Azure. Ultramarine. Indigo.

Beyond that line
where ocean plunges down the edge of the world
and the sky curdles and thickens and follows over,
each yearning to meet the other,
a high-prowed boat with russet sails is moving closer.

Galatea

– woke from a statue's dream
on the night of full moon
(May's Milk-Moon)
her whole body altered:

with the moist gleam of marble
under quarry-dust
like flesh through talcum powder,
caked breasts stone-hard:

a spangled web of pores
patterning the skin
like an astronaut's map
or a fountain of stars.

Phallic Sapphics

Close your eyes against accordion angles
opening out like ivory fans, poker
hands and velvet theatre curtains, or bivalves
to the swirling tide.

Watch instead a runnel of lime-charged water
slowly drip from a stalactite to pattern
the slick wet sides and floor of a karstland cave
with mineral lace.

Remember the bird you once held on your palm,
how it struggled to fly? Its hot hard feathers
in panic-flutter were striped with the same pale
onyx colours as

shingle under almost invisible waves
(or smooth skin sliding through my practiced fingers).
The bird was blinded by fear. But your eyes blur
in expectation.

The Necklace

Someone sent beads for a necklace,
an unexpected gift. When I
opened the bag of soft rubbed chamois
and loosed the knotted leather cord
they spilled across the floor like those
first rolling drops of rain
coated with summer dust that seem to be
quicksilver, or threshed grain poured.

They were jade, coral, amber,
streaky mineral and polished
metal, clear and clouded glass –
beads of every shape and sort.

I peered under the furniture,
crawled through the table legs, trying
to find them among the carpet's tufts
where they nestled like insect eggs.
I searched the hearthstone's ashy corners.
The shards of jetty coal and cinder
and splinters of carbonised wood might have
been beads. I think I got them all.

A man was there, who laughed as he watched.
But I can't tell you who he was
or what happened next. I didn't
thread that necklace in my dream.

Romance

(for Assia)

Every time I fold the laundry
I remember how she told me
it took an hour to put the clothes away,
and that meant every day.

Eyes flashing, she made the list
of her duties into a metaphor.
She looked like a Minoan goddess, or Yeats'
princess bedded on straw.

She seemed to gloat on oppression,
as if it were the fuel and source
of her obsession, and each passionate protest
a further confirmation.

My spirit shrivelled, like fingers
from harsh soap and cold water,
to hear this version of the same old story.
Yet I could not doubt her.

Fairytales are very specific,
almost domestic – tasks to be done,
problems to solve. They tell about bewitched
princesses, toad princes,

and the force that holds them spell-bound.
Smoothing his shirts, she dreamed
of transformation and reward, and being
happy ever after.

I'd gone down that road before,
and knew its forks and sudden twists
where one false step has mortal consequence.
But I was luckier.

Homage

It's not a case of forget or forgive.
Who expects either?
Something different happens.
I haven't forgotten
what you did to me or what I did.
I think about it often.
A steady contemplation
can dissolve the need for action
as acid soil consumes cloth, bone, wood.
After a time, even the metal's gone.
Nor have I forgiven.
Forgiveness would be understanding
why those burials were so elaborate.
To the few surviving rituals
of a lost tradition, I pay homage.

A Mourner

I put my head on my arms on my desk
to weep, and the smell and heat of my breath
remind me of afternoons at school
when the teacher made us stop our noise
and running around, and take a rest.

Not since then, except in love's
embrace, have the damp intensities
of my own body and feelings so
combined. My pain is this particular
odour, this primeval climate.

The teacher talked about an endless
age of fire and flood and earthquake,
everything changing, life-forms dying
and being born. In all the confusion
and turmoil, there should be a mourner.

Lark

Lark, lift my pain
above the rolling tide
and restless grey sea,
the yellow poppies blowing
on the dunes, into
the bright stormy clouds,
the sky's darkening blue cone.

Lark, ease my heart
as you soar and disappear
on a beaded thread of sound.
Let each pulse and throb
become a purer note
on the stave of your song:
music which forgets its source.

Until You Read It

Like music on the page
which has to be played
and heard, even if
only by one person,
this word, this phrase,
this poem, does not exist
until you read it.

III.

Bird and Worm

The bird pulled at the worm for a while,
got it half out of its hole, then hopped off,
in that bright-eyed mindless way birds have.

The worm rested after the ordeal, feeling
perfectly safe. But the bird wheeled round,
to where it wriggled, confident.

The beak bobbed, only once or twice,
but enough to drag the worm's full length
clear of the earth. Then gobble it down.

The Old Dog

The faint sound of a drill
somewhere down the street:
an old dog wheezing and snoring

under a kitchen table
scrubbed until its grain
stands proud as Braille

and the wood between
damp and soft and worn
as washday hands that grope beneath

toward the old dog's head
and twitching flanks,
to soothe him back into his dream.

The Fish

Trying to think it through,
force my mind to hold one specific
thought, makes my brain convulse and twist in my
skull like a fish in a net, with a fish's vigour.

I see the fixed glare of its eye – blood,
jet and mica – feel the rasping touch
of fin and scale against my hand, the tail's
last spiny flick and panic-thrust as it
wrenches free; and I am left wondering
what it was I tried to think about, depleted

yet glad that now I can follow it through
                    all the way to the sea.

Visitation

A foam-crimped wave clear and silent
as a sheet of glass slid across
the shingle that wets your feet before
you notice then dulls and vanishes

or a sigh of wind under the door
that lifts the carpet's corner a single
moment and lets it settle as if
nothing happened although you know it did.

Reflection

I write with my left hand, but
the one in the mirror
holds a pen between the fingers
of the hand on her right. Her smile
slants lop-sided, her hair is combed
the wrong way, she stands so badly:
reversed and changed and all contrary.

I want to see photographs
(my own face and its reflection,
unlike each other
as matter is from anti-matter)
and contemplate resemblances,
opposites: me, not her –
the person they mistake me for:
all contrary, changed, reversed.

Part of the Crowd –

      – means not only
going with the current, but also
pushing against it: that almost
ecstatic fear.

      Above the surge
of bodies, anxious eyes
demand a confirmation.
Others, already surrendered
to the greater being a crowd is,
are vacant disks of light
on the flood's surface.

And sometimes
it soothes me: drifting through
sale-crazed department-stores or
carried like cargo down escalators
at rush-hour, onto the platforms
of underground stations:
                part of the crowd.

The Law

Like someone walking a tightrope
or trying to stay upright
on a heaving platform – first
one foot, then the other,
backward, forward, swaying,
arms stretched shoulder high.

Never before have feet
and fingers felt so alive,
reaching out to sense
the slightest shift in balance
and position, like the growing
tips of trees or vines.

For things to stay the same
they must keep changing. So
the best way to change your life
is to be still and do
nothing, while everything else
follows the law of change.

To Whom It Pertains

To create, to God alone pertains.
SIR JOHN DAVIES

'Stop creating!' is said to a tiresome child
who's half-hysterical with tiredness
from survival tactics, waiting
for the boredom of childhood to end.

Or said to the girl who insists
there must be a meaning to actions and words
the other wants to ignore and dismiss.
She keep worrying away at it.

So the child makes a drama involving
whoever, maybe the whole family
at a party or a public place
like a restaurant or a railway station.

And the girl leaves her hearer so weary
with the story that finally he agrees,
'Yes, yes, how right you are. That's exactly it.'
Then she contradicts herself and starts again.

Making something from nothing:
a definition of creation
generally alarming except
to the one (having fun) to whom it pertains.

The Plastic Bag

If I imagine this plastic bag
(innocuous stripes of blue and white)
being blown along the pavement
exploding
as I step on it; imagine shrapnel
penetrating my flesh;
the primary black white and red

of metal, smoke, glass and blood;
am I easing into this dimension
what need never happen?

Some say: even to allow
such images to mushroom up,
as ink clouds water,
uncages only pain and terror.
Others claim
that language can defuse danger.
There were nightmares
from which I woke gasping with relief,
disasters not yet suffered,
with nothing remembered.

The flimsy bag billows,
looking strangely full, packed
with all the grand categories,
endless problems,
disregarded warnings.
It skitters across the path
I can no more not follow
than the one who chose
the code-word for revelation
can stop before action.

The Problem

I

The problem of what to do
with radioactive waste
is not yet solved.

There are deep-sea canyons
off the continental shelf
where sealed cans are dumped,
caves under the Alps,
Cyclopean bunkers

to store the glassy blocks
(their deceptive dullness
like quiescent magma
in a lunar crater)
fused and annealed
from the residue.

II

The problem of what to do
with this new being,
slick with scar-tissue,
this mutation, this survivor
of injury and alteration
by archaic pollutions,
pressures and forces
that gnaw into the marrow,
the cell's blueprint,
the soul's structure,
until fear of future
irreversible error
becomes the critical factor,
demands a solution.

III

What to do and how to move
beyond this moment
which seems so final,
detoxify and heal
each molecule
of earth and air and water,
of soma and psyche,

how to enact the decision
not to abandon the sinned-against,
the sin or the sinner
but exorcise and absolve,
bring back rhythm and pattern and order
(how to love)
is the problem.

IV

Newborn

From the roof of her under-reef den
a giant Pacific octopus –
whose suckered legs are meters long,
who changes tone when curious
from glowing white to glorious red –
hangs a hundred thousand eggs
clumped into strands, like clusters
of grapes painted on the ceiling
of Sennefer's tomb at Luxor.

'The rough surface of rock
makes the vine-tendrils and fruit
more realistic. The artist's
experiment has succeeded,'
the guidebook says. I remember
that tomb in the Valley of the Nobles
more clearly than the others.
An arbour of freshness and coolness
lay below its dusty entrance –
a foretaste of the Western Kingdom.

Sennefer was Mayor of Thebes
and overseer of Amon's
temple garden, three and a half
millennia ago – yet
the vivid colours on the frescoes
and ceiling look newly painted,
the lotus held to his nostril
still fragrant, the grapes luscious.
His wife is young and beautiful.
She tenderly touches his leg
as they stand at the offering table
or sit together, pilgrims
on a boat to Abydos.

The third leg from the right
of a male octopus is modified
with a groove for mating.
When its tip is pushed
into the female's mantle cavity
a long tubular bag of sperm
slides down to find the oviduct.
An octopus is a solitary creature –
this rarely happens more than once.

For the next six months the female
stays in her den, stroking
the clusters of fertilised eggs
with gestures I want to interpret
as consciously gentle, even
maternal, shooting streams of water
from her siphon to keep them free
of fungus and oxygenated.
She will not eat again.

Wasted flesh
        Skin
peeling like blistered paint
off a ransacked tomb's mildewed walls
or the weightless husks and residue
of grapes pressed dry –
drifting like a grey ghost
trailing mummy bandages
across the ocean floor.
Now the eggs are hatched
her purpose is achieved
if two survive.

A hundred thousand octopus-
existences break through
the membrane web that sheathes them
and float out to the darkness
of the circling current
like souls departing for eternity
or new-born gods.

The Cranes

Far and high overhead, the cranes
were hard to sight but could be heard
the valley's length. Then a plane
appeared to pass through them, and showed
them clear against the racing clouds
and vapour trails in the mild noon sky.

Each bird marked another point
inside an ever-changing space
or on its surface – like the junction knots
in the mesh of a strong net, where
a huge, half-transparent, half-
imagined being, powered by
its own fierce jet and surging thrusts,
was streaming out glory pennants.

We saw new constellations forming
as patterns altered in all dimensions
and trapped the pale print of an almost
full equinoctial moon.
The cranes veered and banked, following
the river's thermals and currents.
We saw cherubim and seraphim
above the Rio Grande.

Late Low Sun

A late low sun
shone through each small new leaf on the vines.
Rows of gnarled brown stocks
pruned for decades to the same height,
and this year's shoots
tethered along the trellis wires,
sprouted new growth –
foliage translucent as lime jelly,
gaudy as stage jewellery

– as if a flock of butterflies
just emerged from their chrysalides
had landed on the vines and spread
tender, crumpled greeny wings
to harden and dry.

Late low sun,
a fluttering in the air. A double-
headed creature
settles on the stony terrace wall.
Pin-eyes fixed
in opposite directions, antennae
at full stretch
and thread-legs braced,
two thin and downy bodies
almost hidden
by dark-veined wings that keep shuddering.

All at once,
still joined, they lift and veer, erratic,
into the branches
of the chestnut tree, whose ruffles of buds
and half-furled leaves,
where sunset's intensest purple rays
strike through,
are the exact colour and shape
to shelter ecstatics.

Flowing Stream

Shadows of leaves
on the pavement I'm laying
with stones from the garrigue
are drifting across it
like clear water in a shallow stream.

Shadows of chestnut
acacia and elder leaves
ripple like water in sunlight
over smooth pale stones
which might be a stream bed.

The movement of shadows
silhouettes of leaves
speckle the cobbles, the wave-worn
limestone slabs of unclassifiable
lichen-spotted shapes

and alter the pattern
by glittering refraction
as the water eddies
around fallen twigs and pebbles
on the sandy stream bed, on the paving

Until I don't know
whether shadows or reflections
wind or stones or leaves
are the transparent water
in a flowing stream.

Thunder

I am very good at chimpanzee's work:
shelling almonds, picking stones out of lentils,
scratching a smear of food off a sleeve or collar.
I find a satisfaction in repetition,
superstition, and know the myopic's refusal
to look above or beyond the horizon. Half
of my nature is simple as a medieval
peasant. The other isn't, and that's the problem.

It's harder to date the complex of discontents
shared by any metaphysical primate,
who soon learns that pain is surer than pleasure.
A stubbed toe hurts, and the soul asserts itself
by the same token. Such thoughts are as timeless
as wondering how the planets started spinning
and why one cannot live forever.
Elegies must be the oldest art form.

Thunder rolls from the northern hills, and the lamp
on my desk flickers. Once, it would have been
an omen, a god's voice or seven-league tread.
Now it's only a nuisance, or a warning
reminder of how easily the world could end.
There are days in the present when I imagine, far
in the future, someone brooding on first and last things,
keening the dead, and tending her garden.

Buds

From late November until the solstice –
what used to seem the lowest notch
before the sky-ratchet nudged forward –
I have begun to notice, on vines
and shrubs and trees I'd thought were dead,
half-hidden below those few
stiff, discoloured leaves that cling

to dull twigs and dry branches, hundreds
of swelling, glossy new buds.

Such confidence and stubbornness
make one reconsider. Those old leaves
protect next season's growth.
The blackish trunks can still pump,
through months of winter, enough sap
for most buds (their scaly sheath,
their fragile freight of protoplasmic
leaf and pulpy, pleated petal)
tenacious, to survive. Once
you know where to look, confirmation's
omnipresent: not a moment's
hiatus between death and life.

Solstice

A door swings open
slow and heavy
on rusty hinges.

A wheel revolves
clumsy, jolting
against the fulcrum
of its wooden axle.

A round winter moon
disentangles
from roofs and branches

to float above
snow-blanked fields
and rocky mountain peaks
weightless, easy

on the humming pivot
star-gleam flashing
of the new year solstice.

Privacy on Lake Ochrid

(for Elaine)

When I asked our guide
if this was the house
of a rich Turkish merchant
he said, 'No, it was built
by a Christian. Turks
had high walls and windows
facing inward.'

My friend laughed but
insisted, 'Your nature
is secretive –
a primitive who
fears a photograph
will steal her soul.'

She got it right.
I can't resist, early
evenings, staring
into lighted windows –
though in my own room,
black reflecting glass
unnerves me. I always
close the curtains.

I imagine
a house facing inward,
a hidden courtyard
full of flowers
with a blue-tiled
fountain in the middle,
and birds that do not
want to leave,

where women sit –
black hair spread to dry
like capes of glistening silk

across their shoulders –
and watch between the roofs
and snow-streaked hills
the white clouds drift.

On the Coast Road
(north of Dubrovnik, August 1989)

A mosaic of broken glass (halting the traffic)
strewn across the sun-dappled, heat-softened coast
road surface, fills a larger space than when
it was a windscreen; and the undamaged door
of a new bronze Mercedes makes the crumpled fenders
seem ancient and fragile, like a chariot unearthed.

Two men, with movements as rapid as dancers,
cut into the side of the car and manoeuvre
the pieces apart. Is that sound the whine
of an electric tool slicing through metal
or a faint scream from the trapped driver?
The blue plush bear lolling against a wheel
and the red pantalooned clown appear unhurt,
but there's no sign of a child whose toys they were.

A high terrace overlooks the corner
where the local car smashed into the tourist,
like a box at the theatre. The terrace is crowded
with people pressing against the railings to see
everything better. Their faces are concentrated
but calm, like angels watching the damned suffer.

Veronica's Napkin, or 'Nick's Lament'

Veronica was listening to the guitar music. Her loose sweater and thick stockings were the same raspberry colour as her unpainted lips, whose puckering lines, incised by constant shifts of mood, echoed their texture. Her smooth bare neck and face were so white they made me think of St Veronica's napkin. I wondered if she was menstruating.

Outside the window, a pneumatic drill and the irregular thump of a machine almost engulfed the quieter passages. The performer huddled over his instrument. Each auditor leaned forward at the same tense angle in an effort to filter out the jarring sounds. Their eyes showed the alertness of people waiting for a vital message in a half-familiar language. Veronica's darkened eyes were glistening and wary. She yearned for the summons into a larger reality, like the musician, or her namesake.

The evening before, we had eaten Sole Veronique. In the shadowless light of the recital room, Veronica's flesh had the same pale gloss as the creamy sauce and starched linen napkin – or the napkin Veronica had given Jesus to wipe his face as he was prodded along the road to Calvary, on which the image of his features has remained ever since. The flat fish sheathed in sauce might have been the dim imprint of a face, and the pulpy globes of peeled green grapes its eyes, cloudy crystallisations of pain.

If a napkin stained by sweat and blood were stretched and framed it would serve as fit illustration of this lament for a dead young man – a sequence of statements about grief, memorialised from different angles: an aural iconostasis of pietàs and lamentations, with pneumatic drill accompaniment.

'Nick's Lament', composed by Erika Fox

Art

Straightening the pie by trimming the sides of a widening wedge.
I never could get it right. Always an overlap of crumbling pastry,
or a slice of apple, seductive, unbalanced the symmetry –
until the pie was half-eaten.

                              Smoothing the top of the hash
(onions fried soft and translucent, chopped-up meat from yesterday
and mashed potatoes), I pressed the fork to make a pattern of lines.
Between the tines, the mixture squeezed through. I levelled it down
again and hoped no one would notice.

Alone in the kitchen, left-overs cooling under the neon,
the radio audience laughing next door, where my mother listened,
smoking or mending a stocking – neither hunger nor greed
could really explain why I was messing around with the food.

It was freedom, being at home, my good fortune, who and
where I was, an abundance never questioned, that let me use
the stuff of life and death in the same way a child will play
                              with water earth stones paint and words.

Chardin's *Jar of Apricots*

The jar is half-full with the soft gleam
of dark gold apricots, and has a sheet
of parchment tied across the top.
Chardin painted it at the same age
we both are, noting the different
transparencies and thicknesses
of wine glass and jar – and the decorated
cup with a spoon inside, pieces of bread,
crumbs and a knife, the orange or lemon
and paper parcel on the wooden table
pushed against a soft taupe wall
in the oval frame. I look at it

for a long time and the painting opens
into another sort of time,
with its own depth and light and meaning,
like a childhood memory. No!
Make it go beyond the old story,
but keep the timelessness of the child's
first concept of eternity –
which might have come while staring through
the reflecting sides of a half full
jar of apricots on the kitchen table.

Arshile Gorky's Mother

Her death determined his aesthetic:
colours as acid-raw as open
wounds, soft as an embroidered apron.
Shapes biomorphic, protean.

On tilting pavements, clockwork locusts
and dervishes with arms stretched wide
tread out the blueprint of an emerging
image: opaque Armenian eyes.

Surviving every transformation,
the unity between those figures:
the pale calm woman and the boy,
face suffused with a lifetime's remembrance
of when that photograph was taken,
and his engrossing need to paint it.

Twelve Sibyls

(1991)

Squatting at the Womb's Mouth

Swaddled in feathers and cloth
a keen old face peers out through
what could be the entrance to a burrow
or a hanging nest

but she is not that sibyl, so shrunken, so ancient
who pleaded for death

her gaze is too cool
with an abbess's shrewdness, an ambassador's
judgement, the tolerance
and wisdom of the Great Mother

squatting at the womb's mouth
giving birth to herself.

Sibyl Hands

When she adjusts my back or moves my head
and says: 'Come on. Let go. Loosen your shoulders,'
in that calm and neutral tone,
I imagine whole parts of my body –
like embers when a wind blows down the chimney
or the lit-up city
seen under a propeller – would pulse and glow
to every sensor of a thermal scanner
whose arcane colour language
of computer printouts like cubist paintings
in shimmering blocks of orange green blue red
explicates the future,

as she can, by the touch of cool-skinned palms
and long articulated fingers, make
the vital forces flow out from the centre
with her sibyl hands.

Facts About the Sibyl

The total lack of charm Heraclitus stressed:
that she started to utter prophesies
the moment after her birth and drank bull's blood,
are facts about the sibyl I find of interest.

She put the Golden Age far in the future,
not the distant past, and was as hostile
to idolatry as a Hebrew. She refused Apollo
her virginity, and never wore perfume.

She said that when she died she would become
the face in the moon, go round and round like the moon,
released from her oracular ecstasy.
Only a sibyl can outstare the sun.

After Possession

She stands between the bird and silent crowd
with her vulture epaulettes and voodoo hairstyle,

with thick veined hands as stiff and cold as clay
that touch each other, unbelievingly,

and the closed smile of the survivor's perfect
knowledge, total recall. Like a stopped cyclone.

Profiles

I saw three profiles: hers, the bird's
(hawk-familiar perched on her shoulder),
and the image they faced. I heard
those words, echoed by a raucous croak,
emerging from her open mouth –
one part of a dialogue.

Her features mirrored each suave curve
of his, whose bronze and golden crown
was marked with the same plume-pattern
as the wings that framed her head. Then
she turned away. Her eyes rolled inward
and the words stopped. The huge bird
clapped its pinions, shrieked, and chose.
I saw them deny the god.

His Face

This place must seem a larger cage to my birds
than it does to me. The dark passage where
questioners wait on shallow benches and
the cavern roofed with arching rocks it leads to,
the hidden alcove and cool cistern, define
our territory. Only at night, sometimes,
when no one will see, I go outside to watch
the birds' black shapes move against the sky
like a loom's shuttles weaving stars and clouds
closer, and read the text they trace, whose fine
calligraphy encodes tomorrow's answers.

Then, with a special sound between a moan
and whistle, I bring them down to settle.
I am cloaked and hooded. The touch of a beak
on my lips is cold as the serpent's tongue licking
my ears when I was a girl in Apollo's temple

and learned the language of birds. What they whisper
has a trickster's glamour, but their night-
patterns between the planets incarnate
the god. For one moment, before the first
beams of the dawn sun pierce that image,
my flock of wheeling birds becomes his face.

Dreamy

Since early this morning
the big blonde sibyl is dreaming,
hunched over, clasping her knees,
like a girl at the edge of a field
staring into the tall grass
toward a distant line of trees,
remembering where she came from,
how the look and smell of everything
was different.

One of the temple birds
has settled on her back.
The dusty weight feels comforting.
She senses it is just as mournful
and dreamy as she. The bird
is brooding migration,
a river glinting direction,
hearing again the raucous cries of the flock.

They know they will not leave
this place. They both belong to the god
now, forever.

Weighty

There is such rage in her tilted head and distorted mouth.
She'd thought of mythological births, from the brow or thigh,
not a wet gag of bristles and feathers stuck in her throat,
vomited out. Anomaly between giant and dwarf.

Like a shift in the structure of matter, that creature, small
enough to hang around her neck among the amulets and
other jewels, became weighty as the densest metal.
They sank down through temple pavement and limestone strata,
rivers' sources and roots of islands, to a dark region
where she must serve and worship at his altar, forever.

Of the hundred mouths to the sibyl's cave, not one had gaped
wider than hers when Apollo's goad bit into her brain.
She had foreseen it all. But there is nothing that will change
the future. Not even this impotent fury, endless pain...

Inward

Her eyes are staring inward
into a space as endless
as the distance from here to the mountains

she has forgotten. Between
those peaks and this high cave
lies the drowned valley floor where it happened –

whatever gave her the look
of a violated woman
or a bird that clings to a storm-struck mast

and made everything fade –
like being formed from clay and breathed
into life. Or a god's visitation.

What Greater God...

What greater god possessed her god
(they wrestled hard, like two screaming hawks
till they became one gross bird)

and made him change his sibyl
to a faulty copy of what she was
(shoulders hunched and hands too large

and that new expression,
threatening yet uncertain)?
– useless now for any purpose

but as the evidence and trophy
of his triumph over the other
and her unimportance to either.

Elegant Sibyl

Having become an expert at false tones
as the voices slide lower or higher than intended
out of control, having heard so many lies
seen so many faces altering crazily
trying to hide their real motives,
having pondered the fate of those who came to consult her
and how little difference any words make,
her gaze is now withdrawn and watchful as a diplomat's.
Her lips, though still full, meet firmly in a straight hard line.

But her feathered cloak and tall head-dress of glorious plumage
are so elegant, no one can resist her.
The Emperor comes to hear her pronounce almost daily.
All the rich men's wives copy her style.

Alone at last, she strips off her regalia
lets the fine cloak drop to the floor
pushes strong fingers through the stubble of cropped hair

and climbs into the deep stone bath of water so cold
that even at the height of summer she shudders, and in winter
the effort of will the action demands
has become her greatest indulgence.

Only then is she able to think of the god and wait his pleasure.

The Egg Mother

In the same soothing tone the god uses
before he mounts her, she whispers
secrets that the stars and trees have told her
against the bird's warm neck
then grips him firmly around feathery sides.

His strong wings raise them high above the coast
and follow the river's trail
glinting up the valley to its mountain
source. Brought on the backs
of their oracular birds to a rock-strewn field

below the summit line, sibyls gather:
the Delphic and the Persian,
Cumaean, Erythraean, Tiburtine,
and those from even further –
sudden green oases, weed-fringed islands.

As if it were the Orphic World Egg,
a silver moon floats up
to signal her arrival, and all the women
turn to watch the bird
settle, and catch her first words and smiles.

Using the same tones their gods do,
gentling them into submission,
she strengthens her sisters for their stern duties.
She is the oldest now.
Her time has come to be the Egg Mother.

Sugar-Paper Blue

(1997)

I.

Agua de Colonia

The sharp smell of cheap eau-de-cologne,
agua de colonia, will call it back:
every aspect of the lonely summer
in that other era, when I was young.

Watered pavements of narrow streets between
old buildings. Dim high-ceilinged cafés blue
with smoke from yellow-papered cigarettes.
The almost neutral taste of almond *horchata*
in a tall glass beaded with moisture. I pressed
my wrists against its sides to cool my blood.

Molten sunlight through the shutter slats
corrodes the floor-tiles' lozenges and arabesques.
Insomnia under a mosquito net.
My scent. My languor. My formal clothing.

The Bowl

She was like a bowl filled with liquid
pushing against the meniscus, up
to the brim, waiting
                    for something
to tip it over, let all it holds
flow freely,
                for someone who knows
that however rich and rare, unless
spilled out its contents must stagnate
decay and parch.
                    But the bowl sits so
well balanced, as if nothing less than
a cyclone could budge it,
                        and the other
grows doubtful, while the weather stubbornly
stays in the doldrums, unbearably calm...

Pomegranate

Its twisted stem is rough as hessian twine,
its skin taut as the head of a drum,
its angled form an ancient box streaked by
metallic lustres green and red and bronze.
The seeds inside are chunks of ruby crystal
that grit between my teeth like broken glass
and melt like lumps of sweetened ice, the mesh
of pith that holds them, jewellers' chamois wrapped
around a garnet necklace, or worn suede gloves.

*

Two pomegranates, one larger, one smaller
grown from the same stem, close to each other
like two sisters, mother and daughter.

It took several tries to get them down
from the highest part of the tree –
the long-handled fruit-picker just not reaching
or pushing the branch further away.

Proud of their orchard, their rabbits and chickens,
Luisa and Catalina had already gathered a cluster
of green lemons and the first ripe clementines:
lemons, clementines and pomegranates
I brought back to London.

Persephone and Pluto and Demeter
were names unknown to the sisters
(so many teaching stories
for outrage, grief and compromise),
but they told me of their mother's death
and gave me pomegranates, saying,
'If you eat one, we shall meet again.'

*

No one knew where it was,
when I tried to find their street.

'Somewhere up there?'
        'Near the market?'
                'Sounds familiar.'
Even the townhall guard wasn't sure.
I wondered, had it been renamed?
couldn't understand why
people who lived in such a small place
didn't know their neighbourhood geography.
But I had gone so often to that house,
twenty-five and thirty years before,
with lengths of cloth
for tryings-on and final fittings.
(I still wear clothes they made.)

Ten years sooner,
might someone have recognised me?
In cafés and shops, market and square,
the welcomes I'd imagined did not happen.
The irrelevance of disillusion.
But I wanted to see Luisa.
That much I knew.

Starting again, I let instinct guide me
down narrow streets past wooden doors
half-open onto fern-cool courtyards.
Then an old woman, black-clothed
and bent over, rounded the corner.
I felt a tightening in my chest.
It happened so quickly.
In less than a moment.
Absolute recognition.
'Luisa? Is it Luisa?'
The same soft cheeks, gone slacker, creased,
and those uncertain, affectionate eyes
peered through the decades.
'Señora! Is it really you?'

*

Luisa, who used to be wary, seemed skittish,
effusive – but fragile. I was nervous.
I didn't want to distress or exhaust her.
Catalina, the simpler, still smiled eagerly.

Withered convent girls
who today must be aged about sixty.
No brothers, no other sisters, no nephews or nieces.
Luisa nodded toward garden and livestock.
'No one to help now, or live here after –
we'll have to decide what to do.'

My hand clutched with playground urgency,
I was hurried to the rabbit hutch.
'Eleven babies, and her first time!'
She lifted one to show me.
A tender, work-stained finger
stroked the velvet squirmer.
From the terrace, Luisa watched.

Catalina never learned about Persephone,
but had other knowledge just as ancient –
would not take a doe to the buck
at the lunar waning.
Low-angled afternoon sun slanted dusty rays
through fruit and leaves of the orange trees,
burnished them to Fabergé toys
or an emperor's grave-goods,
and magnified her meagre frame
clothed in a not-too-clean housedress
to the dimensions of a mother goddess
as she explained how every sort
of seed grows better and stronger
if planted under a waxing moon.
'Everyone knows it,' she said, matter-of-fact.

*

Turning off the coast road
from olive down through orange groves,
first sight of the valley –
     morning haze, encircling mountains:
     that exact line against the sky
     prototype for every horizon
     etched on my mind's eye
     annealed into my memory
     in another age, an endless time...

Driving away at sunset,
as the car climbed loops and bends
I noticed how the road was widened;
looking back, saw new apartment blocks
and houses; behind Luisa's orchard
the dusty squalor of a building site.

That particular gesture remained unaltered:
the way her head would slant to one shoulder
and a hand deprecatingly fall
while she gently complained
of the cousin who had sold his garden.

*

Empty pomegranate husks discarded
when I split the fruit to suck its juices
strewn across my table
like corroded armour, tarnished goblets
or the casing of an archaic bomb
burnt and rusted by earth's ardent acids
only now exhumed.

*

Whatever stayed forgotten,
memory, more cunning
than the finest tailor
had stitched decades and moments
truth and confusion
unrecovered facts
pious error
into a seamless garment.

Was I as unchanged (the same
friendly foreigner) to Luisa
and her sister (my two chosen
innocents) as they were for me?
Stranger yet closer.
Until we meet in Pluto's realm
to share our pomegranate seeds
I shall not know.

The Lizard

A lizard's agile scuttle
to clear their speeding car,

then her gesture, later, back home,
urgently crumpling a letter

into her pocket, insisting
no mail had come, none at all.

Linked determinations
to save something vital:

its life, for the lizard – for her,
the freedom to enjoy

anything on offer,
whatever else got spoiled.

*

The lizard's action was focussed,
total, its dull green body

and legs splayed wide were fixed
on survival. She was also.

Yet her manner seemed more
ambiguous, not quite

guilty; annoyed would be
a better word, he thought.

A shame he's so observant –
he wonders just what's worth

this much anguish. (Though
she veered to avoid the lizard.)

The Same

The same wound you made
now you want to cure –
yet when the torn and bloody
tissues, soothed, begin to mend
you tear the scarf-skin off once more.

The same dagger, thrust
into my flesh, you use
to trim new bandages –
then rip away the half-formed scar.
And healing hurts the most of all.

The same gentle words
and acts – or cruel, cruel.
Which is worse to bear?
The tape reverses, but still spools
the same tales of love and war.

The Old Typewriter

Every time the letter 'O'
was struck on the old typewriter
you lent me last summer,
it punched a hole in the paper.

I wondered what pattern of lace
the punctured page might weave
on a jaquard loom, what tune
play out from a pianola,

and if, when held to a lamp or
window it would read in code;
whether the poems I typed
last summer sent another
message, contradicting
what I thought I wrote.

Friends' Photos

We all looked like goddesses
and gods, glowing and smooth, sheathed
from head to foot by a golden essence
that glistened and refracted its aura
of power – the wonderful ichor called youth.

We moved as easily as dolphins
surging out of the ocean, cleaving
massed tons of transparent water
streaming away in swathes of bubbling
silver like the plasm of life.

Still potent from those black and white
photos, the palpable electric
charge between us, like the negative
and positive poles of a battery,
or the fingers of Adam and God.

We were beautiful, without exception.
I could hardly bear to look at those
old albums, to see the lost glamour
we never noticed when we were
first together – when we were young.

Young Men

Young men disturb me as they never used to –
a sharply physical disturbance, with full
awareness that stiff joints and slack flesh
no longer could perform what I imagine;
mind and body
                    moving further apart.

I feel a tenderness and sympathy
for old body, that poor donkey, most

burdens too heavy now, though once little
seemed beyond it; ruefully acknowledge
how only rage and lust
                                augment with time.

Whether mind becomes more tolerant
to repetition of the same absurdities,
nothing learned, is a moot point.
But those young men – ought I to want
the day ever to come
                            when they don't disturb?

Maenad

Once upon a time
I ranged the mountains
with the rest, the best, arms
raised high, head thrown back,
bright brief breast bare, etc,
etc. They said I looked
as if I had danced off the side
of an Attic vase. My legs
were strong. My nails were sharp.
My laugh was wild.

What happens next, after
frenzy and consummation,
after stumbling home to swab
away the blood, pick
dark hairs from teeth and tongue,
vomit gobbets of fat and skin?
Time works the changes:
maenad – matron – crone – (who
still remembers how it felt;
everything).

Silly

Age also brings its silliness.
I watch two white-haired sisters
in my train compartment

features blurred and faded
worked over by the seasons
as dolls forgotten in the garden

who once were stern brunettes –
daughters, wives, mistresses
a suburb's heartbreakers –

flirting with the ticket-collector
and simpering for approval
as I used to – Daddy's little darling.

Whatever

This urgent impatience comes with getting older.
I'm sure I once was able to hold out longer,
pace my pleasures and accept postponement.
These days though, I crave them instant, constant.

I thought it was supposed to slow by now.
But this fear of being about to scream or cry,
goad someone dear into a fateful quarrel
by pointless vicious words, or gulp down a tumbler
of vodka, doesn't conform to the model
I'd hoped was possible: self-control.

I want events to be closer together,
things to keep happening, one after another,
like the dizzying progression of yellow-painted
warning chevrons on the oil-stained macadam or
the fluttering blur of pennants and trees in the wind
at the auto-route's verge; as if perpetual change
and movement against whatever background – that
unaltering horizon – were my sole protection.

Eyeliner

How long ago? it's hard to remember –
this time of early evening, late
September, days shortening, the same
traffic sounds – I'd be making up,
painting a careful line under
each eye, smudging the upper lid,
getting ready...

One could almost say, nothing
has changed, the same excitement,
the same styles come round again –
except that I was starting then; now
I've learned that though the traffic
and the parties carry on,
there will be other hands, harsh
or kind, to get me ready, under-
line and darken my eyes
before they close them.

Milky Way

Under the spout of the shower,
lifting an arm to soap the armpit –
recurrent gestures
                that open onto
a flickering continuum,
like a zoetrope...
              The girl in Virginia
who lay on her back in the bathtub
to let the water needle her body
deliciously and the woman
in England, meditatively washing,
enacting the same movements...

                              One
remembers, the other puzzles why
she feels the moment returning,
streaming before – behind –
                              circling
as water spirals, clockwise, counter
clockwise – as a cloud
of dust and gas coagulates
into a galaxy...
                    While the shower
patterns her body, scalp to footsole,
with a pelt of irridescent foam
like a map of the Milky Way.

Chained Angel

Since I stood it outside my front door,
this almost life-sized wooden figure,
I've questioned visitors on their opinion
of my angel's gender – whether it more resembles
a Duccio virgin or Uccello warrior.
The angel's attribute: a branch of palm,
its dress: a simple robe, and hair curled
to the shoulder, are not specific to either.

At first you think it's there to guard the door.
Then you notice a length of chain attached
between statue and floor – how else to defend
my captive, so ambiguous and helpless,
whose plumy wings are shackled, pinioned,
who cannot protect me nor itself from harm?
It has another purpose. I fear my angel
soon will utter what I do not want to hear.

II.

The Mercury Vapour Moth Trap

I

He always put it out before dusk:
some moths are crepuscular.
Metres of electric cable,
like power lines for a pop-concert,
were strung between the trees
to the furthest part of the garden,
to keep the light as far away as possible:
white light and ultra-violet light
from a lurid, incandescent bulb
whose central purple pulse and throb
was not to be looked at;
(u.v. is the primary attractant).

II

How to describe a mercury vapour moth trap?
Imagine a black plastic drum
with the circumference of a tractor tyre,
and a funnel shaped baffle –
an entomological lobster-pot –
channelling down to empty egg boxes
like the grey cells of a brain cross-section
for the moths to roost on.
He said they found it comforting.

III

That summer
my schoolboy son
commandeered a shed
normally used for storing tools or wood.
Every morning
from the kitchen window
I watched him (he had grown that year
to almost the size of a man)
stumble into the yard
clutching the dew and grass-smeared object

high against his chest,
twist half-around to get a hand
near enough to press down the latch,
then loop back a foot to close the door.

IV

Some days there were ten; others, hundreds.
If he moved gently, he proudly told me,
not more than a quarter flew up.
He would log them all in his notebook,
numbers and species,
ease anything special
carefully into the killing bottle,
then carry the trap to the brambles
at the end of the orchard
and watch the swarm disperse
into the bushes and long grass,
under every leaf and stalk.
He could stand there and muse for hours.

V

Once only I ventured into his realm –
a dim space thick with layers of movement
like the swaying of dirt-stiffened curtains
in a half-demolished house:
last year's spiderwebs and coaldust,
this day's filaments, antennae, scales;
confusing and, yes, I'm sure I heard a sound –
the beat of panicking wings,
an ultra-sonic wail of distress;
and my own shriek: shocking, immediate,
as the fulvous dusty mass
like a drench of slush from a cornering car
flapped against my face.
Until evening I snorted and spat
fragments, the bitter smell and taste
from nostrils and mouth.

VI

Specimen boxes, carried
since then from loft to loft.
Rusted pins and faded wings.
An excellent collection of moths.

Hendon Central

Driving north past Hendon Central parade –
which doesn't look much changed – I have a flashback
to the cotton fabric: loose weave, pale green, white
floral print, of my first-year summer uniform.
(My parents sent me to the local private school.)

Dressed in the same quaint gear, class-mates and I
would stop to look each way (good children!)
before risking what was not yet a dangerous
junction where two four-lane main roads meet
but a suburban crossroad, and race to the sweetshop.

Its small-paned window level with the pavement,
dark steps down to the narrow space between counter and
shelves jammed with stock, even then seemed outdated,
a story-book illustration. My favourites were
the liquorice straps rolled round sugared almonds –

though when I had to choose (and could resist
the candy-lure) I'd use my pocket-money –
coins as blackened as if long buried,
pale images and letters barely legible –
for packets of Japanese paper flowers.

In a plain jar of clear water, scalloped
scraps and folded strips of coloured paper
would soften, open, spread, miraculously,
into the abstract forms of leaves – petals –
blossoms – and air bubbles cling like diamonds

to the creaking, glittering branches of the midnight
forest in *The Twelve Dancing Princesses* when
the gardener's boy followed the one he loved.
The cunning of it! I longed to know what really
happened – how everything was done.

Nature

'It's natural,' my mother would say,
as though the word had power to justify
and was the highest praise.
'Natural!' I scoffed. 'Like a cancer eating up someone.
Like war and death and pain.'

Nature meant flowers and babies
to her, not a slaughterer but a shepherdess.
She wouldn't have been out of place
at the Petit Trianon, with Marie Antoinette.
Remembering her panic-struck face

when I protested against
such Panglossian blindness to the indifference
of Nature, God, Fate –
whatever one called it (I was so infantile) –
still makes me itch with shame.

A girl of my age
should have known better, stopped tormenting her mother.
But when she went on about Nature
I refused to listen. She admitted nothing.
Not even gas chambers.

Horns

Before my walk
I went to look
at the trusting calves,
their onyx eyes.
Instead, I saw,
livid, red,
between whorled hairs
white and black,
raw shallow wounds
and bloody clots
where budding horns
had been cauterised.

Then full recall –
the school playground:
its asphalt surface
gritty, harsh,
to knees and hands
of the one downed
by a press of children
daring each other
to push thick fingers
through springy curls
above her temples
and find the horns.

(This refers to the old belief that, as in Michelangelo's 'Moses', Jews are horned.)

Evacuee

The secret of life had some connection then
to the ivory sprout of a flat pale bean –
pointed tip and crumpled seed-leaf straining
up between a moistened wad of cotton
wool and the curved shine of a glass jar
in the airless classroom where our teacher
prosed on nature's wonders. The glow it shed.

Or the hot throb of a bird in my hand –
a fledgling, fallen from its nest, rescued
from the crater of a cowpat; the shock
of its raucous protest, its open
amber beak and pulsing throat bright
as crocus petals; the globule of dung
that slid like an egg onto my unnerved palm.

Or the long wicks of white pith packed inside
the clumped hard green stems of rushes I'd split
with the nail of my thumb – which pricked my legs
as I ran – and the thick runnel of blood
from my knee the day I tripped, reading a book,
not looking where I was going. The scar,
tattooed by coaldust, which marks it still.

Dinah *(Genesis 34)*

*High-spirited and martial men among all nations and throughout
history have often yielded to blind cruelty when dealing with
an outrage of this nature.*

(note to Genesis 34.31, SONCINO: *Pentateuch & Haftorahs*)

Holding up my hands in warning,
I want to call, 'No! No! Don't do it!',
to Shechem and Dinah, to Simeon and Levi,
but most of all, to every able-bodied male
of Hamor's tribe. 'Don't consent, it's a trap.'

Swollen tender flesh:
Shechem's, aching with lust and love
(he told his father, 'Get me this damsel to wife',
he 'spoke comfortingly unto the damsel');
Dinah's broken maidenhead;
Hamor's guards, weakened by pain,
three days after circumcision.

That was the moment chosen to destroy them,
spoil the city, take their flocks and herds,
enslave their wives and little ones, while
Dinah's brothers led her back to Jacob's tents,
ancient honour satisfied.

Jacob chided his sons, fearful
that Canaanites and Perizzites
would now combine against him.
Not until he lay dying
did he curse them for that wild vengeance.
What Dinah thought of Shechem's death
is never mentioned.

'No, no, don't do it!',
I want to call out,
palms upward, heart pounding.
'Choose another future!'
But it's always too late or too soon.
So much still must happen.
The story has just begun.

Fatima

Fatima put down the broom
to lift the blue-eyed boy
(who crowed with joy) from his cot
with strong dark hands and arms,
to show him the bright blue sky,
the pine-coned branch that over-
hung the terrace, boats
on the glittering sea. Her smile
was broad, yet poignant.
'So blond and fat! So red and white!'
Her gold tooth gleamed. 'Little
turnip! I'll gobble you up.'

Fatima sat in the playground
at Kensington Gardens
watching the foreign children.
She wanted to try it all:
slide, roundabout and swings,
had never dreamt such toys
existed, when she was small.
But everything was different
here – like the slant-eyed man
with yellow skin, who followed
one afternoon, as she pushed
the pram, to see where she lived.

Fatima locked in a room:
the first months of marriage
for a frightened thirteen-year-old.
After the ceremony, as
was customary, her husband
only arrived for meals;
ate, smoked, pulled her onto
the bed, then disappeared.
For hours she would look
at the patterns of flaking paint
on the lime-washed wall and
the houses opposite.

A group of women used to
sit on that roof and henna
each others' hair. She tried
to catch their words. It was worst if
they laughed. She imagined their names,
what their children were called, but
no one came except the man
and his mother, until the midwife
they brought when the pains began.
Two weeks later the fever
broke and she heard them say
the baby, a boy, was dead.

Fatima had three daughters.
When too much *kif* killed her husband,
she sent them to her sister's
village and their throng of cousins.
Whatever hurt, she ignored or
forgot – a trusted servant
and nursemaid now in other women's
families. The best were *Nasrani*.
One Madame took her to London.
(The little turnip had cried
and screamed and clung.) Some days
she knew he was her son.

Two Pictures by Judith Rothchild

I *Three Jars*

Tall jars, red earthenware vessels
held together by a network of pale mastic,
swirls of green and yellow glaze
dribbled down from the incised double lip
to the high-waisted swell of the fullest part,
    handles like the small ears of archaic
    Cycladic crop-haired athletes' statues,

are standing against a grainy wall
    (which could have been built by Cyclops),
    each lichen-blotch and roughness
    in the pitted cemented surface softened
    by centuries of sun and storm;
whose blunted edge presses into the sky
(harsh blue with a few high strato-
cumulus clouds) the same firm line
as the mountains behind, like another horizon:
an almost primeval landscape
of small peaks, threatening to erupt,

    as if these jars had been brought
    from the cindered slopes of Santorin
    to the side of a scarlet lake
    at the foot of the Massif.

II *Queen of the Nile*

Black Sarah, the gypsies' Virgin,
Queen of the Nile and
the three Marys' servant,

with the Virgin Mary, Mary Magdalen,
and Mary her sister, after the crucifixion,
was put in a boat lacking sails and rudder

but which found miraculous harbour
under the cliffs of Les Baux
when storms drove them far inshore.

Now, an agapanthus lily,
the blue, African, 'Queen of the Nile',
flowers on a Languedoc terrace

as if Sarah, worshipped as a saint
from Sete to Agde to Aigues Mortes,
turns proud dark eyes toward

the long view down the littoral,
where her tomb is guarded, all night through,
by fishermen and wanderers.

Vendange

(for Mark Lintott)

The hollow thud as a bunch of grapes,
bloomed like new-dug minerals
in every shade of grey from dark
to pale – jade, bloodstone,
malachite – lands in the bucket,
the rustle of wind through leaves
already crimson and purple-stained.

Every vine is different:
this one's clusters glossy,
heavy and easy to cut. On that,
each stem is trapped, twisted
around another, and must be clipped
in sections; the centre is rotten,
powdery, mildewed and black.

Plunging your hands into some
you feel like a midwife at a difficult
birth, a butcher doing
a disembowelment. You touch
the Bacchic source. With the best
you become a châtelaine
culling her orchid house.

Dry and harsh as wire,
teasels and burrs – tenacious
little hooks like centipede
claws, almost impossible
to detach – infiltrate.
Whatever you wear for the job
will be ruined, or chafe for weeks.

Vendangers' hands are filthy,
varnished with pulp and juice and earth,
stained in every pore and crease.
When I saw what went into the vat,
I thought I'd never drink
another glass. But soon, I'm sure,
this bottle will be empty.

Ancient Egyptian Couples

Ancient Egyptian couples
standing or seated side by side.
Plaited wigs and pleated robes
breastplates and bracelets patterned
with lotus and papyrus buds
in wood, stone, plaster,
meticulously worked and incised.

Signifying separate realms,
his skin is painted
earth red, hers gleams soft
and golden as the sky.

Sometimes, the wife has placed a hand
upon her husband's shoulder.
They stare at us, not at each other,
from enormous kohl-rimmed eyes.

That surge of affection
across millennia, like
the sudden return of desire
which haloes the head, the whole
body, of the one confirmed
again as beloved, brings them
close as you and I.

Woodman

You cut some branches, also a bough
from the tree outside my room
to widen the view and let
me see as far as the vineyards,
but a stiff and sullen mood
would not allow one word
of thanks or pleasure.

Something is wrong with my eyes –
they only recognise the past,
with my heart – it only beats
nostalgia or remorse,
with my mind – which cannot learn
until too late, too late,
only values what is lost.

Afterwards, I could look
across the vines to the lone tree
not quite at the top of the hill
and the square Saracen tower
the village doctor was rebuilding –
none of which had been visible
before you played the woodman.

Woodman, will you trim the lilac,
the hawthorn and the hazel
in another garden,
reveal the line of hills
behind another house? Now
I know how little time is left
to prove I'm grateful.

III.

The Corset Lady

How long is it since I noticed one of those discreet corsetry shops on a leafy side street off the main boulevards, small show-window lined with dull-toned grosgrain drapes against which the sole identifying object on display was the plaster figure, half or quarter life-sized, of a female torso topped by a modestly pretty head and face whose demure vacuous gaze evaded every admirer? The surprisingly full and shapely body would be clasped by an elaborate girdle: boned, hooked, bound and strapped – all the skills of corsetière-proprietor exhibited like a sampler stitched by an 18th-century girl, and the truncated lower parts veiled by a frill of faded écru lace. How delightful to have a little lady like that at home, for my very own. Preferably alive.

My mother would laugh indulgently as I elaborated the fantasy. But later, older, arm in arm with some uncertain young suitor, if I stopped entranced before such an illuminated display, I sensed a certain uneasiness, even alarm, to hear this wish expressed.

By the time I came to appreciate their miniature allure, these figures were anachronisms. Their worn appearance testified that no replacements existed. Chips and knocks inflicted while being moved in and out of the window for trappings to be adjusted or changed, revealed dead white (or crumbling, porous, dirty) plaster under the painted surface. Through the slow effects of time and dust, their painted features darkened into a curdled puce and mottled ochre that evoked the complexions of those plaster heads with antique coiffures and missing noses – like saints in post-Reformation churches – which still survived in occasional hairdressing salons of the outlying suburbs, or the powdered faces of their increasingly short-winded clientele.

Sometimes, between glowing globes of green and purple liquids in shabby pharmacies, I would sight the plaster figure of a man – proportions similar to those of the corset lady, but usually with all limbs and parts intact – garlanded by bandages, trusses, and splints. The two of them seemed to form a pair: a devoted couple maimed and cruelly separated by the exigencies of survival. But I do not recall any urge to reunite them, nor ever wanting to take the little man home with me.

Hand Shoes

She is a honey-skinned hazel-blonde, faint laughter lines radiating from sleepy, witty eyes, and dimples at each side of full un-painted lips compressed as if about to smile – a mouth around which, in certain lights, through the mesh of her veil, pale down glistens: the woman wearing fine tanned leather 'hand-shoes', (or gloves, as English terms them). They are chestnut coloured and slightly stained at the palm by her moist, perfumed skin, with elaborately stitched gussets between each finger and flaring over the wrist. *Der Handschuhe.* She is walking on her feet, in polished high-heeled boots, and not on her hands, towards the city's best café to meet her Hussar and drink a cup of coffee. I half expect her to stretch and arch that supple spine, raise to the sky then lower to the ground tight-sleeved, stiff-elbowed arms, slowly roll back her head, and paw the earth as if those small shod hands were hooves and she the mate of a centaur.

The Tooth Fairy

She liked watching him at work – the concentrated expression, the clean-shaved skin, every pore visible as if under a magnifying glass, the well-trimmed nails and immaculate tunic and smoothly pelted arms. She registered his scrupulous odourlessness, the trimmed nostrils and perfectly maintained teeth. And there were more intimate aspects of contact: the faint but definite pleasure as he slid a finger along her gums and the responding desire to bite or lick it, or those times when, struggling to extract the recalcitrant shards of a shattered root, his body cantilevered across hers as if they were wrestling or making love.

Her brother loved to touch her teeth when they were children, which had irritated and disturbed her. She remembered his avid expression, and unsuccessful attempts to evade his hands. 'Of course you smash your own teeth,' a friend commented. 'There's nothing else you can let yourself smash!' She wasn't aware of anything unusual about her bite. Sexual pleasure makes the teeth melt. In the extreme of sexual spasm, not only hands and feet but even teeth seemed to dissolve into pulpy plasm, like the primal stuff of a half-term embryo, or the curdled liquid inside a chrysallis where an insect metamorphosed to its final state. There were dreams in which every tooth in her head fell onto the ground.

Conflicting odours of mouthwash, impression plaster, amalgam and abrasive; the stink of charred bone and infected tissue and their taste in her mouth; the high-pitched whine and whirr of drill or aspirator; the focused beam of the chair lamp and the glare and glitter of overhead neon reflected from smooth white surfaces and the line-up of probes, mirrors and instruments whose name she had never learned; the fine spray of water which cooled the drill and beaded her face; the flutter and nausea as the anaesthetic hit; the ache in her back; the sometimes barely tolerable restlessness and tension – or a flaccid languor compounded of discomfort, boredom, and fear; and those rare occasions when a part of herself floated towards the ceiling to observe benignly what was being done to the body which normally contained it: such were the pains and pleasures of their meetings.

In a small painted box on her dressing-table lay two recently extracted molars. There had been a certain surprise and even (she wondered) disgust at the request for these bloody souvenirs as soon as she was able to speak again, but they were wrapped in cotton wool and put into an envelope for her to take home. The fanglike curve of their roots and rough surface to which a faint meaty residue of gum tissue still clung, and the smooth enamel with its golden inlay of filling, made them resemble shamanic amulets, and for a time she thought of wearing them on a chain around her neck, to mark her thralldom to the tooth fairy.

Bruises

At first my face looked smeared
with dust or earth or soot, like
bread when it starts to go mouldy.
Then slate-blue brightened to purple
and a curdled green tinge
flushed up like the underpainting
on a Byzantine ikon
or a ghostly Duccio Virgin.

After the swelling's gone,
the bruises faded, I certainly
hope there won't be another
occasion – though watching the changes
(there must be a fixed sequence:
something to do with rates of decay
of bloodclots or protein?)
was interesting.

Pain

The track of an electric
storm sparked and jagged
and bounced across my body,
through every limb and part,
but settled nowhere;
as a bird trapped in a room
veers and darts from one wall
to another, ceiling to floor.

Heat flared in my back:
a firework arching out
its tentacles – molten
ores and golden jets,
fading flakes of light
from earlier explosions,

a meteor shower sifting down
a black summer sky

– or a rose, wide
open, suddenly past
the crucial moment, letting
all its petals fall.
A thick, hot, blindingly
bright fluorescent tube
is pressed into my spine.
Then everything goes dark.

Jade

My toe won't heal,
for months needs dressing.
Maybe the cure is jade
with its gift of renewal,
a piece from the burial suit
of a Chinese emperor, which
he hoped would make him immortal.

Whole lives used
to quarry, slice, abrade
the precious stone
mottled green as a bruise,
a rare mouldy cheese,
into small rectangular plates
     like the counters and chips
     for a game no one alive
     can play, or the scaly
     back of a dragon-god
linked with gold wire
into a suit of armour
absurd and awesome
as a Lilliputian attempt
to gird Gulliver
or the determination
to survive aeons.

How long before a new
toenail grows from the root
to replace the damaged disk,
opaque as jade? What
did they see, what did they find,
that first moment when
the tomb was opened? Tarry
ochre-streaked remains and
the scattered, broken parts
of an empty jade suit.

IV.

Signs and Wonders

Maps of million-year-long moments
when the poles reversed, the planet lurched,
shuddered, groaned and swung,

stripes of alternating magnetism
that show where molten rock, iron magma, rose
then flowed and still continue to spread

forever symmetrically outward
from mid-ocean ridges, core to surface,
script of a language no one yet can read

– or the perfect pattern of fingerprints,
clear marks left by the touch of whatever
unimaginable consciousness

will create and destroy with the same blind joy
new elements, continents and climates
forever. Its signs and wonders.

Spider Plant
(for Bertrand)

Is the spider plant an ordered or
chaotic system? Diagram
of bifurcation, binary network,
cascading complexity, it asks:
                        which path
will the energy take?

Like the aerial view of a river
augmented by shifting tributaries,

a wide slow delta altering
its palmate pattern, no way to know
where the next oscillation
                    will start,

which fine node on the pale stem
will swell and bud and open
a new growth of almost luminous
leaves – faintly striped tender
plasm, nor when
                    it will happen:

a further demonstration
of the random element, strange
attractors, act of God or
force of gravity:
                    symmetry
perfected into harmony.

Black Plastic and Poplars

The hard-edged clarity of plastic sheeting
stretched across a mound of winter fodder
weighted down by worn-out tractor tyres.
Behind that super-realistic foreground
stands a fourteenth-century village church,
its yew tree sifting arrows and prisms
of sunlight on eroded gravestones –
watercolour of a vanished perspective.

Further into the picture a curving line
of poplars halfway up the hill – a northern
windbreak, vibrations of light and colour
against a cloudless, baby-blue sky. A lingering
autumn thins the foliage, spreads a deceptive
golden tinge of spring over the sharp tones,
the ammoniacal earthy stink of death,
bundled into black plastic bags.

Driving IV

A group of standing stones.
Men with hands stretched out
to touch each others' shoulders
blindly treading their slow dance
until the circle forms.

A twig studded with hard green buds
gripped by a blackbird's amber claws.
A clump of ivy thickening
a tree trunk to the shape of a body,
head slumped forward.

Four small planes in a hangar.
The dark propeller cones and gleam of
cockpit windows are the moist black snouts
and gentle eyes of four cows
watching from their stall.

Somerset August

A man stands silhouetted,
pondering his allotment,
against a flat horizon.
One hand rests on his spade,
the hip on the opposite side is raised
in the balanced diagonal slant
of a classical statue.

*

Arching from their banks, lianas
of brambles and tangles of nettle, hogweed,
wind flower and rosebay willowherb
darken the lane. It is still too soon
for their downy seeds to clog the hedge
like froth from a receding tide.

The trees have altered shape –
branches sunk, spread by the weight
of apples, hazelnuts and plums.
Across the valley, straight rows of maize,
with reddened tassels, could be vineyards.

Vague clouds, like milk dissolving in tea,
process from south to north – their shadows
dull the separate tones of the fields
then fade, and colours sharpen again.

*

A plane flew low and loud over the village
and flocks of birds bounced and whirled and swung
above the windbreak of poplars behind him,
the television aerials, the pantiled roofs,
the churchyard yew, the breast-shaped hills –
then circled back.

Next year, everything will change.
No more cabbages or runner beans.
Now the children have left home
he can grow flowers.

Autumn Crocus

Anomalous bright blossom
in late afternoon shadow.

Mercury-pale stems
surging out of the dark
earth: Halloween candles.

Mauve flowers with amber
yellow pollen-swollen anthers.

Each clump is bordered
by a halo of rotting
petals like votive objects
around a damaged ikon
or a martyr's statue.

Morpho

Blue like bolts of slubbed raw silk –
a fan unfolding flung across a counter
summer lightning coruscating
in the darkest corner –
   like lapis, Persian enamel
   neon violet flashes
   from the deepest mica strata
   smeared rainbow prisms
   across the freeway's puddled asphalt
   a peacock's flaunt and shudder
   the burning sapphire antarctic heart

is the sky reflected
by the colourless transparent wings
   their pulsing beat
of a morpho butterfly
which moves through a haze of weightless scales
   like sequins loosened
   from a dancer's bodice sparking
   in the footlights' glare
   a yacht ringed by the foamy
   tarlatan skirt of its wake

to flare like a splutter of phosphorus
into the noonday zenith –
   ignite and vanish.

His Things

From the kitchen window
his wife watches
the old poet
stumble across
his windy garden

and well knows
that he pretends
such interest
in his frostburnt trees
their damaged bark
and seared foliage

to hide the tears
seeping down
his ashy cheeks'
unshaven stubble

his back to the house
and far enough
so she won't hear
him groan his grief
his rage and fear
of death aloud, as
he mourns his mother.

The Bench

(for Harry)

There used to be a wooden bench
under those trees –
this glade of chestnut, maple, flowering
thorn. It was more
than a decade ago, the day I sat there
after the call announcing your death.

Since then, the trees
have grown as much as trees will do
through several years.
Trunks have thickened, crowns of branches
spread and filled.
For months, I felt compelled to sit there
and think of you –
choosing the place, perhaps, in contrast
to the mood evoked, remembering.

The trees grew taller
the glade seemed darker, the bench collapsed.
But even now
the empty space vibrates with emotion
and I try to avoid it –
when I don't forget.

Those Trees

It must be the dawn chorus –
or are the birds that just woke me
perched on those trees:
my lost garden burgeoning beyond
the window, years receding
like scrims of painted scenery,
flimsy curtains drawn across
and closing off the street outside?

Those trees, here, are fuller
and taller than they were there and then.
Their branches are thicker, reach further now –
changed by how many years' growth?
Some part of my being stayed
with them, witnessing time
alter the shapes
of bushes and hedges, adding, subtracting,
substance and meaning. Are real birds
really singing this early, this winter
city morning – a dawn chorus –
or am I in that other house?
For they are more immediate
than memory: those trees.

Whatever It Was

I go to fetch something
but forget what it is
before I get there
        wherever that is
then go back again
two or three more times
before I remember

as a bird – is it a swallow?
circles darts and skims
round and down
across and up again
until the moment of contact
    to scoop
        out of the air
the spinning winged seed
the bright buzzing insect
the one glittering perfect object
– whatever it was.

Where and There and Here

Where did the mind swoop,
rapt and helpless, for what felt aeons
but it seems was only minutes?
(Time is different there.)

This has to be explained
in the language of science-fiction:
flashing stars and comets
scary, spongy blackness
the pulsing rhythm,
Superman & Wondergirl

teleported somewhere else,
another dimension, total transfer
toward that giddy angle of entry
which is the sense of return.

How long was I there,
absorbed and distracted,
where exactly was it?
(Though I know 'exactly' is a word
which doesn't belong –
any more than I do – here.)

The Gates

There is the labour of giving birth.
I have known that – at times even
remember the effort to be born.
Still to come is the work
of leaving life. I have seen how hard
it is for some, while others,
who one moment were present, the next
are gone. I have passed the gate
of flesh. Now, the wait – how long? –
to learn the final task, before
I am let through the gate of earth.

The Point of It All

Duplications and perspectives, like mirrored
halls or corridors in tourist hotels.
Static-sparking nylon carpets. Walls
a paler version of the same exhausted
colour under neon-strip illumination.
Smoothly-swinging double doors, marked
'Anarchy Storeroom', 'Betrayal Department'.
The usual anxiety dream
including it all.

This time, another actor on the scene:
someone I hoped might be the very ally
to help reduce the tension that oozed its poison
through weeping eyes and skin. Alone, I knew
how I would lose control at the worst moment
and foolishly encourage and confirm
the malice and pleasure of my tormentor
(now also present) – who had to be
the cause of it all.

Wearily, we quartered every corner,
exploring spaces musty as cupboards, huge
and drafty as shopping precincts   stumbled
across an empty office whose wide windows
opened on a sunset sky and showed how high
above the street we were. But it was always
the wrong place and time for easy answers.
The next part of the dream I forget:
the point of it all.

Poetry

I

Something reminds you of something else
of something that happened and what you felt
and then the memory reminds you
of something to make a comparison –

412

like the flight of birds which wheels and turns
here, today, against the clouds
outside the window like that web of birds
coordinated as a single creature

veering low to skim the poplars
and almost disappearing in
the noon dazzle – a farewell banner
flared across a brilliant sky –

above another garden for the last time
that last day. But even a memory
which only reminds you of something then doesn't
go further, might be the start of a poem.

II

A spider on its lengthening thread –
which I just noticed – is a reminder
of that still potent childish wish
to tug one end of a thick rope
passed through a pulley's grooved wheels
or an iron hook fixed high on the wall
of a bare whitewashed room (the other
end knotted around my neck),

to haul myself up like a sack of meal or
pannier of grapes, evade the limits
of matter's laws like a god who plays
at changing shape (stretched to a cord,
pressed spider-small, cut with the grain,
crushed with the grape): do the impossible –

while imagination, intoxicated,
veers through role, form, time and space
like a spider web's patterned versions
of what there is, what might be.

                                        Its poetry.

V.

Sugar-Paper Blue

I

Trying to describe a colour
by comparison and metaphor
is as futile as the attempt
to hum the tune I hear in my head.
But I thought everyone knew
what was meant by sugar-paper blue.

Sugar-paper – that thickish, stiffish
somewhat-grainy-surfaced, mottled
faded-navy paper glued or folded
into bags for sugar: the next image
is my aunt and mother sticky-fingered
in the family grocery store.

After school, pushing a metal scoop
through the shifting granular dampness
inside a hairy sack of jute,
they'd fill those bags, then do their homework.
        You understand, there is no proof
        this actually occurred.

I was trying to describe a room
in Leningrad (in '65
still the city's name), walls painted
the traditional nineteenth-century tone
I called sugar-paper blue,
to a friend in New York, years later.

II

It was the study of my guide's parents,
two polite Petersborgians
who had survived the siege,
their daughter said, with bodies gaunt
and eyes enormous as Rublev saints
on icons at the Hermitage ('That's

how we all looked'), and now, proudly,
showed books, albums, pamphlets
guarded through terrible years.

I turned the pages of thick or flimsy paper,
thought of those writers and artists
gone to the gulags or Paris, and knew
that I was touching holy relics.

'Here's Mandelstam's first published verse,' Galya
translated. 'These woodcuts are by Goncharova.
And look: Blok. Bely. Gumilev.'
'The Acmeist who married Akhmatova?'
(I was such a show-off.) 'Yes,' they confirmed.
'And this is the book with the cycle of poems
dedicated to her by Marina Tsvetaeva'
        – who titled them *The Muse*, and later said:
        'I read as if Akhmatova
        were the only person in the room.
        I read for the absent Akhmatova',
        – who didn't hear them, but carried the manuscript
        in her handbag for years, until
        it split at the folds and fell apart.

   III

I was probably not more than twelve when,
in my aunt's glass-fronted mahogany bookcase –
        dusting its elaborate clawed feet,
        the swagged garlands of leaves swathing
        the hips of the female torsos
        that surged from the columns each side
        like naked caryatids or
        twin figureheads with the fixed eyes
        and stern faces of implacable Fates
        on the vessel of expectation
        which that bookcase (the same piece now
        in my London apartment; the one object
        whose look and contents, I suspect,
        formed my taste in everything) became –
I found what can only be called
'a slim volume', with limp covers,
in an unknown script and language.

I don't remember Aunt Ann translating
one line from its pages, nor ever
explaining how she came to own it.
But she told me some facts about the woman
who wrote it – the first time I heard
those words: Anna Akhmatova –
     later, I wondered how important
     the coincidence of name might be for her,
     my aunt, who since the sugar-bagging days
     saw herself an artist-manqué.

    IV

'You are an admirer of Akhmatova?'
It was a loaded question, then.
Faces gleaming white against the dark
blue walls and shelves of books
as marble busts in a library,
all three watched me closely.

'You know I don't read Russian. But
there are a few translations – '
I couldn't go on. I felt ridiculous.
'She's ill now,' Galya said,
'but still in touch with everything.
And what a good neighbour.'

A neighbour? Hard to imagine her
in such a mundane situation.
Like the taut silk of a parachute
collapsing inward, billowed out,
by contrary winds, the barriers
of time and space changed shape and meaning.

'Do you hear that sound?' My gaze followed
Galya's to the ceiling. 'She must be
better today, she's walking around.'
'Anna Akhmatova lives upstairs?'
My awestruck, disbelieving voice
creaked like the floorboards.

V

Incredulous questions:
as if needing to hear the simple fact
reiterated yet again;
pleading that somehow they help me
to meet the famous poet,
the witness,
the sacred monster,
the old, dying woman —

                   or at least
    help me to see her —
    even if only over the shoulder
    of one of them — who could knock
    at her door and let me look
    even if only a moment —
    just to see her — a glimpse —
    Anna Akhmatova:
                  my obsessed
demand exceeded decent behaviour.
But they firmly insisted, repeating,
as many times as I asked, that what
I wanted could not happen.

VI

I have scanned encyclopaedias
and dictionaries, read every entry
under 'sugar' and 'paper' and 'blue':
endless, tedious searchings. But no one
acknowledges the relevance
of those qualifiers, or recognises
the description, though I see it
so clearly: a glaucous sheen
on the cheap, thick sheets of paper.
    Mandelstam — I hadn't read him
    then — might have written
    of sugar cones from North Africa,
    but eating blue grapes
    under 'the burning blue sky'
    of Tashkent, did Akhmatova notice
    one wrapped in blue paper?

(As for 'papier bleu', in *White Flock*
I found it: 'the blue copy-book
with the poems I wrote as a child'.)

There are other more poetic blues:
azure, cerulean, lapis lazuli,
ultramarine, cornflower, indigo;
(the colour of rivers and ocean,
the shadows on ice and snow).
But my imagination
stubbornly returns
to my aunt and mother,
Feigele and Channah – Fanny and Annie –
unhappily filling packets of sugar
(while sucking the crystal residue).
     It's not as if they came from Russia.
     Somewhere near Bukovina
     was where they were born.

Is it impossible to say:
standing side by side in the damp room
behind the store – like sisters
in a Dostoevsky novel –
that their chilblained hands and feet
burned as blue with cold
as Anna Ahkmatova's
heart, mind, soul, body,

or allude to the janitor's blue cap,
or the blue lips
of the woman who whispered,
'Can you describe this?'
as she stood in line
three hundred hours
with the other mothers, wives and sisters
outside Kresty prison.
Is it shameful or shameless
that I can't disentangle the stories?
     How they all must have yearned
     for something to sweeten their mouths,
     or had they forgotten
     even the taste of sugar?

VII

Poetry, maternal figure. Sugar syrup, blue paper.

The Muse: a veiled girl with pipes in her hand.
Cassandra: '…my words prophesied those graves.'

    sugar syrup, blue paper

'Not quite a harlot, burning with passion;
not quite a nun, who can pray for forgiveness.'

    sugar syrup, blue paper

Orthodox Russian village women pilgrims.
Michal, Rachel, all the daughters of Israel.

    sugar syrup, blue paper

'They are very nice when they are courting.'
The face of a child with divorced parents.

    sugar syrup, blue paper

'Hiding her heart' from her husband,
drinking to 'loneliness spent together'.

    sugar syrup, blue paper

'Everyone looks through a foreign window.
One in Tashkent, another in New York.'

    Poetry.
    Maternal figure.
    Sugar syrup.
    Blue paper.

VIII

I wanted to see her.
I wanted to be initiated.
Like a hungry animal
wanting to push its muzzle
into the sticky, blue-sugar secrets
of suffering and poetry,
to lick the gritty essence of love
from the palm of her hand:
such were my ignorant, urgent demands.

The vibration of footsteps,
the sense of a body's bulk and weight
displacing space, the mystery
existing, alive and breathing
above my head, were maddening.

> That was when – my first trip to Russia –
> after letting me talk, and spin a rope
> of hopeless platitudes more than
> long enough to hang myself,
> a stranger said: 'If you ever come back,
> then I'll tell you how it really is.'

> Glad to join our party – the table already
> covered with half-empty bottles and glasses –
> he then revealed he'd last seen his father
> in the witness box at the Doctors' Plot trial.
> To make quite sure I understood,
> his wife murmured, 'Murdered,' in my ear.

Remembering this, I had the childish wish
to take the misery of the century
compact it to a small black stone
with the density of a neutron star –
hundreds of million tons per cubic inch –
wrap it up in blue sugar-paper
then cast it into the core of a black hole
from which nothing can ever escape
from which the signals would come
dimmer and redder and fainter
until they stopped forever...

IX

What I wanted would not happen. What
I wanted made the rest of my visit awkward.
Quite soon, Galya and I
were saying goodbye to her parents –
and that beautiful blue-papered study –
and walking down the stairs.
          The same stairs, etc. etc.
          All the obvious thoughts.

I stopped to look up at the grey façade
(a handsome building, as I recall) and,
thinking I was very cunning, casually asked,
'Which window is yours?' Half-reluctant,
half-amused, she gave the answer I hoped for.

There was a time,
in the forties, after the war,
when guards were posted
in the street outside her house,
and Anna Akhmatova
was obliged to appear,
morning and evening, at her window,
to confirm that she had not escaped
or killed herself.
                    Though I stood
for a long time next day
on the opposite pavement
and stared at the window
hoping to see, behind
the spun-sugar lace of the curtain,
the pale blur of a face
which might be hers,
no one was there.

Sugar-Paper Blue
NOTES TO SECTION VII:

'a veiled girl...': As in Akhmatova's poem, *The Muse*.

'Cassandra': So Mandelstam had called Anna Akhmatova. In that 'persona', she wrote: 'Oh grief / my words prophesied those graves.'

'Not quite a harlot, etc...': From the critical essay about Akhmatova's work by G. Lelevich (1923).

'Michal, Rachel, all the daughters...': In the early 1920s, Akhmatova wrote about Old Testament heroines. She had already used the figure of the Orthodox village woman as a symbol of Russia, and of staunchness, etc.

'They are very nice...', 'Hiding her heart', 'loneliness spent together': Quoted from poems relating to Akhmatova's relationship with Nikolay Punin.

'child with divorced parents': Reference to Anna Akhmatova's son Lyova (Lev Nikolaevich Gumilev), her only child (by her first husband, the poet Nikolay Gumilev).

'Everyone looks through a foreign window...': Quoted from Akhmatova's *Poem without a Hero* (1940-1962).

Burning Wire

(2002)

Burning Wire

I *The Medium*

Rein back from thought until
you are its medium – or
force mind forward like
a burning wire into the core
of question, explore the process
of release and tension.

The medium is ink
and paper, the product, you hope
– holding your breath before
you dare to judge the simplest
word or metaphor –
is something like a poem.

II *The Nightingale*

I was hoping the nightingale would go somewhere else, sing
outside another window – then

had to laugh at myself, as I groped for my earplugs. I tried
to get back to sleep, but the nightingale

forced its song like a cauterising wire into the dark,
demanding a poem.

In the Dream

In the dream I was an old, smiling woman
– like one of those Japanese wise men
you might find in a woodblock print,
squat-bodied, knotty-limbed, head tilted back
as if to make eye-contact with something
only he can see above him in the sky.

In the dream I was as free as they.
Decades of tension and vanity had slid like
a silken cloak off my shoulders. Now,
the coarse weave of my dress was faded and worn,
garb of a pilgrim or hermit (though others
moved beside me on the road, through the market),
and I knew this was a crucial moment: when
I woke I could choose – for the rest of my life
if I wished – to be that woman.

Song

The brush of something heavy and wet
                    against your leg in passing
a rustle behind your back a flicker
                    in the corner of your eye
like an uneasy awareness you don't
                    want to acknowledge
a weariness and impatience
                    with the repetition
of energy and ambition, always new
                    theories, life-forms, styles...

It's like the ocean, processions of waves
                    cresting the horizon
moving towards you. If only you could sink
                    down through the gritty sand
and opalescent pebbles
                    deep enough not to return.
The dirty foam at the edge of the tide
                    is the hem of a coat
dragged across the beach by a figure
                    who might be from the future
receding with a courtly flourish...
                    better to smile than cry.

Transience

Like a flock of pigeons
settling on the roof ridge
opposite before they
lift and wheel around
again: the raucous flutter
the shimmer of wings and eyes...

Like a flush of fruit flies
in the momentary season
of their existence...

Like coals in a furnace:
that throb as if a giant sighed,
the low rush of breath
through massive lungs
and the halo of burning gas
colourless at the surface,
mercury white, then
methane blue and yellow
as it flares and dulls...

Like a surge of water,
prismatic reflections and
widening circles on the
rocking meniscus shivered
when the tension is broken
by one of the stones: each
a different shape and colour...

Like the compulsion
of the one who throws it...

...Whichever image,
contrast or analogy you
choose, for transience.

Ephemeral Lives

This year seems an interlude
between two events, though I don't yet know
what those events are. The first
must already have happened (at the time
I didn't notice), but until the second,
whenever it comes, the future stays obscure.

A week now is as short as a day,
a month no longer than a week used to be.
The only way to stop acceleration
(this hopeful theory still needs testing)
would be to concentrate my attention
on the smallest details of a fly, a mouse,
a flower. Compared to such ephemeral lives,
my own will proceed with glacial slowness.

Beetle

In the sealed gap between the inner and outer
window (neither of which can be opened)
of the downstairs cloakroom – a large dark beetle.

For a long time I watched this investigation
of a prison's limits, the effort to climb
the thin leaded edge of the bar dividing
the outer window into smaller panes.

But impossible to get a purchase on
glass or metal: after each effort, straining
a few inches upward, it topples back.

At last, after the six thin jointed legs
had flailed, bicycling helplessly, like the limbs
of bodies falling through space, somehow
it rights itself and struggles back to its feet.

There is a pause, as if mustering strength,
a posture of tenacity, what seems a stare
of stubborn hope. Then the process starts again.

I do not want to monitor its death.
But unless I break the window, I cannot
release it or myself. Then the beetle-god
blesses us both; next morning, the space is empty.

What

What was God doing
through cycles of aeons
as the planet steadied and cooled
elements were captured
matter shifted and fused,
before even the first amoeba,
first creature, first mammal...

Was he brooding on the waters
face turned away, endlessly
patient, secure in his purpose
between storm and eruption
while the heavens formed and
evolution slowly produced
the consciousness of worshippers...

The faith demanded from humans
is nothing, compared to
the fissions of energy needed
to sustain belief
in his own existence, endure
the darkness, the silence
the purgatorial waiting, waiting...

Imagine the moment
that affirmed his being, when the first
prayer rose to his gratified ear,
smoke and fumes
from the sacrificial fire,
as his doubts were banished
his obstinacy justified...

And what, since then, has God been doing?

Thankful

Nothing ever happens more than once.
The next time is never like before.
What you thought you learned doesn't apply.
Something is different. And just as real.
For which you might be thankful after all.

The Tree Surgeon

Pressing against the trunk, he twists around
and back to test the resilience of the branch,
the rope, the safety of his position,
then crawls along a bough – a primate
in his habitat. When he stops to rest and
contemplate the distracting criss-cross of last
season's twigs, plot his next move and where
to cut yet not harm the tree's structure,
he becomes a modern human.

Next spring it will start again. By autumn,
when this year's leaves have fallen, the space
he's cleared will be filigreed with new growth.
The pressure of a tool on his palm, the timeless
repetitions of toil, seem part of the same
process: something more important than
an individual life. He's caring for trees,
not carving a sculpture that will immortalise
him; would never conceive such ambitions.

At ground level, two men, helmeted,
their ears muffled against the sound, feed
fallen branches through the mouth of a hopper
that spits the shredded stuff into the open back
of a truck. The tree surgeon, gracefully
stretching toward the tip of the tallest branch,
is only not an artist because he knows
that what he does could be done as well –
or maybe even better – by someone else.

Ordinary Sorrow

'Mozart touched that piece of paper,' he said,
'wrote music on it, and now I touched it.'
This was a young man talking – awestruck,
overwhelmed – feeling another power
for the first time. His excitement was touching.

Mozart, in *Cosí*, Shakespeare in the *Dream*,
knew enough not to judge such miracles,
call this one a hero or villain, nor
think themselves more immune than kings, lovers
or fools to ordinary joy and sorrow.

They shared the objectivity of gods
towards their own lives as much as others',
the tender amusement that defines wisdom.
Beauty's vivid favourites, and death's
levelled ranks, were what touched them most.

Potatoes

A young woman sits in the stone-flagged kitchen, the bowl of potatoes she is peeling for the family dinner in front of her on the scrubbed wooden table. Like every other day, she is meticulously cutting away the eyes and specks of rot from their pale raw flesh.

In one chilblained hand, chapped fingers and split thumb-ends engrained with kitchen dirt, she holds the angular half of a peeled potato, in the other, a small steel paring knife so old that it had been her mother's favourite, the blade worn thin and crescent-shaped.

Lifting both arms high to her narrow chest and pressing them against the ache inside as she stifles a cough, she moves into the patch of wintry morning light that lies like a frozen puddle below the small high window, squinting myopic eyes with the effort to see more clearly.

Her sister peers around, then softly shuts, the kitchen door. Too abrupt a waking might block the soul's re-entry into its vacant body. She knows that Emily is far away, out on the moor.

Prosody

Tone alters. Words sound different
now, transmute in the alembic
of iambic, trochee's fused
aggression, pyrrhic's fluid
modesty – whichever structure
the image chooses as its form.
Thought is fractured into dactyls
or confirmed by anapaest,
while special pleading, argument
and rhetoric prefer spondees.
Slowly, you become more fluent
in this new language. Springing
rhythms lift your limbs in dance.
Ancestors speak through your mouth.

This Visitor

A white night, a cold dawn, London
mid-October. After months
of blindness, dumbness, this visitor
and her confirming song.

She stood tranquil and tall
strong toes gripping the ground
head wrapped in a pale green cloth
wearing a faded blue gown.

The sidelong shrewd glance
of grey eyes under smooth brows
assessed me but was not hostile.
I knew I had passed a test

when she stepped forward, away
from the others, laid
a small warm hand on my arm,
came into my house.

After months of blindness, dumbness,
such confirmation.

Footprint

You are cast away
in a damaged boat, the unmapped ocean
empty to the horizon

to glide beneath a wall
of ashy cliffs, till past a headland
a harbour slyly opens.

Quickly, swing the tiller
press the paddle deep and hard
push through the reef towards

that track of smoother water
marked like moirèd silk or oil-slick
on a darker surface

across the waves' rhythm
calm against their raucous tumult
the current's counterpoint

until the splintered boat
is safely beached. Your footprint
will not be the first.

Insistence

I never thought I would be writing about the moon
                                        at my age
nor that a full moon could still keep me awake,
                                restless, excited,
all through a summer's night, like the old days.

But this insistent moon, bright rock in a dark sky,
                                blatantly present
when the curtains are parted, demands response.
                                For one moment
I am confused, uncertain, a girl again.

Then confident as she, return that gaze.
                                While she insists
her kindliness, I realise that nothing has changed:
                                to be the watchful,
solitary sister of the moon is still my fate.

Black

A crow
in the middle of the road
a brushstroke marking a word
on an opened scroll
in a script I cannot read

that only lifts
as I approach
at the last moment
with a sudden clap of wings
abrupt, its mission done:

to search me out
on this empty stretch
of pale winter road, with
a summons from a black-
beaked, bird-masked god.

La Chaise Bleue

(for Judith Rothchild & her picture 'La Chaise Bleue')

Shadows are moving across a wall
of pale stone and crumbling mortar –
an image of coolness, like running water
or darkness inside an open door.

The rustle of wind through dusty lime leaves,
a shutter's intermittent creak
and the cicadas' stridor, seem
voices choiring the noonday heat.

Upstairs in the bedroom, under
a beamed ceiling, two lovers,
smooth bodies pungent
with sweat and perfume, turn from each other.

Poised between the house and terrace,
its angled legs as delicate
as an insect hovering above the threshold,
the blue chair stands empty.

Feathers

You came back from the market
with a fresh-killed chicken,
barely plucked.
It still felt warm.

Inside the carcass,
the butcher had stuffed
feet, head, heart, crest,
liver and gizzard
and other bits I didn't
recognise: raw
crimson, watery pink
and livid blue, already
varnished by death-fluids.

The yellow skin, pale
as a sodden lemon husk
in a glass of cold tea, was pocked
and shadowed by horny sheaths
of half-extracted quills
and dark filaments
of broken feathers,
like an unshaved face.
I worried them out with tweezers.

When my mother cleaned a chicken,
after she'd sluiced and patted
it dry, she held it over
the gas stove's burner
for a final singeing.

I remember the stink
of scorched feathers. Now,
above a glowing brasier,
we tried to do it right.

Later that night, in bed,
a pillow split. The air
was thick with down and feathers.
They stuck to our lips
floated up as we laughed
and would not settle. You said
I seemed to have wings. I wanted
every bristle of your beard
to sprout a feather.

Our Song

Stripped vine-stocks, leaves gone red and yellow
and every beaten-copper, crumpled-leather
shade between: the beauties of decay.
(Sweetheart, that's our song! Play it again!)

Primrose Cottage

A rattling latch against a dark oak door
at the bottom of the crooked stairs.

Swathes of misty rain blown from the west
blurred the panes until we barely saw

early windfalls rotting in the uncut grass,
fly-infested doilies of Queen Anne's lace.

Thorn needles and heavy 78s: 'His
Master's Voice'; a wind-up Victrola in a

dusty corner. A Turkish carpet with
faded motifs and tangled fringes, worn at the edge.

We tried to light a fire in the low-ceilinged bedroom's
shallow grate with the last slack but it made us choke –

so kissed, laughed, and dragged each other back
into the sagging bed and damp sheets.

Sunday Afternoon

A Sunday afternoon in late July:
the leaves look tired, the sky is clouding up,
pressure falling. The couple
in the next apartment are arguing
about how much he does or doesn't help.
Eavesdropping from my terrace,
I am jealous of how it's bound to end:
the stuffy bedroom, moans and love-cries muffled
so the baby won't wake.
I remember every detail of
the misery there is in marriage –
and then making up.

Four Pheasants

Where the road curves sharp left, it dips,
and after heavy rain, a glisten of wet –
what might be the bed of an old stream or
an overflowing spring – marks the surface.
The water sinks into the dark earth
deepened by centuries of rotting leaves
and decomposing creatures, and the trees arch.
Their top branches meet above the gap.

When the leaves are russet and gold, the wet road,
fitfully lit by weak sunlight filtered through
interlaced twigs, seems to lead somewhere important.
From a bank of bronze and copper bracken,
dew-beaded, frost-softened, four pheasants
emerge, one behind the next, and stalk across.

The Drive Back

A line of speckled white and black cows
evenly spaced: baked Egyptian funerary beads
strung on a necklace.

The tenacity of hedges
which keep growing back,
no matter how drastic the treatment they get.

Spiky rows of pale stubble
shifting angles as we round the corner.
A house of cards collapsing on a brown table.

Ragged grey clouds rear up over a road sign:
Welcome to Wiltshire.
The sun goes in like a light switched off.

Harsh filigree of bare trees
at the top of a hill. When the sun shone,
mottled patterns of bark and leaves and

green stains of moss on their trunks
clung soft as camouflage-net, but a change of light
hammers them to iron silhouettes.

Passing Stonehenge. Last week, it stood squat
and black under anvils of cumulo-nimbus.
Today, rises pallid from a surf of tourists.

The English Country Cottage

A Jewish poet in an English village:
incongruous and inappropriate
as a Hindu in an igloo, a Dayak in
Chicago, a giraffe at the South Pole.

That shadowy yew in the churchyard, only
a few steps away from this cottage door,
was planted in the centuries between
the Lincoln pogrom (when little St Hugh,
they claimed, was murdered by the Jews, and all
Christ-killers left alive were banished)
and the year when Oliver Cromwell changed the law
to grant honourable men of Israelite persuasion,
with their prudent wives and obedient children,
the privilege to be legally present in England.

As a youth, my father was a patriot,
a Labour-voting true blue. But though
he felt entirely English, the problem was:
to certain natives of whatever class
he was a wily, greasy Levantine
and always would be. His solution was
to leave the country, go far enough away
to 'pass for white', somewhere he could play
at being pukka-English through and through.
(Yet still more proud to be a Jew.)

Maybe because she came from Bukovina,
my mother had no illusions. She was used to
rejection, born to it. First, the shock
of Ellis Island: another world, another
language (I knew how hard she tried). Then
further uprooting; though the nineteen thirties
were not exactly propitious, her restless husband
– handsome, dreamy, unpolitical –
felt the lure of home, dragged her to England.

I ran straight into the fire's centre,
towards the focus of trouble, glamour, danger;
danced, like Esmeralda, on the Round Table
as desperately as if to save my life.
Such were my tactics in those distant times.
Now (though mimicking the locals dutifully),
thatch and cruck-beams cannot camouflage
the alien. The carillon rings mockery.

Sometimes I wonder if I should have known better:
to sweetly smile and eat the mess
of pottage – but never sell my birthright
for an English country cottage.

Green Tomatoes

Down the high street, past the post box,
Doris, whose husband suddenly died
at the weekend, called me over. She was
mowing the lawn to make it all tidy
before the funeral. Arms and legs
bare in the heat, skin sagging
like washed-out, faded longjohns,
she led me into the steamy warmth of
a greenhouse crowded with green tomatoes
as hard and vivid as malachite.
'Would you like some?' she asked.
                    'They won't stop ripening.'

An Encounter Near Ladbroke Square

A windy, rainy night, about eleven o'clock.
A small moon half hidden by ragged cloud.
He puffed a cigar, strolling back from the club
along a new-made road in what were still
the western outskirts, pondering adventure.

In the long intervals between the gas lights
he wondered if he were safe. Then he saw a policeman
and called a loud goodnight. The fresh coarse gravel
on footpath and carriageway crunched under his feet.
The noise disturbed him. He stepped onto the meadowland.

At the end of the lamps, an empty row of new-built houses.
Their garden walls loomed gaunt above the open field.
He turned the corner sharply.
Out of the blackness a woman approached.
He slowed, and clinked the coins in his waistcoat pocket.

She wore a big round hat with a dirty feather,
a dark dress with a small shawl across her breast,
a clean white apron, white stockings, and strong boots.
She was tallish, thick-set, and looked about thirty,
like a woman who sold things from a barrow in Notting Dale.

In Ladbroke Square

The oldest trees have
boughs strong as elephants' legs
bark gnarled as their hide.

Under their branches
generations of children
and flowers, wide-eyed.

(In the trees' shadow
children tear daisies apart
rip the wings off flies.)

The Begonias

I

Don Carlos de Begonia,
grand old navigator,
the monarch's favourite –
his wattled neck is weathered
by salt and sun to the red
of watered blood and glistens
with stubble like silver
filigree or Aztec crystal.

II

Doña Angel de Begonia
wears a long collar
spotted with white and pink
rosettes. With lowered eyes
and folded hands, she prays
that sober demeanour and secret
penance will gain remission
for her father's sins.

Lisbon Faces

The cats on the azulejos
of the Fronteira palace,
the putti, birds and satyrs –
cobalt blue and manganese
black, with yellow eyes,

the fishermen and monks, Jews
and courtiers, the royal pair
with ornate rich-toned robes,
honouring São Vicente
in Nuno Gonçalves' painting,

have a subtle resemblance – that
shrewd, mournful, watchful expression –
to people I passed in Alfama
this morning: they all share
the same Lisbon face.

Peruvian Views

(for Mimi and Moisés)

I *Over N.W. Peru*

Are those clouds, or snowy mountain peaks?
I think they might be both. And
the thin, white, broken line I see,
peering through the smeared plane window
to where a heaped swirl of dun rock and
sand, streaked by the dry trails
of ancient meanders, meets green ocean
must be moving surf – though from
thirty thousand feet seems as fixed
as the horizon's distance
      and bright immensity.

II *Amazon*

Glare then darkness. Indurated lianas.
The feel of shallow laterite underfoot.
The clammy heat the racket

and that other pressure: totally focussed existence
one thing clutching onto growing into another
a tree's tensed roots thrusting out from its trunk
like buttresses to arch over reach further
straining to claim some untouched patch of ground
to draw whatever nourishment has not
been leached yet by the rain – the crazy
struggle for *lebensraum*
for light and air and space.

Mottle freckle iridescence maculation
on strident insect furtive reptile raucous
brilliant bird or scurrying hot-blooded creature.
Whistle. Grunt. Moan. Roar. Shriek.
The code and language of compulsions
you will not confront
    cannot ignore
        are not allowed to forget.

III *At Huacachina Oasis*

Tamarisk, bamboo, eucalyptus, palm,
an opal-green lagoon. How soft the air seems
here – not like the parching desert glare
of wind-paled dunes that rear above the trees.

Scrape mud from the water's edge, take it
back to Lima to make a mask for your face,
and you will stay – perhaps even become,
the legend goes – as beautiful

as the Inca princess who drowned herself
for love in these smooth oasis waters.
Now, she rises with the moon's reflection

to sing her story and lure young swimmers
under the opaque oily surface towards
her embrace: the mermaid of Huacachina.

IV *El Niño*

A thousand years used to seem nothing,
the blink of a pterodactyl's eye.
I could cast my mind back an epoch or two
without even having to try.

Now I find it hard to imagine
more than a decade into the future.
Is it the end of the century, the world,
or my own life that blocks the view?

Apocalyptic dreams and fears confuse the issue,
while a steaming dragon-tongue of ocean laps Peru.

Montevideo

Cabbalistic calculations and lists of numbers on the pasteboard back of a photograph – pencil scrawls in a rapid hand; and up toward the right top corner a faded blue, oval-shaped stamp: '*The Hughes Business College and Academy of Languages*, 1476 Treinta y Tres [1833: the date of a battle in the independence wars, commemorated by the name of the boulevard], Montevideo.' But when she looked for that address, that street and building, fifty years later, she could not find them.

She recognises him at once, on the edge of the group. That pretty girl is his sister Fanny. Whether the stocky man nearby is her grand-father she can't be sure. No one is still alive who could tell her what they were doing, why they are included, whether teachers or students. Serious-faced, swarthy and fair, respectably dressed and combed, children and women are seated in rows, men standing behind, posed against a wall on a wide terrace: perhaps the picture taken at the end of each school year, or as the souvenir of an excursion.

Her not-yet aunt and prospective father already show the family face: the shared curve of lips and wary, attentive eyes, a combination of arrogance, insecurity and charm. Not having noted such a resemblance before, she is shocked by how much they look like her son, as he turned to say goodbye, then left for Montevideo.

Shocked

(i.m. F.M.)

How few expressions a face adopts,
are even possible. Muscles
tighten or relax in combinations
of the same features – whether
to laugh or groan or sob. To read
its meaning, you need the context.

That look of amazement
brows raised and eyes rounded
mouth held pursed forward
with closed lips presenting
for a kiss or to repress – what
wordless recognition?

I hadn't seen that face since we met
forty years before, days
after her marriage, until here
in a hospital ward, after
the operation, where she waits
for the biopsy results.

The same expression: shocked
by fear or delight (now she
has met the gaze of both
that pair, Love & Death), back
to the core of her obstinately
unalterable self.

The Clarinettist

Pale round arms raising her clarinet
at the exact angle, she sways, then halts,
poised for the music

like a horse that gathers itself up before the leap
with the awkward, perfect, only
possible movement

an alto in a quattrocento chorus, blond head
lifted from the score, open mouthed
for hallelujah

a cherub on a ceiling cornice leaning out
from heaped-up clouds of opalescent pink,
translucent blue

a swimmer breasting frothy surf like ripping through
lace curtains, a dancer centred as a spinning top,
an August moon

alone, in front of the orchestra, the conductor's
other, and unacknowledged opposite,
she starts the tune.

Opera in Holland Park

Raucous peacocks like abandoned babies
counterpoint the final chorus of *Tosca*, Act I.

Every table in the café is occupied
by drinkers halted in the posture of listeners:
abstracted gaze, alertly lifted head.

The fumy blaze of flowerbeds, smouldering braziers
in the summer dusk. Vortices of midges
vibrate above the hedges like heat mirages.

To stare at the waterfall in the Japanese garden
for more than a few moments alters the scale:
a thousand-metre plunge down an Andean precipice.

In the interval, the audience eat ice cream, stroll
past the orangery. Violinists tighten their strings.

I have never been so close to a peacock before.
It struts, stops, opens its beak, emits a creaking,
tentative call and makes me jump with fright.

The small blue head swivels, crowned by feather-antennae
searching a signal. Precise articulation of
spurred legs like precious mottled enamel, clawed feet.

Massed trees darken into carbon-paper silhouettes
against the glassy tension of a paling sky
perfecting its spectrum of yellow, mauve and red.

Scarpia's room in the palace. Magnificence.
I can hear Tosca singing. The anguish starts again.

La Traviata in 2001

(for Suzette and Helder)

Hearing the broadcast – a live performance
from the New York Metropolitan Opera –
first in the kitchen, cooking then eating,
then in my study. It has just finished.
So much can happen, while listening to an opera.
The mind inhabits so many parallel worlds.

How angry that story always makes me.
Piange! Piange! The crucial problem:
as angels calmly view the damned soul's torment,
art is also the contemplation of pain's beauty.
The experience is called catharsis. (The same
response can be produced by news reports.)

I was eating, reading the paper, yet listening to Verdi
in a darkened theatre, watching the singers
from somewhere not very close to the stage –
which looks as small as a television screen –
the image distanced, as in a camera's (or a sniper's)
viewfinder, smaller and further away than from
the highest tier of the "gods". Imagined visions
flow into the present's urgent forms.

The tiny, vivid figures gesticulate.
The hollow vessel of the theatre
resonates with instruments and voices.
An audience in thrall – like the poor *traviata*
to Alfredo's love and Germont's power.

I was there in the theatre, also in the kitchen
and in Afghanistan, which I was reading about.
I don't know if – before – minstrels played and sang
comparable romantic sagas there.
Under the burqas are beautiful women;
a grainy agency picture of one of the first to unveil
showed a face with the complex glamour
of a prima donna. And so many handsome fighters:
more than enough protagonists
for a repertoire of tragic operas.

449

I first heard *Traviata* – Saturday matinee
live from the Met (long may it continue) –
as a schoolgirl in Virginia, at the house
of my opera-struck aunt. Is it possible
that this announcer whose voice sounds so familiar
now, in London fifty years later, could be
the same man who introduced it then?
His description of Violetta's flowered dress
resurrects, yet overlays, the memory
of every Violetta I have seen.

I am listening to an opera, reading an editorial
and thinking about *La Dame aux Camélias*:
remembering how the woman it's based on
always wore a spray of white camellias – except
for those days of the month when she wore one of red.

Dinner is finished and I have moved to my study.
We are each in our study, both radios at full volume
in the almost empty building (it's the weekend before
Christmas, nearly everyone has gone away already)
blaring out Act III – resolution and death – and a friend
in an unhappy marriage has chosen this moment to call.

I can't bring myself to say I don't want to talk
yet surely she can hear the singing behind me.
I haven't lowered the volume. But she only remarks
that she has never understood how
anyone can listen to opera, that caterwauling,
then plunges back into her own story.

Piange, piange, dear friend. Suffering
is a stimulant. A hateful realisation.
Another stratum of thought: that the sexual aspect
of our culture is still unbalanced; and the music
rises to a climactic duet and Violetta's
ecstatic dying words: Joy, joy – it's the end.

My friend wishes me a happy new year.
I listened to her and to Violetta
with equal attention while thinking about
the many different strands of thought
a human brain can plait into the same moment –
and about that film which begins with a man
in a jester's striped red-and-yellow costume, running
through a field of tall grass in northern Italy
in the year nineteen hundred (even though he died
in nineteen hundred and one), shouting, 'Verdi is dead!'

Spiralling

The sigh and scratch and drag
the rustle and swish –
like the hiss of surf
down a shingle beach
as the tide pulls back
and foamy water
slides and sinks
between cold stones, topaz
quartz and malachite,
spiralling – like

the train on a narrow dress
heavy with metal beads,
vitreous glint
and gunmetal glow,
scraping along the floor
then nudged aside by
the tip of a velvet toe
as the music starts
for the next dance
– spiralling…

Shawl

A heap of snow, shovelled
to the side of the road, hardened
by weeks of cold, is netted
in a web of filth like a shawl
of tarnished metal lace
that slid from naked shoulders,
unnoticed, onto the pavement –
to be found and worn till she tore
it or left it in a doorway
by a homeless woman (or did she
drag it from the waste bins
behind an apartment house?).

Such an intricate pattern –
like tire-tracks from that low
slung limousine churning
its wake of freezing slush
and rush of sound: the radio's
raucous blare as a dark
window slides down for a moment
to toss the shawl out, then snaps
back shut, throttling a shout.

What exactly happens
in that smoke-fouled car,
already lost in a murky
vanishing perspective
of tramrails, wires, telephone
lines and blurred neon signs?
– as if the whole district
was deep under water, cruised
by spiniferous creatures
with bulging luminous eyes,
their speckled pleated gills
and accordion-fins swathed
in shredded nets and fringes
of unravelling shawls.

The Constellation of the Jacket

The room seemed layered and latticed
with feathers. The faintest movement
of air – a sigh was enough –
would start a slow swirl
of floating feathers:
    receding constellations
    in deep space.

           *

He could imagine feathers
glossy as satin ribbons
stitched into a magic jacket
with narrow seams, archaic cut,
    that will never get wet
    always deflect
    arrow, stone or swordstroke

made especially for him:
    youngest son, unacknowledged
    prince – favourite – idiot –
    unwanted one
sent into the world to find his
princess and his palace,
to be a hero,

           *

despite the wish
(would he fulfil it?) to refuse
the jacket, deny all duty
to that starry constellation
pattern behind the moon –
    – then open the door wide
    and let a great wind blow through.

Feathers and Jug

Last night I heard the peacocks scream
      from the park.
This morning I found three feathers
      on the wet grass.
They are here now, two upright, one
      curving back
toward the rim of the green and
      yellow jug
which always stands
    at the corner of my desk.

The Second Page

The fact that the feathers stretch
from downy base and webby vanes
to speckled tip along the curving
quill, across the two separate panels
of this wide sheet of creamy paper
from the crowded left-hand side

to where their shadows are absorbed
into the empty, sooty darkness (softened
by streaks of light refracted through
a bottle of milky transparence
and a bowl with vitreous-glinting rim)
of the almost empty second page

is more than sufficient matter
to delight in and to contemplate.

The Screen Door

What I remember best
is running up the path
through the humid August dark
past the scary bulk of shrubs
the glow of pallid flowers
drooping and shedding their petals
the exhalation of plants
in neighbours' backyards
watered an hour before:

how I'd vault the wooden steps
push against the screen door's
creaking spring and hinges
onto the shadowy porch
where light from the house, open
from cellar to dormer to any
current of air, diffused,
and the grownups lounged,
too relaxed to talk:

how when the screen door slammed,
from every angle of its
cross-hatched metal mesh
a tiny bead of moisture
iridescent as spray from
the sprinkler, bounced, my face
reflected on its surface
clear as a cameo or
a family portrait: how much
that resemblance confirmed.

My Mother's Eyes

My mother's frightened eyes.
What did she expect?
I never wondered.
In most of the family photos
she is younger than I am –
but seemed an old woman,
already out of the picture.

A picture of my mother.
She wears a fur around her neck
a felt cloche hat with a metal clip
yet isn't elegant.

Maybe it is her posture, hunched,
and the way that handbag is clutched
against her chest,
her frightened eyes.

Every picture of my mother –
alone or with others,
as a young girl or
just before she died –
shows the same wide gaze
desolate and stoic
as a punished child.

When she first saw my baby
and later, during visits
I grudgingly accepted,
her eyes did not alter.

A grandmother's eyes
are meant to show delight,
but the sight of the child
who makes her child a parent
can be another sign
of how little time is left,
of death, not life –

or so I interpret
my mother's expression
in answer to the question
the rankling problem the unsolved
puzzle of what she feared
and expected, as I gaze into
my new-born grandson's eyes.

Even Captain Marvel

My grandchildren are Spiderman and Barbie.
How could they evade the archetypes
any more than I? – who once upon a time
was Wondergirl or even Captain Marvel.

December Moon

Like the web of a leaf – fine as the mesh
of a moth's crest or a filigreed
blade of coral – that I'd stoop to peel
from the damp pavement and carry home
(another object for my collection)
in spite of Mother's protestations

like a scrap of lace on the blue carpet
of her cool bedroom, that lay unnoticed
since I cut a veil for my doll's new hat
from a torn scarf (or perhaps to knot
around my neck for dressing-up)

like the wrinkled skin my mother would scrape
so carefully with a little spoon
from the top of my cup of boiled milk
(which unless she did I wouldn't drink)

and watch her drop it onto that plate –
my favourite – with a painted line
around the rim like autumn trees
against a sky (it's not that long
since the leaves fell) of the same

rare December blue as the morning sky
I see today here when I draw
the curtains apart, and this pale moon,
half consumed by the last month
of another year, floats into view.

Cousins

The little boy straddles the eldest cousin's shoulders,
silenced by pride. The two of them become
the mythic figure of a Christopher,
a triumphant monster-warrior, a Mayo composite.
Back at ground level, he giggles and
clambers into the basket-crib of his baby sister.

Soft hands pat his naked buttocks and tuck him
under the covers. Petals around a flower's centre,
the cousins cluster and tease:
'Baby, baby, look at the baby.' His eyes like
chips of sapphire slide from one rosy face to another.
He squirms onto his back and grabs his small white penis.

His mother shifts the baby from breast to shoulder.
'You're a big boy now. That's the baby's bed.'
He can tell by all their expressions that it has to end.
He climbs out of the crib and starts to play with
something else, then drops the toy and rushes
across the room, to clutch his father's legs.

Those Days

What were my thoughts, those years
when I had my hair set every week
and wore court shoes with high heels?

The shoe store was on a corner,
opposite 'Your Crowning Glory' –
which seemed important,

though I never knew the reason
why. It was, I recall, the era
I first feared I might reach

a point of no return between possible
alternative futures –
and choose wrong.

Those irrecoverable days
of doubt and joy and pain
were my youth. What more can I say?

Prescience

Long ago, when I was a girl,
constantly, obsessively, I drew
faces of uncertain gender:
philosophers who'd lost conviction,
blocked, bitter artists, or ageing
women with the deep eye-sockets
and bony structures I aspired to,
strong vertical lines marking each
side of a mouth that once was softer,

a face which only now (flinching from
the prospect of what's still to come)
I recognise reflected back
from the mirror – and must acknowledge
the prescience of that young girl
whose hand, as though it held a wicked
fairy's wand or Clotho's spindle and
not a brush or pen, unerringly
created this face, that future.

Brush and Comb

Untwisting hairs from my brush,
tugging them loose, I think
of the cruel princess who stood

on an outspread sheet and charged
her femme-de-chambre to dress
her hair with so much care that
when she stepped off, not one
curl or coil was visible
on the smooth white cloth.

I never imagine being
the princess – always the maid.
I must prefer the role
of victim. (Though sometimes not.)
Best to forget that tale
and use a comb; the shoulders
of my peignoir show
I'm losing too much hair
to my own harsh brush-strokes.

Essential Equipment

The steel stays that pushed through frayed seams from
her grubby corsets – their strange lingerie colours:
soap-greyed white, watery sepia black or
the livid mauve of fading cabbage roses;
and the desert tones: henna, ochre, terracotta, of ointment stains, cosmetic smears
on greasy crumpled tissues and wads of cotton
that blurred her dressing-table's glassy surface;

the enema bag on the back of the bathroom door
its ridged rubber tube and metal clip,
the raw red bulb of her douche syringe and
her shiny leather bunion shield, the tweezers,
scissors, curling tongs like torture instruments;
all those tool and objects – appurtenances
of the female – were the burdens she assumed,
the gear she used: her essential equipment.

Knives

The little mermaid
is stepping on knives,
her song was sacrificed
to gain true love
and win a prince's heart

– knives that carved
two shapely legs
through flashing scales and fins
so she could walk; knives
to mute her tongue.

Now she is halved
to human – woman /
wife / silent one:
roles that she assumed,
knowing the price.

Stranger

Meeting strangers
I lack discrimination
become too familiar
as if greeting a lost relation.

I don't know how to keep my distance
or not feel rebuffed and rejected –
exposed, foolish, pathetic – when
by the second or third occasion
it is perfectly apparent
there is nothing left to say.

I often wonder which one,
in a bus or train, if
disaster came, would pass the test
and save me. Another stranger.

The Mechanism

Jump off the merry-go-round
whose jangling roar and varnished glare
jolt you awake

Veer out of the path of those plunging
creatures with flaring scarlet nostrils
vacant insect gaze

The whirling sheets of printed paper
rhetoric and propaganda
blown into your face

A desecrated dream-world, gone
from pastoral to derelict
to post-disaster waste

Then force yourself back on and seize
the lever of the mechanism.
Now hard-brake.

In Illo Tempore

(for Ana Maria Pacheco)

The elegant mother, ocelot coat draped
across her shoulders, face masked by a ram's
head with curved gold horns, and the almost
naked daughter in acrobat's regalia
(standing on a box which makes her taller),
their sharp profiles clear against the darkness,
are each holding a burning wire.

One wire seems to control the brake
of their trolley, the other, the hidden pulley
which keeps that fiery bag suspended
like a token of danger, judgment, fortune,
a god's visitation, floating above them,
lighting their way forward or
blinding them to what is still to come.

SHEBA AND SOLOMON

I *Their Words*

A dark winter day. The end of an afternoon.
A young girl sits in the empty school library
reading *Solomon's Song*. She thinks of an orchard:
almond / apple / etrog / pomegranate / fig.
She stares down at the whorled grain of the table,
the same pattern there on her fingertips,
and reads again: 'My beloved is unto me as
a cluster of camphire in the vineyards of En-Gedi.'
She sees a fountain, its jets and conduits,
the marble basin carved with rampant lions
and dragon-headed cherubim. Around it
grow flowers and spices: crocus / roses / lilies.
'I am my beloved's, and my beloved is mine:
he feedeth among the lilies.' The words disturb
and excite. Myrrh / spikenard / frankincense.
Her whole body goes icy-hot, imagining
that caress. Under sleeves and stockings,
at the back of her neck, the soft hairs lift.

II *The Hoopoe*

Imagine somewhere so far from Jerusalem
not even the Temple-builder Solomon
knew about that country with a queen.

When the hoopoe, to excuse her absence
from the canopy which all the birds of the air
formed to shade the king's head

and save herself from cruel punishment
or execution, explained she had found
a place where a woman ruled

and the One God was not yet worshipped,
Solomon gasped with disbelief.
He had to see this woman.

III *Solomon*

Solomon understood the language of birds.
He spoke with animals. Djinns obeyed him,
angels praised his words.

He had seen heaven and gehenna, earth's molten
matrix, had watched the elements transmute
and fuse into gold.

He knew the secrets of life and death. No man
knew as much. He had been a shaman.
He had been a woman.

   *

When Solomon needed water, he summoned
his hoopoe, who could see through sand and rock
the secret rivers running underground.

Where the hoopoe marked the place with her beak
(her beak marked with the name of God) his servants
dug, and drew sweet water for Solomon.

IV *Sheba's Marriage*

Sheba despised the local princelings, as
her haughty father, King of all the Yemen,
rejected human women and chose a demon's
daughter for wife. With such a mother, Sheba
would not endure a life of spinning cloth,
weaving carpets – nor submit to marriage.
She was born to be the natural successor.
But for reasons of tactics, and to gain
the tribes' allegiance, she needed a consort.

Courtiers and nobles found it hard to accept
the one Sheba proposed. He also was astonished,
shamed (fearing refusal) not to have spoken
first, as the man should. She talked about
passion and acted besotted, rolled her eyes
and grinned. He was so easy to deceive.
Later, alone, before he could touch her
or understood what was happening,
she reached for the hidden sword.

v *The Invitation*

Sheba worshipped the sun,
but sight of the rising god
was blocked that day by the hoopoe
who perched in her eastern window
bearing Solomon's letter,
an invitation – or command –
to visit him. How could
a woman so sceptical
worship what disappears each
night, is eclipsed by a bird?

Sheba got her husband drunk
on their wedding night, then cut off his head
and hung it from the palace gate.
She had no problem after that –
until Solomon's hoopoe opened its beak
and dropped a letter on her neck
in the same place the sword had struck.
His words were as smooth as his penmanship,
but she sensed a threat. She sought advice
from her wisest men – and then ignored it.

vi *Sheba's Tests*

First she sent him treasure.
If he kept it, like any lesser king,
that would prove her the stronger.
When he sent it back, she understood
he was a man of power.
Yet she had to test him further.

　　*

She sent five hundred girls
five hundred boys, dressed in each others' clothes
to try his subtlety and intuition
to see if he would notice.

She sent an unpierced pearl
a moonstone hollowed in a twisted spiral.
Was one a symbol of virginity
the other, of violation?

　　*

When he solved her riddles –
could not be deceived by disguise, but recognised
the difference between the children,
the essence of male and female

and, to meet her challenge,
commanded that an earthworm and a fruitworm
pierce the pearl and thread the moonstone –
she confirmed his wisdom
                    and went herself.

VII *Sheba's Journey*

Once she had decided to accept his invitation, Sheba ordered her
caravan to be assembled outside the walls of Kitor. There were horses,
camel-trains and teams of asses with their grooms and drivers, soldiers
and courtiers and all their servants, her advisers and attendants. They
were thousands.

This is the list of gifts for Solomon:
brilliant-plumaged birds and pearls from Kamaran island, where the divers
        go in the cool of dawn to the oyster banks, then under the shade
        of sails from their dhows rigged on sticks in the sand, sing and
        play their drone and pipes through the hot afternoon
myrrh and frankincense from Hajja and Suda
translucent flasks of alabaster oozing perfume: spikenard and benzoin and
        terebinth
jars of honey from the hives of Hadramhaut
fragile rolls of cinnamon and cassia bark
robes and carpets woven from the silky hair of mountain goats and fleeces
        from her finest flocks
silver chains and artefacts of gold from the mines south of Taif: brooches,
        bracelets, buttons, earrings, necklaces and pins; tripods, boxes,
        goblets and bowls, the best examples of her craftsmens' skills,
        carefully packed and crated into the great baskets for which the
        region was famous.
It took more than three months for all to be made ready.

Once they set out on their journey, this is what they saw:
the great dam of Marib, its walls so tall and grand, the story was it had
        been built by giants
granite peaks of the desert range

shafts of purple light between bare yellow crags
red volcanic cones and dark grey lava fields
strata of pale marl and black basalt columns
the vapour of hot springs rising from craters
piled towers of cloud, thunder and hail, cold or burning winds
a mountain that glittered, as if clothed in mail, after a heavy rainstorm
dry and flooded wadis in their different seasons
scorpions, vipers, awl-headed snakes to avoid
bustard, quail and larks to soothe their eyes
hedgehogs and foxes, jerbils and spiny mice, the smallest desert creatures
gazelles and lions
sandstone monoliths eroded by windblown grit
salt mines and rocky ground brittle with iron ore
endless dunes of the empty quarter, the horizon shifting like a slowly
       flicking whip
the rare oases
blasts of heat from sun-scorched stone and sand
glare bounced back by every smooth surface
brilliant starlight and moonlight after vivid sunsets, the maw and roaring
       furnace of the fiery heavens.

Through all the seasons, Sheba and her retinue moved northward over
mountain passes, into shadowed valleys between massifs, across dusty
tilted tableland and unmarked desert, until at last they reached a low,
monotonous, pebbled shore. This was the border of Solomon's kingdom.
A final climb through the Judaean hills would bring them to Jerusalem.

VIII *Sheba and the Trees*

When Sheba entered Jerusalem
with her gaudy, caparisoned caravan, she
stopped at the bridge on the river, refused
to put one foot on that sacred timber,
but bowed down and wept and worshipped it.
They say that Sheba was the link between
Adam and Jesus. This is what they tell.

Like the ripest fruit on the tree of life,
dying Jesus hung on a cross
of wood from the great tree on Adam's grave:
tree sprung from the seed of a fruit of the same

tree that gave knowledge of good and evil,
the fruit Seth begged from the fiery angel
who stood at the gate of empty Eden.
To taste that fruit again, its mingled flavours
of death and sin and pleasure,
was his dying father's last wish.

The germinating seed split Adam's coffin
and grew to be the noblest tree in Judea.
Centuries later, King Solomon,
building his Temple, had the tree felled.
But the beam hewn from its trunk was rejected
by the workmen, and used instead
as a bridge across the Kedron river.

Some tell how Sheba warned Solomon
of the sorrow his race was doomed to suffer
and therefore wept, how she revealed
that the tree which would redeem mankind
was the same by which all had been damned:
the tree from which the beam was cut.
Solomon believed each word she said.
He had it carried to the Temple's
Treasure House, to wait the hour
her prophecy should be fulfilled.

IX *Their Meeting*

Solomon sat on a crystal throne
as wide and tall as an elephant
on the far side of a glittering court
which his djinns had conjured in less
than a moment, its glass floor invisible
above a pool of clear cool water.

When he beckoned her close, Sheba
approached, dazzled by such splendour,
but wary. Why were fishes swimming
there between them? Thinking to keep
its fine threads dry, she slowly raised
the hem of her embroidered skirt.

Solomon stared. The tale was true –
she was only half-human, an efreet's child,
with the face of a girl but the hirsute legs
of a youth. 'You're beautiful,' he said,
'but this is wrong. Here in my kingdom,
women and men must be different.'

X *The Sweat of Horses*

In this story, glass and water
signify deceit. Sheba's riddle
is: what water comes neither
from below the earth nor falls from heaven?
One answer: the sweat of horses.
Horses and water are the desert's wealth.
(Another answer: the tears of women.)

Water beneath the glassy floor
of Solomon's court, where he sat on his throne
like a painted pope, was meant to confuse,
so she would lift her robe to show
pelted feet and ankles, smooth
as the coat of a fine horse. (But
Sheba never wept for Solomon.)

XI *Water*

Through transparencies of water
like shifting panels of broken glass,
rocking reflections of golden carp
fins swirling out then narrowing
like fans, Solomon imagines
Sheba's ankles as if she stood
in a stream immersed to the knee –
how a film of air would coat her legs
with silver stockings, and a cluster
of bubbles cling to each hair along
the shin around hard-muscled calves
like a sheath of seed pearls.

470

XII *Solomon's Desire*

Her name is a red word like a red flame to burn the tongue that speaks it.
The bitter rust of desire is eating my breast. It is blinding my eyes with
    red dust.

Sheba among the women is a vine plant among acanthus.
Sheba among the women is a date palm among wild plum trees.
Sheba among the women is a cypress in a grove of tamarisk.

Her voice is a jet of water lifting to the sky, a river falling among the
    rocks.
For her I would climb the black mountain of the sky from peak to peak
    and pluck the lily of the moon and the stars' buds.
She is silver and gold hammered together.
She is the wine of my mouth, the water of the well preferred, the
    cleansing and assuaging water.

She is a statue of white salt, the fringes of red belts, she is my carpet of
    dark wool, my bright fountain, my cool garden.
She is like the naked summer moon. Her beauty is hot as amber.
Her jewels press blue and crimson kisses upon her body. My lips will
    double their number.
The wet fruit of her mouth. Her skin as soft as bread.

I desire her as the sky desires the mountain, as the mountain the plain, as
    a new-sown field the first rain.
All the men who passed their turn in her bed are no more to me than
    clouds passing before the moon.
And all my wives and concubines are no more to me than vapours of the
    dew to the sun who makes them.

XIII *Sheba's Mistakes*

What were Sheba's three mistakes?

The first mistake:
When Sheba stopped outside the walls of Jerusalem,
Solomon sent water to wash away the dust of the road
and an envoy to receive her. Dazzled by the young man's
beauty and splendour, she thought he was the King himself.

The second mistake:
When, to prove the story false or true
that the Queen's legs showed a growth of hair like a goat or
an ass or a demon, Solomon used his magic arts to confuse her
so she would see the floor of his court as a pool –
Sheba raised her skirts to wade through the water.

The third mistake:
When Solomon made her swear that if she took even
one thing of his, he might come to her bed – then
fed her spicy meat and potent wine so she would thirst –
she did not think a single cup of water broke that oath.
But, 'What is more precious than water?' he asked,
and claimed the right to do as he wished.

XIV *They Break Their Oath*

Solomon slept with eyes half open,
but when he was awake he closed them.
No one guessed that, like a spy,
he saw whatever they did. Sheba,
who had eaten and drunk too much
and only reluctantly agreed
to share his chamber, was amazed.
He seemed to fall asleep at once.

Hours later, the queen lay wakeful
and thirsty. She'd forgotten their oath.
All she craved was a sip from the jug
he'd filled with cool water then placed
between them, its curving sides slick
with oozing moisture. Her only thought
was not to disturb him. She moved across
the darkened room as soft as a cat.

Runnels of delicious water
trickled down her throat and wet
her robe; then she gasped, spluttered,
choked, to feel one hand clutch
her hip and another, her breast.
The dropped jug shattered like shrapnel
and sprayed them both as Solomon groaned
and pulled her onto his bed.

XV *In Solomon's Garden*

Under bright clusters on a grape arbour, silvery
leaves of the oldest olive tree in Jerusalem
and the thrashing shadow of the tallest date-palm,
Sheba and Solomon lounged by a great pool
thick with white and yellow water-lilies, sipping
pomegranate juice and admiring his garden.

She'd brought roots from her own orchards: storax
and cistus, whose bark exudes a balsam for incense.
He'd plant them near the almond tree (its pale wood
made Aaron's rod, its pale flowers resemble seven-
branched candelabra), the myrtles and oleanders used
for Tabernacle booths to celebrate the harvest.

'Your kisses are the drowsy juice of white poppies,
your scent the essence of jasmine and narcissi, you are
as beautiful as scarlet tulips from Galilee.' But then
he teased: 'Look where that hyssop grows from the wall.
Its sharp berries and dark shaggy stamens are like
the taste of your nipples, and my first sight of your legs.'

XVI *Legends of Sheba*

Sheba was called Balkis in Yemen;
by the cabbalists, Lilith,
riddle-poser, dark sister
of the Shekinah; in Abyssinia
Candace or Makeda the Southern Queen.

She was named the mother of many:
Nebuchadnezzar, who wrecked
his father's Temple; the magus kings
who worshipped Yahweh's son;
and Menelik, first Lion of Judah.

Like a sibyl, Sheba
prophesied the coming of Christ.
A pagan, yet she foretold
Islam's triumph. She acknowledged
Solomon's true wisdom.

Thirty silver coins
among the gifts she brought
to Solomon, were looted
from the Temple's treasure-
house by Nebuchadnezzar,

but reappeared
as the same ones offered
to Jesus by the three wise men;
then played a further part in
the story as payment to Judas.

And always, in every legend,
those hairy legs.

XVII *Another Version*

Queen Makeda and her dear friend Sawneth,
like jaunty girls craving adventure,
set out from Tigré and sailed up the Red Sea
to the tip of Sinai to learn for themselves
if all they had heard of the wealth and wisdom
of great King Solomon was really true.

Makeda braided her hair to look like a man,
Sawneth did the same. They helped each other
wrap the thick dark plaits around their heads
and tuck them under long-fringed shawls,
placed the jewelled coronet, then tenderly
smoothed damask robes over bound breasts,
shoulders and back. Now they were ready
to enter Jerusalem in regal splendour
as King of Abyssinia and his Prime Minister.

Because they ate and drank so little
at the welcome-banquet, Solomon guessed
they were women. That night, he tricked them
with a bowl of honey and watched them lick it
when they thought he slept. From one bed
to the next he crept, without a word

embraced them both, one after the other.
Makeda laughed, and Sawneth shouted:
'My deflowering has been accomplished!'

Solomon gave the queen a silver mirror
as a parting gift, so wonderful
she thought it had been made by demon smiths.
Years later, she gave it to Menelik,
'Son of the Wise', when he set out –
with Sawneth's boy as his companion –
to find the place of his conception,
present himself at last to Solomon.

Makeda knew how devious
the king could be. But once he saw
his own reflection: Menelik,
his replica and image – though Solomon
might hide among his courtiers
or wear disguise to test the boy, she
was quite sure the son would recognise
his father, the father not deny
his own blood, and her flesh.

Menelik stole the Ark of the Covenant
from the Sanctuary of Solomon's Temple,
then persuaded twelve young Israelites
from the oldest priestly families
to follow him across the desert and
beyond the mountains to Ethiopia:
a rebellious farewell. His kingdom
would become the second Zion,
and he, Makeda's cub, be Judah's lion.

XVIII *Hair*

Why was Solomon obsessed with body hair? (No more obsessed than I.) The pelt on Sheba's legs connects, like the strands of a web, so many points and tender nodes of the past: resurrects the shame and pride of those curled tendrils in armpit and groin, the fascination with hairy moles on my father's neck; my aunt's warning not to shave my legs or the hairs would thicken and coarsen, I'd be forced to do it forever. Hard to imagine forever. Of course I ignored her. All my friends, the girls in my class, set the example. But under strata of rebellion and conformity lay the half-conscious, dubious pleasure of being stupid. It overpowered me then; only now can I understand what was happening: collusion with the process of becoming a woman.

Solomon knew that until Sheba accepted his demons' depilatory formula (she was their first client), and unless she submitted to such symbolic gelding – to put it bluntly – she would not be appropriate for his attentions. He lusted for her, but those legs were too much like a man's. It was a problem.

I am sure that ceremony did not seem very important to Sheba. The novelty of being smooth, like the nights that followed, had been part of it all, another among the memories she pondered, later, back home in Ethiopia, with Menelik at her breast – or was it the Yemen, and Nebuchadnezzar? The skin felt rough and itched when the hairs pushed through, but then the bristles lengthened and softened. (My aunt was right but also wrong.) She preferred her legs like this.

Moon Wheels

(2006)

Apogee

A silent wary cat, prowling the hall
end to end, in the blanched light that pours
through uncurtained windows and open door
a glaze of silver hoar-frost across the floor,
in tune with traffic-murmur and aircraft-roar
I tread soft, to mute the creaking boards.

Alert and feverish in the cloudy dawn
of the first chill autumn night before
the exact apogee of its orbit
between wax and wane – as the moon alters
course and turns its high, hard, wide, bald
brow toward the dark, I wait for morning.

Moon Wheels

The sky is clear and dark, the moon's disk
far away and small and silver-bright.
Its cold beam probes through my window:
the torch of a seeker, invisible
behind a cone of wavering light.

Too much on my mind to let me sleep.
A disk of rubbish, half-submerged
in foamy surf, swirls through pier-struts.
Then I remember: full moon tonight.
I cannot hide from this disturbing muse.

We lurch together, drunken lovers:
two sides of a coin which can never
see each other – sky-disk, world-rubbish –
one sharply incised as if new-minted,
the opposite worn smooth, illegible,

or two wheels which cannot stop grinding
between them the coarse stuff
of existence, images and words,
into a substance called poetry. The process
is indescribable. And its purpose.

Moving

Sit down among the boxes and write a poem,
he told me; obedient, I'm writing.
Moving house, he said, is such an ordinary
thing to do – a regular activity,
especially for you – no obligation
to unpack at once or be too dutiful.

Find a vacant corner and there among
half-empty cartons spilling crumpled paper,
piles of sofa cushions and rolled-up carpets,
dining chairs like acrobatic couples
or swimmers, chest to chest, one pair of legs
trailing through water, the other flailing air,

and think about important things – not builders,
plumbers, electricians. I try to remember
how it began, this restlessness: a lifetime
trying to feel at home. A need and hope, he
hints, which might be programmed in my genes,
bred in the bone – nothing to do with him –

and makes me realise again those complex
ties that hold us together: everywhere,
both of us are strangers. Then: 'Let's open
a bottle of wine and drink a toast to life,'
he smiles and holds me close, 'then go upstairs.'
Why not? I ponder, putting the poem aside.

Blankets

The stuffy ground-floor bedroom
at the back of our flat. The bed,
covered with blue Witney blankets
bound with paler blue velvet.

Measles, scarlet fever,
influenza, whooping cough.
The night I tripped over the oil-stove
Mother lit to warm the bathroom.

From hip to heel, burning
paraffin splashed. Weeks in bed
under a sort of cradle made
to hold the weight of the blankets off.

Bunches of flowers, orange and red,
climbed the faded papered walls
up to the ceiling. My eyes rolled back
in their sockets, counting the nosegays.

Nightmares under the blankets.
Like sodden tufts of moss
bulging virulently green,
mounting the window ledge

and oozing through the open gap,
its sooty spores clogging my
nostrils and mouth, the touch
of velvet would make me scream.

I still sleep under those blankets
(their velvet binding rubbed bare)
the self-same ones I pulled around
my shoulders and hid beneath:

now potent and dangerous
as plague-infected blankets thrown
over the walls of a city besieged,
or exchanged for the sacred land

of people with no more immunity
to the pathogens they carried, than I
to the fevers of memory in the folds
and the weave of these old blue blankets.

A Bowl of Apples

A painter looks at a bowl of apples
on a wooden table pushed against
a roughly plastered wall, and sees them
in the same instant as particular
fruits picked from a tree in the garden
or bought at the corner store, noting
yet ignoring the implications
of fading tones and softening forms –
and as abstract ideals of apples.

But whichever I choose, whether
the most elaborate metaphor
or barest statement, words
are too specific. Language
forces definition. Impossible
to write a poem impersonal
as a still-life, or to articulate
the essence of apples, and not
expose my true nature.

My fingers crave the firm touch
of craftsman's tools, pencil or brush,
my nostrils, the reek of size and paint.
I want to understand and feel
through my own flesh the roundness
and bulk of apple pressed against
apple in the bowl's shadowy cradle;
that fierce joy a god must know,
contemplating his work.

What You See

Remember, draw what you see,
you said, not what you think
should be, but what is there.

*

Although the dance of atoms
creates illusions – the picture's
perspectives and solids nothing

more than patterned surface,
metaphoric symbols
for duration and feeling –

yet how to set the scene
and tell the whole story
is not the only problem.

*

A pebble can obscure
the widest view – and you
loom large as Everest.

Almost Immortality

       Almost immortality: to be
remembered for centuries
       like Azade, slave-girl
of Bahram Gur in Firduz's *Shah Nama* tales

mounted behind, arms tight around his waist
as they hunt gazelles
       on a gilt and silver plate

which survived fire and earthquake
       warfare and plunder
through the long Sassanid dynasties;
to be admired by you and me today.

A Lost Painting by Balthus

A large blond Siamese cat
with the grave face and stern eyes
of an old Don Juan, stretches full length
along the body of a red-haired girl
on a blue chaise longue, her arms thrown back.

They lie as close as the two sides,
fur and skin, of a smooth sable pelt,
two slices cut from the same apple, or
the tender, perfumed, overlapping disks
of 'Gloire de Dijon' rose petals.

Lovely Hands

'…a terrible thing, to fall
into the hands of a living god.' A fierce hound
bounded toward me. I was the quarry.
The phrase thrummed through my head.

A terrible thing, to fall into such hands.
I knew the god must be Apollo
and the hands not his but those of Marsyas,

darkly varnished by his own blood,
twisting in pain as his skin is flayed, and
the dog the little one in Titian's painting,
lapping the drips congealed below the head
of the challenger, strung upside-down from a tree,

who lost his contest with the master of poetry:
the god who sits on the ground, eyes raised
to the sky, mouth open to sing his triumph,
strumming his golden lyre with lovely hands.

Gothick Fingernails

As a girl, I bit my nails to the quick.
Through my twenties, to feel their tips beyond
my finger-ends was maddening. These
days, my nails resemble those opalescent,
polished, women's nails which decades ago
were elegant ideals I could no more
envision on my own fingers than
the silver-sheathed and tallow-coloured
five-inch fingernails of a Chinese mandarin.

When I am really old, desensitised
by age and time, I have decided not
to cut my nails again. Pre-empting Death's
indignities, I'll let them grow until
they terrify whoever looks: overwhelm
my mind and theirs with images
of cemeteries, bodies disinterred
from open coffins crammed with filthy hair,
and fingernails that twist in horny spirals.

Never Again

Old age means not being able
to bite into an apple
walk the length of a valley
see every detail in a pattern
hear the highest alto deepest bass
or wrap my legs around your waist.

The Nest

Watering tubs of box and pots of herbs,
one early summer afternoon, I was startled
by an agitated fluttering under
the slatted lower shelf of the wooden table
in the corner of my terrace. Unexpected,
a pigeon (one of the millions of London birds),
scrambled upwards in a flash of grey and white
to fix carnelian eyes upon me and circle
the narrow radius between neighbouring buildings,
but when I went inside, returned at once.

Next time, I stooped to peer under the table
and found the hidden nest. Huddled, silent,
she was brooding her clutch of eggs: two of them,
glowing with potential life, like oval
sections of a perfect arm or breast
from an archaic marble statue. She must
have scavenged every twig and scrap of weed
from nearby gardens. Our gazes met; I knew
she would not budge, now I had seen her eggs –
would rather die than leave them unprotected.

Late September, I watch a pigeon strut
across the terrace tiles on puce-pink feet.
Everything about this bird is fresh and
young and bright – the clean white tail-feathers,
the neon-vivid green and purple ruff
around its neck. Another lands; they bicker
like adolescent siblings, heads darting serpentine.
No sign of the mother – the nest is derelict.
But now it's spring, and here she comes again –
with sappy grass-strands trailing from her beak.

Those Short Seasons

The grim industriousness of trees:
spring leaf and blossom, midsummer
fruit, autumn seed,
all to be produced in a few months –
                    those short seasons.

Crocuses

Pale, bare, tender stems rising
from the muddy winter-faded grass,

shivering petals the almost luminous
blue and mauve of bruises on the naked

bodies of men, women, children
herded into a forest clearing

before the shouted order, crack of gunfire,
final screams and moans and prayers.

Memorials
(for FM, RN & MD)

The tall plant my friend brought from France
still stands in its glazed pot on the steps
by the front door of the house where she used to live
and flowers every summer.

The worn brass candlestick on the kitchen
shelf was my grandmother's (whom I only know
from sepia photographs), that simple object
is her memorial. And

like a bright flower in the wind, the small boy
sways his head as his father's friends play
the tunes, sing the songs, recite the poems
he wrote, praising existence.

A New Book

Cutting the pages of a new book –
the first touch and smell of paper
matt and dense as chamois leather,
the balanced ivory shaft and fine steel
blade of the knife between my fingers.

The feel of the top is rough, pages
half-attached by nubs like knotted
threads in shantung silk. Sometimes
the knife jags and tears a tiny notch
I try to heal with a palm-caress,

then the blade slips smoothly along
the folded edge where two pages join.
Gentle, the pressure of my hand
to flatten and hold them apart. Such pleasure
from your book – before I read a word.

Mosaic

Writing a poem, shifting
words from there to here
is like choosing between
hexagons of tile
for a mosaic, or the next
move in a game of chess.

The final image is clear
in my mind – now abstract
as the Alhambra, then
complex as Ravenna –
kaleidoscope,
jewelled tiara.

But which piece goes
where, which words cohere,
unknowable until
the riddle's solved, the circle
closed, the pattern fixed.
The poem exact.

Deletion

In less than an instant, I can delete dozens
of messages from my computer screen,
watch them vanish as a swarm of mayflies
spirals upward through the hawthorn blossom
in its dance of nuptial suicide,
or iron filings rush towards a magnet.

But those hundreds of words, read then deleted,
do not disappear. The air I breathe
is clogged with them, like pollen in hay-fever season
or prayer that cannot force the heavenly barrier,
the Heaviside layer, to achieve response.
I can imagine them, twisted around each other
like a heavy ball of rubber bands, or
a weightless pale cocoon sheathing the future.

Powder Mountain

What I imagine
as I hear the river ripple
and stare across the flatlands

is a mountain horizon
like a master calligrapher's brush-stroke
between earth and sky

each receding ridge dissolving
into gauzy veils: mauve/ taupe/ grey/ beige
and behind the furthest crest

unseen valleys
brimming with emptiness
where the last slant rays of setting sun

draw back from rock-strewn slopes
and sift down from the peaks
gentle as powdered talc.

Sinking

I was slowly sinking
through a thousand layers,
through darkening washes
of melting topaz-coloured crystals
like onion skins and fish bones
seethed for hours, as slowly
as an aspic thickens;

all that moonless night,
through a thousand layers
of phosphorescent algae-skeins
and hazy plankton colonies,
sinking into darkness
below the deepest currents,
waiting for sleep.

The Fourth Dimension

A slow heave of time, a rupture in space
– like a cold tide accepting a flung stone –
closed over her head. She was lost, gone,
might never have existed.

What difference would it make – even
in the shortish run – if she succeeded?
Stones were hurled, tides rolled in and out,
Space and Time embraced.

The Pool-hall Theory

What happened demonstrates
the pool-hall theory of human nature:
smooth bright shiny coloured balls
banging into each other, then bouncing
off toward the next encounter,
surfaces so hard, nothing
can permeate or be exchanged:
no message, no memory, not an atom.

What at first seemed merely a nudge
across a field of green baize
(like the sheared lawn of a cemetery)
was the perfect move to eliminate
all contenders. But what set them
on course remains mysterious
as explanations of the universe –
or love, trust and forgiveness.

The Jester's Legs

In a field across the valley
the furrows narrow and widen, fold
into each other and vanish – parti-
coloured stripes of green and tan,
earth and crop: the plain and purl
of a jester's fully-fashioned
knitted stockings. And above it,
a row of poplars rustles, shimmers
pales and darkens against the skyline
as every leaf is turned by the wind:
the rapt gaze of an audience
mystified yet captivated
by the chorus-girlish movement
of the jester's prancing legs.

                 And then,
as if an army of hungry
invaders: the harvesters.

Robbery

In the attic of the convent
they found the stockings: fully-fashioned
pale cotton, elaborately
patterned between ankle and calf,
both heels and one toe
meticulously darned, hidden
long ago by some nostalgic
sentimental postulant.

Now imagine two nuns –
a flash of black and white, like magpies
rising from a bare-branched copse –
their high excited voices, the vow
of silence broken
                   by the first lapse
from what they thought forever promised:
mastered by such temptation,
they spent the rest of their lives debating
whether they indeed were robbers
– and how this sin might be atoned.

A Border Incident

Gleaning olives, hard and black as droppings,
green as lizards, leathery or sodden,
where they lay hidden under faded grass
or lodged between the roots of thorny bushes
on the stony ground –
an old Provençal peasant woman, gaunt-faced
as a gypsy sibyl, with sun-stained skin
and work-warped hands, clutched
her back, straightened up, smiled a greeting.

Ignorant, I fantasised
this border territory as archaic,
classical – and wishing I could answer
in Roman Latin or Etruscan, muttered
'Buon giorno'.
I still recall that look of furious insult
as her gap-toothed mouth spat out, 'Bonjour'.
Lucky not to start a local war! (I wonder
if, in forty years, I've learned much more.)

The Anxiety of Airports

Waiting for someone due on a certain plane
and the plane arrives and you strain to scrutinise
every stranger coming through the swinging doors,
wondering if you will recognise him;
your tension increasing, the anxiety level rising;
then only the last few stragglers....
But the person you came to meet does not appear.
(And the explanation only days later.)

Or flying half-way around the world, a journey of
longueurs and transfers stretched across so many time zones –
wakeful hours in hotel bedrooms and the 4.00 AM call –
until, under flickering neon, adrift along
the static-crackling carpets of inter-terminal
connecting corridors, you're not sure if it's day or night.

And after you've struggled to drag your luggage off
the carousel, negotiated Immigration,
stumbled past the barriers where hotel touts
and drivers holding cards with other people's names
surge forward, and family groups, welcome smiles
set hard, suddenly relax and start to laugh and talk –
the one who should be there for you is nowhere in sight.

So you stand to one side, with the suitcase you're obliged
to guard – though you wouldn't care if it were lost or stolen –
dazed by exhaustion, while the Arrivals board goes blank
and this part of the airport empties of staff and passengers
like water draining down a grating, leaving
only twists of silver paper from candy wrappers,
adhesive shreds of clingfoil like sloughed snakeskins,
and mysterious lengths of white and orange plastic twine.

This is more than childhood fear, this is far worse:
an infant's pre-birth terror of falling through space,
endless abandonment or random malice. But
you force yourself to move, join the queue for a cab,
give the driver an address (though it doesn't sound
right); then sit as far back as you can and
stare out at waterlogged fields and grey suburbs,
uncertain what to expect when you get there.

Plans

The Aymara people of the high Andes believe that the future is hidden, unknown and mysterious, as impossible to see as the skin in the middle of my back, no matter how I turn and twist. They cannot feel regret or disappointment, because they do not make plans.

But the past is unalterable: a coloured map spread across the floor or a landscape seen from a plane, the chance-discovered photograph of what at first seems just a group of strangers, between the pages of a book, then the thrill to recognise the family face; a phalanx of memories, actions and their consequences, sounds and images manifesting before me, to be contemplated – if I dare to look.

When I stare at the sky on a clear night, I must remember that this radiance has its source sometimes as far away as the edges of the universe – has passed through vastnesses of space and aeons of time (as I have been taught to name such things).

Perhaps no one will be left on earth to see the light the furthest stars now emit. As the past exists in the present, and the future's latent image on the present's silvered surface is only revealed, like film in developer, by being lived, I almost understand (and admire, and wish I could emulate) the Aymaras' lack of surprise when things do not turn out as they expect.

An Ichneumon Wasp

No tunes in the head, no music of word or phrase. Inspiration dead. Abandonment. And repeating the story, crooning it like a murderous lullaby, confirms the process, intensifies the damage. Even to think such thoughts is dangerous. To write them, worse.

Or imagine this as possession, not emptiness: an ichneumon wasp lays its eggs inside the pulpy larva of a moth or butterfly.

The egg hatches, the creature burrows and gnaws through the living food-source like a cancer consuming inner organs, or dementia ravaging brain cells. Then, its host absorbed, transubstantiated to another form, the new life emerges.

But this metaphor for the amoral balance between destruction and creation is still off-centre, far too simple; does not justify such energetic malice and ordinary misery, nor explain the force that controls you and why you allow it to triumph.

Doom of Kings

Sunset, slow glimmering twilight, then night. We must be driving along the coast road because, moving from left to right across the picture frame, like those cowboy or war movies where the "good guys" always arrive from the left, we pass a signpost pointing down a track to the ferry for the Northern islands.

Sooty red brick walls to each side and arching above, garishly streaked by yellow beams of light, as if overhead lamps were swaying in a strong wind, leaving whole sections in darkness: the palette of a Beckmann painting. A woman selling tickets in the foyer of an old-fashioned cinema might be a priestess at the entrance to her temple. We ask her the way to *Doom of Kings*. She says we have already passed the turning. I vaguely recall, among a list of other place-names on a road-sign, the words *Doom of Kings*, but so faded and insignificant I thought I'd misread it.

I tell him to leave me and go back alone to find the turning – fourth on the right, the cashier-woman had said, but he insists it will be safer to stay together. We set out on foot, right to left, the direction of defeat and failure, and enter a zone of what seem the ruins of 19th-century industrial structures or bombed buildings. *Doom of Kings*: that far, northern, edge-of-the-land, end-of-the-world place; its craters and valleys, its dark colours, its frisson of danger; its lure of wisdom and transformation.

A Postcard from Tunis

Although the scale of the image is too small to see the fine powdery dust lying thick on the panels' curved edges, I can feel its silky texture between my fingers, smell and taste it in the current of air which rises whenever the door is opened or shut. I can sense the exact temperature of the spring sun on the dry paint, note the first signs of flaking.

A few steps back and I am on the street. Sunlight slants from right to left down the alley where, head pensively bowed, like the prince with his enchanted friend in a fairy-tale, a young man leads a sheep (half-turned enquiringly toward him) perhaps to be slaughtered – which might be why he doesn't seem to notice its gaze. The shadow of something or someone out of sight stops just at their feet. High on the wall behind, near a roughly blocked-up door, hangs a black-rimmed, white enamel sign reading Rue Boughedir in Latin letters and Arab script. The narrow colour range: a palette of white, grey, green, ochre, and buff, links its plastered stone – stained by rain-splashed earth where it meets the pale rock-strewn ground – to the greasy matted coat of the sheep and the man's dark jacket.

The cross-lane turns a corner, and half way along stand two flimsy yellow chairs, as if outside a café. Just visible on the road behind, in a tiny space no larger than the young man's shirt, are the bright white façade of a house, and a prayer rug hanging from the balcony railing of a shuttered window.

An obliquely angled house-front, faced by small putty-coloured tiles with an elaborate arabesque pattern pressed into their surface, occupies more than a third of the foreground. Its façade is broken by a large wooden double entrance door rising from the bottom to the top of the card. It could be the door of one of the houses around the Mediterranean where I spent years of my youth. Every detail of its appearance is absolutely familiar: the faded chalky green paint pale as lichen, the four squares of the lower panels like the sides of a dice, the horizontal lozenge above them, and the two narrow panels taller than my height, topped by another lozenge. The brass keyhole cylinder is exactly placed between the lower and upper panels, and the two leaves are divided into eight sections: that endless repetition of the number eight, curved back on itself, which signifies eternity.

The Threshold

Nineteen eleven, New York City,
the Triangle Shirtwaist Company fire.

A young clerk broke the locked window
of the top workroom,
then helped the women trapped inside
onto and over the ledge,
launching them into empty space
across that threshold
as if handing them up to a coach
or introducing them, one by one,
to the most important person at a grand ball.

A tall girl hugged and gave him a kiss.
When the room was empty, he followed.
From the street the crowd watched.
A better end than to suffocate in a burning loft.

*   *

New York, two thousand and one.
An ordinary autumn morning.

Flames, explosions, the slow
thickening and curdling of smoke;
who were those couples
hurtling past the grid
of innumerable windows
down the façade
of the World Trade Buildings,
grasping strangers' hands?

Day after day, the same images,
day after day, one of millions,
I watched them on the television,
but dared not imagine
the final words and gestures
as they helped each other
across the threshold.

Fabulous Beings

Hard not to think of the Atlantic
and the Mediterranean as two
fabulous beings, sometimes warring,
sometimes at peace. So many myths
and stories record their encounters
at Tangier, Tarifa, Gibraltar...

But for me, the meeting of those waters
is signified not by flags or statues
but by leaking boats crowded with people
desperate to reach the final border
before being caught by a high-speed
police launch, or drowned in a storm...

What they dream: welcome somewhere
north of the Mediterranean,
far from the Atlantic, is unlikely
to happen. Those fabulous beings
who control their future rarely grant
good fortune – indifferent as the ocean.

The Garden of Eden

(4 February 2003)

It started here, somewhere between
Euphrates and Tigris: the Garden of Eden
where good and evil were first defined.

Now, that appointment with Death –
whether in Babylon, Nineveh or
Samarra – seems unavoidable.

*

At the historic sites, shadowed
by half-eroded ziggurats,
hidden aircraft stand primed

for battles which the six-thousand-year-
old walls of Nebuchadnezar's
imperial city will not survive.

*

The leaders talk of culture-clash.
But all cultures might end here,
where they began – among scattered
body parts and shattered idols.

War Moon

(early morning, 18 March 2003)

It's the night before
spring equinox,
the last day
perhaps, of peace –
and I'm wide awake.

The darkest blind,
heaviest drape,
cannot block out
that brassy glare
bounced back off
the hard stone sphere

of a livid moon
orbiting
our unhappy,
angry world
like a fully armoured
squat, malicious
god of war.

I remember now –
there are languages
where the word for moon
is masculine.

Translations

SOPHIA DE MELLO BREYNER

Midday

Midday. No one in this corner of the beach.
The sun on high, deep, enormous, open
Has cleared the sky of every god.
Implacable as punishment, light falls.
There are no ghosts, nor souls,
And the huge, solitary, ancient ocean
Seems to applaud.

[1944]

One Day

One day dead tired worn out we shall
Go back and live as plainly as animals
Even so tired again we shall flourish
Living brothers of the sea and the pinewoods.

The wind will blow away our weariness
The thousand unreal anxious gestures
And our slack limbs surely will regain
The weightless speed of animals.

Only then shall we be able to move
Through the mystery nurtured and lulled
By green pinewoods and the sea's voice
And let its words grow in us.

[1947]

Day of the Sea

Day of sea in the sky, made
From shadows and horses and plumes.

Day of sea in my room – cube
Where my sleepwalker's movements slide
Between animal and flower, like medusas.

Day of sea in the sky, high day
Where my gestures are seagulls who lose themselves
Spiralling over the clouds, over the spume.

[1950]

Sibyls

Sibyls of deep caves, of petrifaction,
Totally loveless and sightless,
Feeding nothingness as if a sacred fire
While shadow unmakes night and day
Into the same light of fleshless panic.

Drive out that foul dew
Of impacted nights, the sweat
Of forces turned against themselves
When words batter the walls
In blind, wild swoops of trapped birds
And the horror of being winged
Shrills like a clock through a vacuum.

[1950]

Listen

Listen:
Everything is calm and smooth and sleeping.
The walls apparent, the floor reflecting,
And painted on the glass of the window,
The sky, green emptiness, two trees.
Close your eyes and rest no less profoundly
Than any other thing which never flowered.

Don't touch anything, don't look, don't recollect.
One step enough
To shatter the furniture baked
By endless, unused days of sunlight.

Don't remember, don't anticipate.
You do not share the nature of a fruit.
Nothing here that time or sun will ripen.

[1950]

Beach

The pines moan when the wind passes
The sun beats on the earth and the stones burn.

Fantastic sea gods stroll at the edge of the world
Crusted with salt and brilliant as fishes.

Sudden wild birds hurled
Against the light into the sky like stones
Mount and die vertically
Their bodies taken by space.

The waves butt as if to smash the light
Their brows ornate with columns.

And an ancient nostalgia of being a mast
Sways in the pines.

[1950]

Torpid Shoes

Torpid shores open their arms,
And a great ship departs in silence.
Gulls fly at high perpendicular angles,
The light is born, and death is perfect.

A great ship departs, abandoning
The white columns of a vacant harbour.
And its own face seeks itself emerging
From the headless torso of the city.

A great ship unloosed departs
Sculpting head-on the north wind.
Perfect the ocean's blue, death perfect –
Awesome clear sharp forms.

[1950]

In the Poem

To bring the picture the wall the wind
The flower the glass the shine on wood
And the cold chaste clearness of water
To the clean severe world of the poem

To save from death decay and ruin
The actual moment of vision and surprise
And keep in the real world
The real gesture of a hand touching the table.

[1962]

Muse

Muse teach me the song
Revered and primordial
The song for everyone
Believed by all

Muse teach me the song
The true brother of each thing
Incendiary of the night
And evening's secret

Muse teach me the song
That takes me home
Without delay or haste
Changed to plant or stone

Or changed into the wall
Of the first house
Or become the murmur
Of sea all around

(I remember the floor
Of well-scrubbed planks
Its soapy smell
Keeps coming back)

Muse teach me the song
Of the sea's breath
Heaving with brilliants
Muse teach me the song
Of the white room
And the square window

So I can say
How evening there
Touched door and table
Cup and mirror
How it embraced

Because time pierces
Time divides
And time thwarts
Tears me alive
From the walls and floor
Of the first house

Muse teach me the song
Revered and primordial
To fix the brilliance
Of the polished morning

That rested its fingers
Gently on the dunes
And whitewashed the walls
Of those simple rooms

Muse teach me the song
That chokes my throat

[1962]

Twilight of the Gods

A smile of amazement appeared in the Aegean islands
And Homer made royal-purple flower on the sea
The Kouros moved forward exactly one step
Athena's paleness glittered in the daylight

In that time the god's clarity conquered the monsters on all the temple pediments
And the Persians retreated to their empire's furthest limits.

We celebrated the victory: darkness
Was exposed and sacrificed in the great white courtyards
The hoarse cry of the chorus purified the city

Swift joy circled the ships
Like dolphins
Our body was naked because it had found
Its exact measure

We invented: the light inherent to Sounion's columns
Each day the world became more ours

But then they were extinguished
The ancient gods, internal sun of things
Then there opened the void which separates us from things
We are hallucinated by absence, drunk with absence
And to Julian's heralds, the Sibyl replied:

'Go tell the king that the beautiful palace lies broken on the ground
Phoebus now has no house nor prophetic bay-tree nor melodious fountain
The talking water is silent.'

[1967]

The Small Square

My life had taken the form of a small square
That autumn when your death was being meticulously organised

I clung to the square because you loved
The humble and nostalgic humanity of small shops
Where shopkeepers fold and unfold ribbons and cloth
I tried to become you because you were going to die
And all my life there would cease to be mine
I tried to smile as you smiled
At the newspaper seller at the tobacco seller
At the woman without legs who sold violets
I asked the woman without legs to pray for you
I lit candles at all the altars
Of the churches standing in the corners of that square
Hardly had I opened my eyes when I saw and read
The vocation for eternity written on your face
I summoned up the streets places people
Who were the witnesses of your face
So they would call you so they would unweave
The tissue that death was binding around you

[1972]

Cyclades

(invoking Fernando Pessoa)

The frontal clarity of this place imposes your presence
Your name emerges as if the negative
Of what you were develops here

You lived in reverse
Incessant traveller of the inverse
Exempt from yourself
Widower of yourself
Lisbon your stage-set
You were the tenant of a rented room above a dairy
Competent clerk in a business firm
Ironic delicate polite frequenter of the Old Town bars
Judicious visionary of cafés facing the Tagus

(Where still in the marble-topped tables
We seek the cold trace of your hands
– Their imperceptible fingering)

Dismembered by the furies of that non-life
Marginal to yourself to others and to life
You kept all your notebooks up to date
With meticulous exactitude drew the maps
Of the multiple navigations of your absence –

What never was and what you never were stays said
Like an island rising up windward
With plumb-line compass astrolabe and sounding-lead
You determined the measure of exile

You were born later
Others had found the truth
The sea-route to India already was discovered

Nothing was left of the gods
But their uncertain passage
Through the murmur and smell of those landscapes
And you had many faces
So that being no one you could say everything

And yet obstinately I invoke – O divided one –
The instant that might unite you
And celebrate your arrival at the islands you never reached

These are the archipelagos that float across your face
The swift dolphins of joy
The gods did not grant nor you wanted

This is the place where the flesh of statues like trembling willows
Pierced by light's breathing
Shines with matter's blue breath
On beaches where mirrors turn towards the sea

Here the enigma that always puzzled me
Is more naked and vehement therefore I implore:

'Why were your movements broken
Who encircled you by walls and chasms
Who spilt your secrets onto the ground?'

Invoke you as though you arrived in this boat
And it were your feet stepping onto the islands
Whose excessive overwhelming nearness
Was like a loved face bending too close

In the summer of this place I call you
Who hibernated your life like an animal through the harsh season
Who needed to be distant like someone standing back to see the picture better
And willed the distance he suffered

I call you – I gather the pieces the ruins the fragments –
Because the world cracked like a quarry
And capitals and arms columns shattered to splinters
Heave from the ground
And only a scattering of potsherds is left of the amphora
Before which the gods become foreigners

Yet here the wheat-coloured goddesses
Raise the long harp of their fingers
To charm the blue sun where I invoke you
And invoke the impersonal word of your absence

If only this festive moment could break your mourning
O self-elected widower
And if being and to be would coincide
In the one marriage

As if your boat were waiting in Thasos
As if Penelope
In her high chamber
Were weaving you into her hair

[1977]

The Islands

I

We navigated East –
The long coast
Was a dense somnolent green

A motionless green under an absent wind
As far as the white shore colour of roses
Touched by transparent waters

Then appeared the luminous islands
Of a blue so pure and violent
Surpassing the brilliance of heavens
Navigated by miraculous herons

And memory and time were quenched.

II

Abstract navigation
Intent as a fish the plane follows the route
Seen from above the earth becomes a map

But suddenly
We cross into the Orient through the great gate
Of blue sapphires in the glinting sea

III

The light of dawn's appearance
Shone in the hollow of wandering
Sails testing the distances

Here they let down the dark anchors
Those who went seeking
The real face of the visible
And dared – most fantastic adventure –
To live the whole of the possible

IV

Dolce color d'oriental zaffiro
DANTE, *Purgatorio*, Canto I

Here they sighted islands rise like flowers
Those who came by sea heading south
And rounded the cape to face the dawn sky
Steering the thrust of the black keels

And under tall clouds like white lyres
Their eyes truly saw
The sweet blue of the East and of sapphires

V

We saw the visible in all its vehemence
The total exposure of appearance
And what we had not dared to dream
Was real

VI

They navigated from the chart they had to make

(Leaving behind the plots and conversations
Muffled intrigues of brothel and palace)

The wise men had already concluded
That only the known could exist:
Ahead lay only the unnavigable
Below the sun's clamour, the uninhabitable

Undeciphered the writing of those other stars
In the silence of cloudy zones
The shivering compass needle touching space

Then appeared the luminous coasts
Silences the palm-groves' ardent coolness
And the brilliance of the visible face to face

VII

Difficult to face your death head-on
And never expect you again in the mirrors of fog

[1983]

Writing

In Palazzo Mocenigo where he lived alone
Lord Byron used every grand room
To watch solitude mirror by mirror
And the beauty of doors no one passed through

He heard the marine murmurs of silence
The lost echoes of steps in far corridors
He loved the smooth shine on polished floors
Shadows unrolling under high ceilings
And though he sat in just one chair
Was glad to see the other chairs were empty

Of course no one needs so much space to live
But writing insists on solitudes and deserts
Things to look at as if seeing something else

We can imagine him seated at his table
Imagine the full long throat
The open white shirt
The white paper the spidery writing
And the light of a candle – as in certain paintings –
Focussing all attention

[1990]

VICTOR MANUEL MENDIOLA

Your Hand, My Mouth

1. A plate is a hand hollowing with thirst or hunger.

2. A plate is a hand opening its depths to receive or to grasp.

3. Although its kindly aspect gives me hope, the plate – this hand – has no qualms.

4. The plate gives, shams generosity, but the knife is close behind.

5. The plate is a hard and dreadful hollow. In spite of its measured and pleasant appearance, blood and bones lie at the bottom.

6. It does not matter if I am well or badly dressed, it does not matter if I am well or badly behaved, when the plate rests before me, it overpowers me and makes me – whether I become boy or woman – the armed man.

7. A plate on the table is a moon over a ghastly wood.

8. On the hard plane
   of the wooden table
   unmoving, bleeding,
   the moon's plate.

9. A cup is a hollow which cannot decide whether to open or close, to reveal itself or to hide.

10. The cup gambles, balancing between two waters or two continents at the same time. It is pretty, but a liar.

11. A glass is a fearsome hollow; frightened to lose its contents.

12. A glass stretches upward, apprehensive.

13. With its insolent aspect, the glass assumes a false arrogance.

14. If the glass lets itself be carried away by fear or self-importance, it closes, becomes a bottle; a scar rises like a knot. A navel.

15. When a glass totters, who knows the reason why my life oscillates, filled with astonishment.

16. In the narrow neck of the bottle – like a shut purse, a sealed sex – are neither words nor fellow-feeling in common. There is a measure to guard, a pip or seed to keep hidden. The glass seals itself not only for protection. It doesn't want to share, unless they pay the price.

17. When a plate breaks something essential collapses. Love or the family. Whatever promise or pact. Whatever embrace. Even the kiss withers. It knows the worst.

18. To be startled or frightened: to have eyes as wide as plates.

19. On the surface of a plate I can see the sky of my house or of the world. The Tao begins in a plate or in the hand. Then comes the balcony.

20. On the surface of a plate I can find, in white shadow, your face.

21. There is a white shadow on the plate, a pale shadow in the polished depth. A phantom that watches me every day from the glaze.

22. In the measured hollow of a plate are your hollows, the centimetres of your bite, the hidden hour of digestion.

23. Close to the plate, the knife praises the toothed gum.

24. Close to the plate, the fork stays silent, devious and alert, like the devil's gaze.

25. In its innocuous way, the spoon licks the soup with its little gloomy complicit face.

26. In its round expanse, the plate observes you; draws you into it.

27. The plate has the blindness of eyes glazed white. You were the needle of its gaze aimed at the quarry.

28. A plate is the cloud of smoke from a cannon or the glow a corpse emits. Consider this well.

29. In the centre of the plate you place, naively and gently, the meat of a bull, a pig or a lamb. Do you believe it? Do you imagine that the fierce laws of saliva that poisons or teeth that rend and tear do not apply to you?

30. In the centre of the plate you place the speed of a lettuce. The air blows on the greenness.

31. In the dining-room you listen to the hammer, the shudder, the dread, the drum of the plates.

32. In the centre of the plate see how the zebras unravel into black white fibres. On each plate there is an African motif. The lion is on the prowl.

33. The plate supports the bull, the lamb and the large green leaf, revealed between shriek and canine tooth.

34. The plate appears a surface, but it is the snare of a withdrawn purse. A claw like a bloody gauntlet. A belly.

35. From childhood I saw the white shadow of the plate and yearned to plunge into its muddy lake of blood.

36. The plate is a carnivorous plant.

37. By that plant you measure your hunger and thirst; the weight and length of your step; the kilos of pressure in your bite.

38. To sit down to eat with someone, to be at table, to make a gentle or brutal clatter of plates: to represent the digestion inside in the theatre outside.

39. The sounds from my belly and yours at this moment were our words of love two hours ago in front of our plates.

40. On the surface of the table glistens the mute depth of my plate, its blue sound pierces my mouth.

41. I look at your eyes. I look at you hungrily; I look at you with my mouth. I want to contain you; let me embrace you with my belly.

42. When we say 'I love you' or 'I want you' we do not mean the smile or the hair, much less the shoulder; it would be better to speak as we speak in the silence of the bed or the bath. Feelings make me a liar.

43. In the dominion of the plate I can say: I need to smell your foot, taste your sour unfolding armpit, inhale the grave-pits of your hot neck, touch the ring of your body, eat you, eat from your hollows. Gnaw your bone, your inside. Let me.

44. When we no longer love, then we do not eat together nor eat each other. The theatre of outside displaces the interior theatre. We are not a plate that races at the furious pace of its pleasure but rather a glass tightening itself without accent or rhyme.

45. On a plate you do not only put your food; you place the ounces and inches of your body. Your flesh and your bones. Most of all, your hollows.

46. An equation: desire = hunger, or the opposite; but perhaps this would be far better: love = plate = mouth = belly.

47. The plate is an open mouth. Feed it.

48. Under my nose, in front of my eyes, I watched two snails become two mouths on my plate. It was the most passionate kiss in the history of cinema.

49. I think of you and divide you with the cutlery of my tongue. No need for spoon or fork or knife.

50. The plate is your mouth when you come close to me. I listen to the beads of your little teeth.

51. The plate teaches me your most delicious hollow. That is why I dabble my finger in your dinner.

52. When I kiss your mouth, I kiss your deepest hollow. And I know where it starts and where it ends.

53. It is not your eyes, not your nose, not your ears which have this depth, this emptiness which encloses me and fills me. Your cunning words, your tongue, are my evidence.

54. Give me food from your plate, surrender your internal world, give me your hunger.

55. Now comes my mouth to your plate to eat from your hand.

56. I put half a tomato on the plate's surface: I see in you the insolent crest of a white cock inspecting his domain. Complacently counting the cows and chickens.

57. I place a sprig of dill on my plate; I watch your hand grow over my hand.

58. – I go to the market. I snatch olives from the counter; tear off three branches; move my eyes along the immobile swiftness of a salmon, frozen into the oceanic vessel of sweet ice in the Fish and Seafood department. The spur of a shark, the claws of a crab. I order three pieces.

I return, laden, to my house. A full bag.

On a slow fire, for not more than twenty minutes, I cook my catch.

Prepare it for you. Butter. Two sprigs of dill. You will have to try it.

Come, nearer, hear this music of blood and fire, eat with me. Come to my house, sit down to eat at my table. Let me enter into you, before I enter you.

59. Your plate is a delicious grave. Bury me.

SOPHOCLES

Three Messengers

I *Jocasta's death*

FROM *Oedipus Rex* (LINES 1223-85)

2ND MESSENGER:
Honoured nobles of this land
what dreadful thing you are about to hear,
and see with your minds' eye;
what great woe will overcome you,
if you feel kinship to the house of Labdacus!
Not even the mighty rivers, not Istus nor Phasis,
could scour this house clean from pollution.
So much hidden evil exposed,
will it or no. The worst woes
seem those we bring upon ourselves.

CHORUS:
What we know already
is bad enough. What more will you say?

2ND MESSENGER:
The shortest tale to tell and to hear –
our royal lady, Jocasta, is dead.

CHORUS:
Poor wretched woman – how?

2ND MESSENGER:
By her own hand.
But you are spared the worst – you did not see it all.
I'll tell you, though, what I can drag from my mind –
where it's already buried – of her pitiful end.
Frantic, she rushed into her rooms,
to the marriage chamber, slammed the door behind her,
and threw herself onto the bed,
tearing her hair with desperate fingers
and calling on Laius as if he were not dead
to remember the night they lay together

and made the one who would kill him –
then left her to be a mother to polluted children.
Weeping, she cursed her evil double fate:
to bear a husband from a husband,
and children from her own son.

I cannot tell you more about her death,
for then, Oedipus, roaring with grief,
burst into the hall and I could only watch him,
raging around the walls, begging one after another
to give him a sword – and tell him where
to find it, that double-ploughed field:
his wife, his mother, and mother to his children.
One of the gods must have shown him the way –
it was none of us who were near, we were too frightened.
Shouting in frenzy, he threw himself at the great double doors,
tore the hinges apart, and fell into her room –
and we saw, o horrid spectacle, the woman hanging,
her neck entangled in a noose of coiled rope.

Then, with what a ghastly roar he leapt
to loosen the cord and lay her gently on the ground.
Poor suffering man – and the horror,
to watch him tear away the beaten golden brooches
from each shoulder of her robe, lift them high
and plunge them into the sockets of his eyes,
crying out that they should never see him again,
nor what he suffered nor the evil he did,
nor look on those they should not –
but only darkness, forever.
Like a dirge, over and over he chanted,
lifting the pins, striking through his eyelids
until bloody matter spurted down his cheeks and beard –
not drops, but a gush like black rain
or hail drenching him.

All this was their fated doom,
husband and wife – evils doubled between them.
The old happiness was finished,
but it had been real. Now,
anguish and despair, madness, dishonour and death –
every evil assailed them; no curse forgotten.

II *Oedipus enters the Underworld*

FROM *Oedipus at Colonus* (LINES 1580-1666)

(*Enter* MESSENGER, *stage right.*)

MESSENGER:

Countrymen – to put it briefly – Oedipus is dead.
But what was done – that cannot be told
briefly, nor what really happened.

CHORUS:

The poor man has died?
MESSENGER:

You can be sure
that man has left this life.

CHORUS:

How? Was it a blessed and painless death?

MESSENGER:

Yes, now we have much to amaze us!
You were there – you saw
how he set off, needing no guide,
he himself leading us all.
And when he had almost reached the sheer edge
of the threshold, where those bronze steps lead below,
he stopped on one of the forked paths
near the hollow basin where the covenant
of Theseus and Peirithous is recorded,
stood between there and the Thorician rock,
then sat down by the hollow pear tree and stone tomb
to free his limbs from the filthy rags that covered them.
Next, he summoned his daughters to bring
fresh water from a flowing stream
to wash his body, and to make libation.
From the green-clad slopes of Demeter's hill
they brought what he needed, tenderly bathed
and dressed him in the customary linen clothes.
And thus his pleasure was completed,
with nothing left undone.

Then the earth quaked and shuddered like Zeus's thunder.
The girls trembled at the noise
and clutched their father's knees,
weeping and beating their breasts.
When he heard their bitter cries
he took them in his arms to soothe them and said,
'O children, from this day your father ceases to exist.
Everything I was has perished. No longer
need you bear the burden of my care.
I know it was very hard. But one simple word,
I hope, will recompense all your pain and toil.
Never will you be loved
more than I have loved you – of that,
you will indeed be deprived for the rest of your lives.'
Clinging to each other, the three of them,
father and daughters, wept. And when they stopped
there was no sound, only silence – until suddenly
came the voice of someone shouting loudly,
and all the hair on their heads bristled with dread.
It was the god who called to him – many times,
over and over, from every part of the grove.
'You there, Oedipus, what is holding us back?
You delay too long. When will you be ready to go?'
When he understood this was the summons from the god,
Oedipus asked Theseus to move closer.
'Dear friend,' he said to the king, 'give me your hand
in pledge to care for my children –
and you, daughters, give your hands to him.
Promise me never to forsake these two,
but always do the best for them'.
Restraining any show of grief, noble Theseus
reassured his friend and swore to keep his pledge.
Having heard this, Oedipus reached out to touch the girls
with his blind hands for one last time, then said,
'Daughters, you must be brave now.
Leave this place, do not turn back
or try to hear and see unlawful things.
Go now, at once – only lord Theseus
may remain, to learn what must be done.'
We all heard him say this
and, sobbing as hard as the girls,
we left the place together...and quite soon,

from further away, we looked back but
Oedipus was not there – he had disappeared –
and our lord had his hands raised in front of his eyes
to protect them from some awesome sight
which he could not bear to watch. And then,
without a word he bent low and lifted his arms high
as if to worship at the same time
the gods of the earth and the sky.

How that man perished, no mortal but Theseus can say.
No fiery thunderbolt hurled by the god took him off,
nor did a sudden storm rise from the sea and sweep him away.
Perhaps an escort was sent for him by the god
or the world of the dead beneath his feet
split open to receive him lovingly.
He departed with no lamentations or mourning,
without disease or suffering – a death
beyond any other mortal's to be wondered at.
And whoever thinks my words are foolish or mad –
I shall not try to change their opinion of me.

III *The deaths of Antigone and Haemon*

FROM *Antigone* (LINES 1155-1243)

(*Enter* MESSENGER *from the direction of the plain, stage left.*)

MESSENGER:
> Neighbours of Cadmus and the house of Amphion,
> there is no rank or style of human life
> I would choose to praise or criticise.
> A man's bad luck or good fortune
> will change from day to day –
> not even a seer can prophesy what might happen.
> Take Creon – whom I once thought deserved to be envied,
> who saved the Cadmean land from enemies
> and was proclaimed its monarch,
> set everything to rights and gloried in his children –
> now he has thrown it all away.
> It seems to me that when a man loses his joy in life,
> his reason to live, he becomes a breathing corpse.
> No matter how great the treasure and power he achieves,
> I cannot think they would have more worth
> than a puff of smoke, once his joy in life has gone.

CHORUS:
> What new grief for our king do you come to report?

MESSENGER:
> Dead – they are dead. And the living are to blame for their deaths.

CHORUS:
> Who lies dead? And who killed them?

MESSENGER:
> Haemon is dead –
> his blood spilled by a kindred hand.

CHORUS:
> His father's hand? Or someone else?

MESSENGER:
> It was his own act – in fury at his father for the murder.

CHORUS:

    O seer, your prophecy was true, and is accomplished!

MESSENGER:

    That is what happened; now you must consider what should be done.

CHORUS:

    Yes, and look – here comes poor Eurydice,
    Creon's wife. Either she heard us from the house,
    talking of her child, or she arrives by chance.

(*Enter* EURYDICE *through the double doors from the palace.*)

EURYDICE:

    All of you here, citizens – I heard your words
    as I came to the door, on my way
    to offer prayers to the goddess Pallas –
    and as I lifted the bar of the gate,
    about to open it, a cry of evil tidings
    to my household assailed my ears. I fell back
    into the arms of my women, fainting.
    Whatever it was I thought I heard, say it again
    and I will listen. I am used to bad news.

MESSENGER:

    Dear mistress, I was there, and will describe
    what I saw, leaving nothing out.
    Why should I soothe you with words
    later proved false? It is always better to tell the truth.

    As his guide, I went with your husband
    up to the furthest part of the plain, where still
    unmourned, the body of Polyneices lay, ravaged by dogs.
    We entreated Pluto, and the goddess of the crossroads,
    to hold back their anger and show mercy.
    We laved the remains with purifying water,
    broke off branches to burn what was left
    and heaped a high mound of his native earth
    for a tomb. Then we turned towards the maiden's
    stone-paved prison, the chamber of Hades' bride.

    Already, from afar, one of us had heard
    a wailing voice from that accursed place

and came to tell our master Creon.
The garbled anguished sounds grew louder
the nearer we approached. He also groaned
and loudly cried: 'How wretched I am!
How could I foretell I was about to tread
the most unhappy path of all I've walked?
It is my son's voice that greets me! Servants,
hurry, closer, look – go to the tomb
where the stones that sealed its mouth were pulled away
and tell me if I am right to recognise that voice as Haemon's –
or if the gods deceive me.'

Obeying our master's desperate commands
we went deeper into the tomb
and there beheld the girl – hung by the neck
in a noose of her linen veil –
and he, pressed close, clutching around her waist,
moaning and wailing the loss of his bride to the underworld,
the deeds of his father, and his doomed marriage.
When Creon saw him, a horrid cry burst from his lips
and he moved towards him, calling,
'Poor unhappy boy, what have you done?
What passed through your mind?
You have gone mad and destroyed yourself.
Come out, my child, I beg you.'
But the boy glared at him wildly
and kept silent – then spat in his face
and drew his double-edged sword. When his father
ran to escape, the blow missed.
The doomed boy, furious with himself, curved
his body forward and thrust the sword deep into his own side.
Half-conscious, he lifted his weakened arms to embrace the girl
and choking, coughed a stream of blood onto her white cheek.
His corpse enfolding hers,
their marriage rites at last achieved in Hades –
a sight to demonstrate how lack of wisdom
is mankind's greatest curse.

(*Exit* EURYDICE *through the double doors into the palace.*)

INDEX

Index of titles and first lines

(Titles and sub-titles are shown in italics, first lines in roman type.)